Intervention Reader Teacher's Guide

Grade 5

Orlando Boston Dallas Chicago San Diego

Visit *The Learning Site!*
www.harcourtschool.com

Copyright © by Harcourt, Inc.

All rights reserved. No part of this publication may be reproduced or transmitted in any form or by any means, electronic or mechanical, including photocopy, recording, or any information storage and retrieval system, without permission in writing from the publisher.

Teachers using COLLECTIONS may photocopy Reproducible Student Activity Pages in complete pages in sufficient quantities for classroom use only and not for resale.

HARCOURT and the Harcourt Logo are trademarks of Harcourt, Inc.

Printed in the United States of America

ISBN 0-15-312749-X

3 4 5 6 7 8 9 10 082 2002 2001 2000

Contents

Once upon a time, there was a town whose playground was at the edge of a cliff. Every so often, a child would fall off the cliff. Finally the town council decided something should be done about the serious injuries to children . . . Some council members wanted to put a fence at the top of the cliff, but others wanted to put an ambulance at the bottom.

Dr. Robert E. Slavin,
Educational Leadership, February 1996

Introduction

During the past few decades, increasing amounts of energy and funding have gone into remedial programs for students experiencing difficulty in learning to read and write. Yet students who spend several years in such programs during the elementary grades often enter middle school far behind grade-level expectations. Research shows clearly that using intervention strategies is a much more promising answer.

What Are "Intervention Strategies"?

Intervention strategies are the fences we build to protect those students who may experience some perilous "cliffs" no matter how well we have planned our curriculum. These strategies offer support and guidance to the student who is struggling. The strategies themselves are no mystery. They are based on the same time-honored techniques that effective teachers have used for years—teaching students on their instructional reading level, modeling previewing and predicting, conducting guided reading, and giving direct instruction in strategic reading, vocabulary, phonics, and structural analysis skills.

Intervention works best in conjunction with a strong core program. Instruction should focus on specific needs of students, as determined by systematic monitoring of progress. Here is what the research says about the components of an effective intervention program:

Materials

- It is essential that students read texts with which they are successful. Effective intervention strategies can widen the variety of texts accessible to students, but it is also important to provide reading material at students' instructional reading level.
- Guiding the students who need extra support through a preview of the literature—with attention to important vocabulary—will help ensure success.

Instruction

- Successful intervention programs allow students to spend more time reading and responding to texts at their instructional reading level. Students are also taught when and how to use reading skills and strategies.
- Teachers should observe any problems that students have during activities and use flexible grouping to provide more individualized instruction for those who need additional help.
- Phonics and structural analysis skills must be given strong, systematic treatment and should be taught along with strategies for discovering word meaning.

Using the *Intervention Readers* and *Intervention Reader Teacher's Guides*

The goal of the ***Collections*** *Intervention Readers* and the *Teacher's Guides* is to provide the scaffolding, extra support, and extra reading practice that below-level readers need to succeed in the mainstream reading program.

Intervention Readers are student editions comprised of selections that

- are consistently parallel in genre, theme, and content to the corresponding selections in the ***Collections*** Student Editions.
- are written on a level that more closely approximates the struggling reader's instructional reading level.
- gradually increase in difficulty so that by the end of the book, students are reading on-grade-level material.
- systematically apply high-frequency words, ***Collections*** vocabulary, and phonics skills.

Each *Intervention Reader* selection is accompanied by a **Think About It** page and—when a Skill Lesson accompanies the corresponding ***Collections*** selection—a parallel **Skill Lesson**, written with the same vocabulary and on the same reading level as the rest of the *Intervention Reader* selections.

The ***Intervention Reader Teacher's Guides*** give step-by-step support in using the *Intervention Reader* to provide comprehensive instruction for below-level readers. Each *Intervention Reader Teacher's Guide* lesson includes the following resources:

- **Phonics/Decoding Lesson** preteaches basic phonics and word analysis skills essential for reading. Each skill is systematically applied in the corresponding *Intervention Reader* selection and reviewed in subsequent selections.
- **Phonics Reproducible Student Activity Page** reinforces the Phonics/Decoding Skill Lesson. This page can be used as a teacher-directed or independent activity.
- **Introducing Vocabulary** activity teaches additional important vocabulary that appears in the corresponding ***Collections*** Student Edition selection and in the *Intervention Reader* selection. This extra vocabulary instruction increases students' chances of success.
- **Vocabulary Reproducible Student Activity Page** gives students an opportunity to use the *Intervention Reader* vocabulary in context and show their understanding of it. It also provides a preview of the upcoming selection.
- **Directed Reading Lesson** offers suggestions for dividing the selection into cohesive sections that are manageable for students, and then using a variety of techniques to help students read these sections successfully.
- **Student Response Reproducible Student Activity Page** gives students an opportunity to respond to the *Intervention Reader* selection and show that they have understood it. It also provides further reinforcement of the *Intervention Reader* vocabulary.

Consonants

NOTE TO THE TEACHER Some students may need additional practice with consonant blends and digraphs. To determine which students would benefit from completing the review, you may wish to give the following informal assessment.

Informal Assessment of Consonant Blends and Digraphs

Assess

ASSESS THE SKILL Use an informal inventory to assess students' knowledge and understanding of consonant blends and digraphs. Say the following words, and have students listen for the consonant sounds that are blended at the beginning. Repeat each word, and have students write the consonants that stand for the beginning sounds. Use these words:

stand, block, frog, train, plant, small, snow, clown, drop

Follow a similar procedure for consonant digraphs. Have students write the letters that stand for the sound they hear at the beginning or end of these words:

sharp, thumb, chip, chain, sheep, think; such, path, both, wish, much, wash

If students need additional practice with consonant blends and digraphs, use the following review.

Review of Consonant Blends and Digraphs

Teach/Model

IDENTIFY THE SOUNDS Ask students to repeat the following sentence three times: *Stan and Fran flew a plane past the gray clouds.* Have students tell which words in the sentence begin or end with the same blended sounds as the following words:

clap (clouds), frog (Fran), plan (plane), stop (Stan), grow (gray), flag (flew); find (and), list (past)

Follow a similar procedure for consonant digraphs. Use the following sentence: *Chip and Beth should catch that fish.* Ask students which word begins or ends with the same sound as each of these words:

shell (should), cheese (Chip); this (that); mash (fish), path (Beth), watch (catch)

ASSOCIATE LETTERS TO SOUNDS Write the following sentence on the board: *Stan and Fran flew a plane past the gray clouds.* Ask how the words *Stan, Fran, flew, plane, gray,* and *clouds* are alike. (*They all begin with two consonants whose sounds are blended together.*) As you point to each of the words, ask students to identify the blend and to name other words that begin with the blended sounds. Follow a similar procedure with the words *and* and *past* and final consonant blends.

Follow a similar procedure with consonant digraphs. Use the sentence *Chip and Beth should catch that fish.* Point out the words that are alike because they each begin or end with two or more consonants that stand for only one sound.

Practice/Apply

APPLY THE SKILL ***Initial Consonant Substitution*** Write the word *cap* on the board. Read *cap* aloud, and have students repeat it. Change the *c* to *ch* to make the word *chap*, and ask a volunteer to read aloud the new word. Follow a similar procedure to have students read all the words in each column:

cap	man	bat	tag
(ch)ap	(th)an	(fl)at	(sh)ag
(fl)ap	(pl)an	(sc)at	(fl)ag
(tr)ap	(St)an	(ch)at	(dr)ag
(wr)ap	(Gr)an	(gn)at	(st)ag

Final Consonant Substitution Use a similar procedure to have students practice final consonant blends and consonant digraphs. Use these words:

bad	man	sad	cap
ba(ck)	ma(sh)	sa(nd)	ca(mp)
ba(nd)	ma(tch)	sa(sh)	ca(st)
ba(tch)	ma(th)	sa(ck)	ca(tch)
ba(th)	ma(st)	sa(ng)	ca(sh)

DICTATION AND WRITING Tell students to number their papers 1–10. For words 1–5, below, have students write the letters that stand for the sound or sounds that they hear at the beginning of each word. Then write the correct responses on the board so students can check and correct their work. For words 6–10, have students write the letters that stand for the sound or sounds that they hear at the end of each word.

1. black	2. chick	3. sheep	4. think	5. frame
6. with	7. must	8. dish	9. wind	10. lamp

INDEPENDENT PRACTICE Ask students to write two words for each of the following initial blends or digraphs: *ch, sh, th, pl, cl, fr, gr,* and *sn.* For each pair of words, have students write a riddle in which they use one of the words in a clue and the other as the answer. Invite students to share their riddles.

Short Vowels (CVC)

NOTE TO THE TEACHER Some students may need additional practice with short vowels. To determine which students would benefit from completing the review, you may wish to give the following informal assessment.

Informal Assessment of Short Vowels (CVC)

Assess

ASSESS THE SKILL Use an informal inventory to assess students' knowledge and understanding of decoding short vowel sounds in consonant-vowel-consonant words. Say each of the following CVC words, and have students listen for the vowel sound that they hear in the middle. Have students write the letter that stands for that vowel sound.

tip, pop, mat, fin, wag, pup, run, hot, red, ten

If students need additional practice with short vowels and the CVC pattern, use the following review.

Review of Short Vowels (CVC)

Teach/Model

IDENTIFY THE SOUNDS Ask students to repeat the following sentence three times: *Six men can run but not hop.* Have students tell which words in the sentence have the same vowel sounds as the following words: *lap (can), fox (not, hop), win (six), hum (run, but), net (men).*

ASSOCIATE LETTERS TO SOUNDS Write the following sentence on the board: *Six men can run but not hop.* Ask how all the words are alike. (*They all have three letters; they all have the CVC pattern; they all have a short vowel sound in the middle.*) Remind students that words with the CVC pattern usually have a short vowel sound. As you point to each of the words, ask students to identify the consonants, the vowel, the short vowel sound, and the word.

Practice/Apply

APPLY THE SKILL ***Vowel Substitution*** Write the word *cap* on the board. Read *cap* aloud, and have students repeat it. Change the *a* to *u* to make the word *cup*, and ask a volunteer to read aloud the new word. Follow a similar procedure to have students read all the words in each column:

cap	hat	bat	bad	bag
c(u)p	h(o)t	b(u)t	b(u)d	b(u)g
c(o)p	h(u)t	b(i)t	b(i)d	b(i)g
	h(i)t	b(e)t	b(e)d	b(o)g
				b(e)g

DICTATION AND WRITING Tell students to number their papers 1–10. Dictate each of the following words, and have students write it. Then write the correct spelling on the board so students can check and correct their work.

1. win	2. dot	3. cub	4. but	5. map
6. fox	7. met	8. ten	9. sad	10. dig

Dictate the following sentence for students to write: *Ten pigs sat in the hot sun.*

INDEPENDENT PRACTICE Ask students to write at least two rhyming words for each short vowel sound. Have them use the rhyming words to make rhyming sentences like these:

Look at the cat.

It is sitting in my hat!

What is in your box?

Is it a red fox?

A Fish Tale

by Sydnie Meltzer Kleinhenz **Use with *Timeless Tales*, pages 6–13.**

Preteaching Skills: Short Vowels /a/a, /i/i, /o/o, /u/u; Long Vowels /ā/a-e, /ī/i-e, /ō/o-e, /o͞o/u-e

Teach/Model

IDENTIFY THE SOUND Have students repeat the following sentence aloud three times: *Nat and Nate had yams on a plate.* Ask students to identify the words that have the /a/ sound. *(Nat, had, yams)* Then ask them to identify the words that have the /ā/ sound. *(Nate, plate)* Follow a similar procedure for short *i* and long *i* sounds, short *o* and long *o* sounds, and short *u* and long *u* sounds, using these sentences: *Tim has time to shine the tin. Rob strode up the slope with his fishing rod. Chuck sits on a dune and hums a tune.*

ASSOCIATE LETTERS TO SOUNDS Write on the board the sentence *Nat and Nate had yams on a plate.* Underline the letter *a* in *Nat, had,* and *yams.* Point out the consonant-vowel-consonant (CVC) pattern in each. Tell students that words with this pattern usually have the short *a* sound. Then underline the *a* and *e* in *Nate* and *plate*, and point out the *a-e* pattern in each. Explain that words with this pattern usually have the long *a* sound. Use a similar procedure to point out the consonant-vowel patterns with the sentences above that focus on the short *i* and long *i* sounds, the short *o* and long *o* sounds, and the short *u* and long *u* sounds.

WORD BLENDING Model how to blend the letters and sounds to read the word *plate.* Point to each letter and say its sound. Slide your hand under the whole word as you elongate the sounds /pplläätt/. Then say the word naturally—*plate.* Follow a similar procedure with *Nate, shine, tin, strode, rod, Chuck,* and *tune.*

Practice/Apply

APPLY THE SKILL ***Vowel Substitution*** Write the following words on the board, and have students read each aloud. Make the changes necessary to form the words in parentheses. Have students read each new word aloud.

sham (shame) mop (mope) pin (pine) strip (stripe) plum (plume)

DICTATION AND WRITING Have students number a paper 1–8. Dictate the words below, and have students write them. Point out that all of the words with long vowel sounds are spelled with the pattern in which the vowel is between two consonants followed by the letter *e.* After each word is written, display the correct spelling so students can proofread their work. They should draw a line through a misspelled word and write the correct spelling beside it.

1. glad*	2. case*	3. gift*	4. five*
5. spot*	6. poles*	7. brush*	8. tune

**Word appears in "A Fish Tale."*

Dictate the following sentence for students to write: *Dan and Dale spot five plumes of smoke.*

READ LONGER WORDS ***Introduce Compound Words*** Write the word *homemade* on the board. Ask students which part of the word sounds like /home/ and which part sounds like /made/. Ask what *home* and *made* together sound like. Follow a similar procedure with the words *windpipe, handprint, ragtime,* and *cockpit.* Ask volunteers to read the words and explain how they were able to figure them out.

REPRODUCIBLE STUDENT ACTIVITY PAGE

INDEPENDENT PRACTICE See the reproducible Student Activity on page 3.

Name ______________________________

A Fish Tale

Do what the sentences tell you.

1. Find Dan. He has a *D* on his cap. Write *Dan* on the line by him.
2. Find Mike. He has an *M* on his cap. Write *Mike* on the line by him.
3. Dan has no rod to catch fish with. Make a fishing rod in his hand.
4. Mike likes to fish with a stick and a string. Make a pole for him to fish with.
5. Find Dale. Make a line from one of her hands to the other.
6. Then draw five fish on the line.
7. Make three stripes on the fish.
8. Make some waves on the lake.
9. Draw a big pine on a sand dune by Dan.
10. Find the ring of stones. Make a blaze in it.
11. Make a plume of smoke going up from the blaze.
12. Find the pup. Make some grub for it in its dish.
13. Make a mat for the pup to nap on.

Write a word from above that has the same vowel sound and spelling pattern as each word below.

14. tune dune, plume

15. bike Mike, likes, five, line, stripes, pine

16. haze make, waves, lake, blaze

17. joke pole, stones, smoke

Harcourt

Introducing Vocabulary

Apply word identification strategies.

LOOK FOR FAMILIAR SPELLING PATTERNS Display the vocabulary words, and ask students to identify any words they know. Divide the word *investigate* into syllables. (in•ves•ti•gate) Guide students to identify the pattern of letters that stands for a short vowel sound in each of the first three syllables. Then point out the *a*-consonant-*e* pattern in the last syllable. Have students read this word aloud and tell how the pattern of letters helped them. Then help students read aloud the other words. Use clues as necessary: what detectives do to solve a mystery (*investigate*); means "from another country" (*foreign*); what a hummingbird did when it paused in midair by the bird feeder (*hovered*); means "stood in one spot, like a soldier on guard" (*stationed*); a feeling of doubt (*suspicion*). If students misread a word and then correct themselves, encourage them by saying, for example, **You read ___ and then changed it to ___. How did you know to do that?**

VOCABULARY DEFINED

emerged came into view

foreign from another country

hovered stayed close to

investigate to find out more about; to research as a result of suspicion

stationed stayed in a particular spot

suspicion doubt about something

Discuss the meanings of the vocabulary words. Then ask students to make up questions using the vocabulary words. (Example: *What is an example of a foreign country? Who is stationed by the entrance to the amusement park?*) Have students continue making up questions until all the words have been used at least once and each student has had a chance to respond.

Check understanding.

Ask students to write the vocabulary words on a sheet of paper. Then ask the following questions. Have students name the word that best answers each question and circle it on their papers.

- **If you doubt that a ring is made of real gold, what feeling do you have?** *(suspicion)*
- **What could you do to find out if the ring is real or fake?** *(investigate)*
- **The greeting *bonjour* comes from the French language. What kind of phrase is *bonjour*?** *(foreign)*
- **If the sun suddenly appeared from behind the clouds, what did it do?** *(emerged)*
- **You did this if you stood near a group of other students, hoping that they would say hello.** *(hovered)*
- **Which word means "positioned"?** *(stationed)*

REPRODUCIBLE STUDENT ACTIVITY PAGE

INDEPENDENT PRACTICE See the reproducible Student Activity on page 5.

NOTE: The following vocabulary words from "The Hot and Cold Summer" are reinforced in "A Fish Tale." If students are unfamiliar with these words, point them out as you encounter them during reading: *authority*, *vow* (p. 7); *incredible* (p. 8); *commotion*, *exhausted* (p. 10); *souvenir* (p. 11).

Name ___________________________

REPRODUCIBLE STUDENT ACTIVITY PAGE

A Fish Tale

Read the ad.

Here are Sam, Travis, and Ingrid. Sam and Travis like to fish. Ingrid likes to fish, too. Ingrid is from a **foreign** land. She stands by Travis and Sam. She hopes they will let her fish with them, but they don't. Sam thinks Ingrid is odd. Ingrid can fish. She can catch big ones. But Sam and Travis must find this out.

One time Ingrid **stationed** herself by the pond. She had a big, big catfish in her hands. Then Sam and Travis **emerged** from the brush. They **hovered** by the big catch. Sam had a **suspicion** when he spotted the fish. Did Ingrid catch it or not? Time to **investigate**!

Is the catch a fake? Will Sam let Ingrid fish with them? Find out in "A Fish Tale"!

Write a word from the ad to complete each sentence. Choose from the words in dark type.

1. When Sam spots the catfish, he plans to ___investigate___.
2. Ingrid ___stationed___ herself so that Sam and Travis could see the catfish.
3. Sam thinks Ingrid's ___foreign___ habits are odd.
4. Ingrid ___hovered___ by Travis and Sam. She hoped to fish with them.
5. Travis ___emerged___ from the brush and spotted the fish.
6. Sam had a ___suspicion___ about the fish.

Do you think Ingrid's catch is a fake? Why or why not?

Responses will vary.

____

Harcourt

Directed Reading

Page 6 Have a volunteer read the title of the story aloud. If necessary, explain that a "fish story" is a story that exaggerates, or stretches the truth. Have students view the illustration on page 6 and read page 6 to find out how Sam feels about Ingrid. Ask: **How does Sam feel about Ingrid?** (*He doesn't like her.*) LITERAL: MAIN IDEA **Why not?** (*because she is from a foreign country and she speaks differently*) LITERAL: CAUSE-EFFECT

Page 7 Have students read page 7 to find out how Sam and Travis treat Ingrid. Ask: **How do Sam and Travis treat Ingrid?** (Possible response: *They are rude to her. They don't let her fish with them. Sam tells her to go hug a slug.*) CRITICAL: MAKE JUDGMENTS

Page 8 Ask students whether they think Ingrid is good at fishing, as she says she is. Have them read page 8 to find out what Ingrid does to prove that she can fish. Ask: **What does Ingrid do to prove that she can fish?** (*She buys a big catfish from a store and pretends that she caught it.*) INFERENTIAL: DRAW CONCLUSIONS **Do you think this is the right thing to do? Why or why not?** (Possible response: *no, because it's dishonest*) CRITICAL: MAKE JUDGMENTS

Page 9 Ask students to read page 9 to find out whether Sam and Travis believe that she caught the fish. Ask: **Do Sam and Travis seem to believe that Ingrid caught the catfish?** (Possible response: *Sam seems doubtful, but Travis seems to believe her.*) CRITICAL: SPECULATE **How can you tell that Travis's feelings about Ingrid are changing?** (Possible response: *He seems impressed when she says she can cut up fish by herself; he says they could go fishing together sometime.*) INFERENTIAL: DRAW CONCLUSIONS

Page 10 Ask students to read page 10 to find out if Travis and Ingrid go fishing together. Ask: **Do Travis and Ingrid seem to be friends now?** (*yes*) **Why do you think Sam is mad when he sees them fishing?** (Possible response: *He's jealous; he and Travis had made a vow to keep the pond to themselves.*) INFERENTIAL: CAUSE-EFFECT

Page 11 Have students read page 11 to find out how the story ends. Ask: **How did Ingrid's fish story get printed in the newspaper?** (Possible response: *A reporter saw her with the big fish and took a picture. Then the picture and story were put in the paper.*) INFERENTIAL: DRAW CONCLUSIONS **What does Ingrid plan to do at the end of the story?** (*tell the people at the* Lakefront Times *the truth about the fish*) INFERENTIAL: SEQUENCE

SUMMARIZE THE SELECTION Ask students what Sam, Travis, and Ingrid might have learned about each other in the story. Then have students retell the main events in three or four sentences.

Page 12

Answers to Think About It Questions

1. Ingrid just moved to Kansas from Finland, and she wanted to be friends with Sam and Travis. SUMMARY
2. Possible response: By that time, they are pals with Ingrid. INTERPRETATION
3. Accept reasonable responses. Newspaper stories should give a brief description of Ingrid and the big catfish and should be written from the third-person point of view. WRITE A STORY

Page 13 For instruction on the Focus Skill: Prefixes and Suffixes, see page 13 in *Bright Voices.*

Name ______________________________

REPRODUCIBLE STUDENT ACTIVITY PAGE

A Fish Tale

Write a sentence in each box below to help you summarize "A Fish Tale." Be sure to write the events in the correct order.

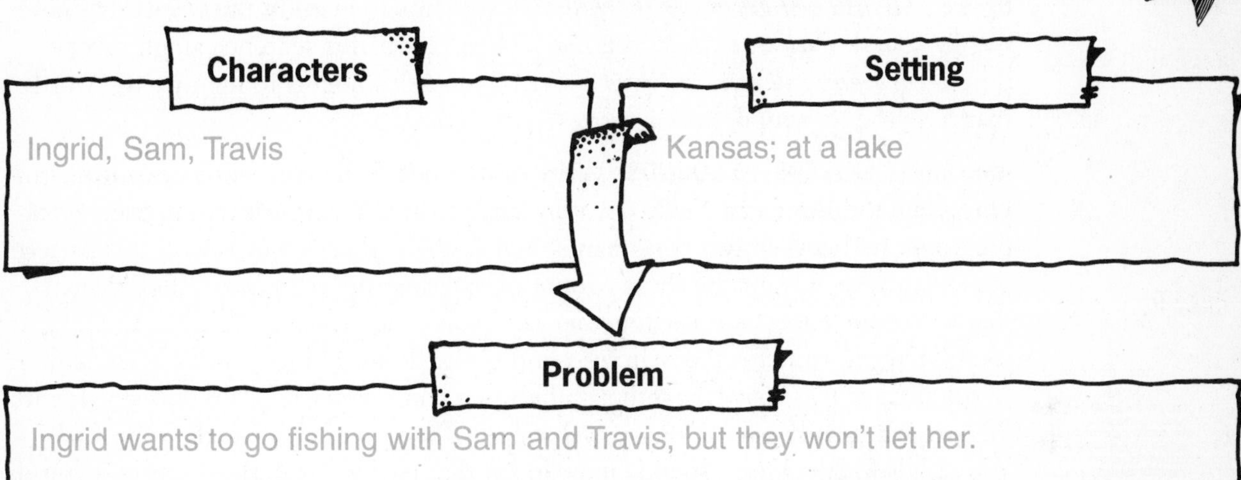

Characters

Ingrid, Sam, Travis

Setting

Kansas; at a lake

Problem

Ingrid wants to go fishing with Sam and Travis, but they won't let her.

Important Events

1. Ingrid asks Sam and Travis if she can fish with them.
2. Ingrid buys a catfish and pretends she caught it.
3. A man takes a picture of Ingrid and her fish for the newspaper.
4. Travis invites Ingrid to fish with him.
5. Ingrid tells the truth about how she got her fish.

Solution

Sam and Travis have so much fun with Ingrid that they all become friends.

Now write a one-sentence summary of the story.

Possible response: Ingrid wants to fish with Sam and Travis, so, to impress them, she pretends that she caught a big fish.

Harcourt

The Quiver

by Sharon Fear **Use with *Timeless Tales*, pages 14–21.**

Preteaching Skills: Short Vowel /e/*e*; Long Vowel /ē/*ee, ea, ey*

Teach/Model

IDENTIFY THE SOUND Have students repeat the following sentence aloud three times: *Nell's red vest got wet in the shed.* Ask students to identify the words that have the /e/ sound. (*Nell's, red, vest, wet, shed*) Then repeat this sentence aloud three times: *The teams will meet at Green Valley Camp.* Ask students to identify the words that have the /ē/ sound. (*teams, meet, Green, Valley*)

ASSOCIATE LETTERS TO SOUNDS Write on the board the two sentences above. Underline the letter *e* in *Nell's, red, vest, wet,* and *shed.* Point out that in each word, the *e* appears between two consonants. Tell students that in words with this pattern, the *e* usually stands for the short *e* sound. Underline the *ea* in *teams.* Tell students that when the letters *ea* come together in a word, they usually stand for the long *e* sound. Do the same for the *ee* in *meet* and *Green.* Point out that *teams, meet,* and *Green* all have two vowels together in between consonants. Explain that words with this pattern usually have a long vowel sound. Then point out that the *ey* in *Valley* also stands for the long *e* sound, and explain that in this word, the *y* acts as a vowel.

WORD BLENDING Model how to blend and read the word *green.* Slide your hand under the whole word as you elongate the sounds /ggrrēēnn/. Then say the word naturally—*green.* Follow a similar procedure with the words *vest, teams,* and *valley.*

Practice/Apply

APPLY THE SKILL *Letter Substitution* Write the following words on the board, and have students read each aloud. Make the changes necessary to form the words in parentheses. Have students read each new word aloud.

fed (feed) dell (deal) fell (feeble) kept (key)

DICTATION AND WRITING Have students number a paper 1–8. Dictate the following words, and have students write them. After each word is written, display the correct spelling so students can proofread their work. They should draw a line through a misspelled word and write the correct spelling beside it.

1. west*	2. telling*	3. deep*	4. trees*
5. team	6. speaking*	7. hockey	8. jockey

**Word appears in "The Quiver."*

Dictate the following sentence for students to write: *I went to greet the hockey team.*

READ LONGER WORDS *Introduce Breaking Between Double Consonants* Write the word *getting* on the board. Point out to students that when the ending *-ing* is added to a word that has a short vowel sound, the final consonant is usually doubled. Also point out that two-syllable words that have a double consonant are usually divided into syllables in between the doubled consonants. Draw a line between the two *t*s in *getting,* and read each syllable as you point to it. Then read the word naturally—*getting.* Follow a similar procedure with the words *puddle, letting, wedding,* and *glasses.*

REPRODUCIBLE STUDENT ACTIVITY PAGE

INDEPENDENT PRACTICE See the reproducible Student Activity on page 9.

Name ______________________________

The Quiver

Write the word that makes the sentence tell about the picture.

1. Janet has a ___pet___ finch named Flute.
   vest pet jet

2. She puts ___seeds___ in Flute's dish.
   seeds feet weeds

3. Flute likes to hit her bell and ___keys___.
   keys honey jockey

4. She ___tweets___ a nice tune when it's time for lunch.
   tweets jeeps beets

5. Sometimes Janet must ___clean___ Flute's home.
   leap clean deal

6. At bedtime, Flute ___sleeps___ on her swing.
   weeds speeds sleeps

7. Flute ___seems___ to like her home.
   speeds seems bees

Harcourt

Introducing Vocabulary

Apply word identification strategies.

LOOK FOR FAMILIAR SPELLING PATTERNS Display the vocabulary words, and ask students to identify those they know. Remind students that they can sometimes figure out new words by looking for familiar spelling patterns. Frame the first syllable in *solemn*, pointing out the familiar CVC pattern. Call on a volunteer to read the word aloud and tell how she or he was able to figure it out. (*When a vowel is between two consonants, the vowel usually has the short vowel sound.*) Help students use the sounds that letters stand for to read the remaining vocabulary words aloud. If necessary, provide clues: normal (*ordinary*); not seen clearly (*blurry*); a picture of someone or something (*image*); stopped an action midway (*interrupted*); to tell people that they did something wrong (*criticize*). If students misread a word and then correct themselves, encourage them by saying, for example, **You read ___ and then changed it to ___. How did you know you needed to do that?**

VOCABULARY DEFINED

blurry not seen clearly

criticize to tell someone that he or she did something wrong

image a picture of someone or something

interrupted stopped for a while; got in the way of

ordinary regular, not special

solemn serious

Discuss the meanings of the vocabulary words. Then have students invent a story using each of the vocabulary words, with each student adding a sentence to build the story. You may want to begin the story with this sentence: *It began as an <u>ordinary</u> day, but soon things became strange.* Continue building the story until all students have had a chance to respond and all the vocabulary words have been used at least once.

Check understanding.

Ask students to copy the vocabulary words on a sheet of paper. Have them name the word that best answers each question and circle it on their papers.

- **Which word names something that is not special in any way?** *(ordinary)*
- **What do you call a picture of something?** *(image)*
- **Which word names what people do when they tell someone that he or she has not done something well?** *(criticize)*
- **Which word describes someone who is very serious?** *(solemn)*
- **Which word tells how things look underwater if you are not wearing goggles?** *(blurry)*
- **Which word tells what happened when you were talking to someone and that person began talking before you were finished?** *(interrupted)*

REPRODUCIBLE STUDENT ACTIVITY PAGE

INDEPENDENT PRACTICE See the reproducible Student Activity on page 11.

NOTE: The following vocabulary words from "Sees Behind Trees" are reinforced in "The Quiver." If students are unfamiliar with these words, point them out as you encounter them during reading: *quiver* (p. 14); *sternly* (p. 15); *moss* (p. 16); *composed*, *tread* (p. 17); *exaggerate* (p. 20).

Name ______________________

REPRODUCIBLE STUDENT ACTIVITY PAGE

The Quiver

Read the story.

A broken wagon wheel **interrupted** the trip. That's when Will ran into the trees. He spotted a quiver.	In the trees, he picked up what seemed to be an **ordinary** quiver. Then he went to the creek. When Will checked, he was lost.	Will's dad was **solemn** when he said that Will mustn't panic if he got lost. But Will did panic.
Will was weeping when he glimpsed an **image** in the trees. Because of his tears, the image was **blurry**.	Then Will could see that a boy had stopped. The boy seemed to be hunting for the quiver, so Will gave it to him.	The other boy wishes to help Will get back to his wagon. Are his ma and pa going to **criticize** Will for getting lost?

Write a story word to complete each sentence. Choose from the words in dark type.

1. The trip was ___interrupted___ when a wagon wheel broke.
2. In the trees, Will picked up an ___ordinary___ quiver.
3. Will's dad was ___solemn___ when he told Will not to panic if he got lost.
4. Will could see an ___image___ in the trees when he was weeping.
5. What he could see was ___blurry___.
6. Ma and Pa might ___criticize___ Will for getting lost.

Tell what could happen to Will in "The Quiver."

Possible response: Will is going to find his way out of the trees and back to his family. His parents will be upset with him.

Harcourt

Directed Reading

Page 14 Read aloud the title of the story. Help students identify Will and the quiver he is holding. If necessary, explain that a quiver is a portable case for arrows. Have students read page 14 to find out how Will winds up in the woods. Ask: **What do you think Will will do next?** (Possible response: *He will try to find his way back to the wagons.*) INFERENTIAL: MAKE PREDICTIONS

Page 15 Have students read page 15 to learn the advice Pa gave to Will and whether Will follows it. Ask: **What had Pa told Will to do if he ever got lost? Does Will follow Pa's advice?** (*Pa had told Will not to panic and to stay in one place; Will doesn't follow his advice.*) INFERENTIAL: IMPORTANT DETAILS

Page 16 After students read page 16, have them look at the illustration. Ask: **What is the blurry image that Will notices?** (*another boy who is looking for something*) INFERENTIAL: IMPORTANT DETAILS **Why do you think the other boy begins to weep?** (Possible responses: *He has lost something important; he also is lost and afraid.*) INFERENTIAL: DRAW CONCLUSIONS

Page 17 Have students read page 17 to find out what happens when Will and the other boy meet. **How do you think Will knows the quiver is special to the other boy?** (Possible response: *He sees how disappointed the boy is.*) INFERENTIAL: DRAW CONCLUSIONS **What does the author mean when she says that Will and the other boy have "seen" each other's feelings?** (Possible response: *They each know the other is sad because they have seen each other crying.*) CRITICAL: AUTHOR'S CRAFT/APPRECIATE LANGUAGE

Page 18 After students read page 18, ask: **How does the other boy figure out that Will is lost?** (Possible response: *Will draws a picture of a wagon and a team of oxen in the mud.*) INFERENTIAL: CAUSE-EFFECT **What do the other boy's actions tell you about him?** (Possible response: *He cares about others and is helpful.*) INFERENTIAL: DETERMINE CHARACTERS' TRAITS

Page 19 Have students read page 19 to find out whether the other boy is able to help Will find his family. **How is Will able to spot the wagons?** (*Will sees the deep ruts of wagon wheels on the land. The ruts help him find the wagons.*) INFERENTIAL: DRAW CONCLUSIONS

Page 20 Have students read page 20 to find out how Will's ma and pa react to his return. **How do you know Will's ma and pa were very worried when he was lost?** (Possible responses: *They do not criticize him for not following their advice; they tell him how glad they are to have him back.*) METACOGNITIVE: DETERMINE CHARACTERS' EMOTIONS

SUMMARIZE THE SELECTION Have students think about what happened to Will after he got lost in the woods. Then help them summarize the story.

Page 21

Answers to Think About It Questions

1. Will gives the lost quiver back to him. He helps Will find the wagons and his ma and pa. SUMMARY
2. Accept reasonable responses. Possible response: No, Will does not feel bad. Will is very sad, and the boy is sad and weeping, too. INTERPRETATION
3. Diary entries should recount Will's getting lost and his initial fright and then relief at meeting the other boy in the woods, all from Will's point of view. WRITE A DIARY ENTRY

Name ______________________________

The Quiver

Complete the sequence chart about "The Quiver." Write a sentence in each box. The first one is done for you.

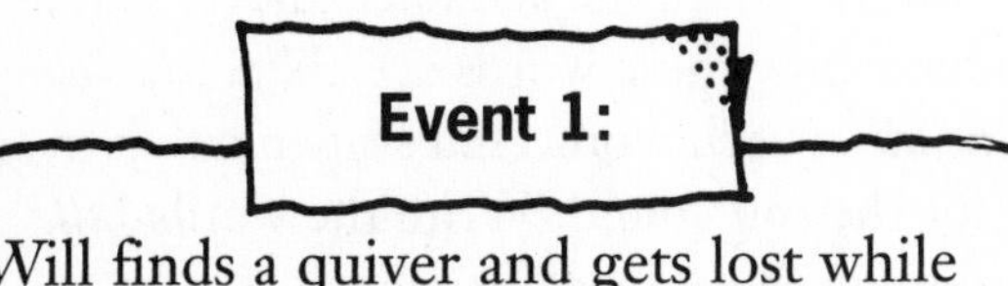

Event 1:

Will finds a quiver and gets lost while looking for more things.

Event 2:

Possible response: Will sees another boy looking for something.

Event 3:

Possible response: Will realizes he is looking for the quiver and gives it to him.

Event 4:

Possible response: The boy helps Will find his parents.

Now use the information in the boxes to write a one-sentence summary of the selection.

Possible response: Two boys help each other find the things they lost.

____

Harcourt

The Audition

by Susan McCloskey   Use with *Timeless Tales*, pages 22–29.

Preteaching Skills: Vowel Variant /ôl/*al, all*

Teach/Model

IDENTIFY THE SOUND Have students repeat the following sentence aloud three times: *June called to ask if she could get a malt at the mall.* Have students identify the words that have the same /ôl/ sound they hear in *halt.* (*called, malt, mall*)

ASSOCIATE LETTERS TO SOUNDS Write on the board the sentence above. Circle the words *called, malt,* and *mall,* and ask students how these words are alike. (*the /ôl/ sound;* al *or* all) Underline the letters *al* or *all* in each word. Tell students that in these words, the letters *al* and *all* stand for the /ôl/ sound. Write the words *fall, salt, tall,* and *false* on the board, and underline the *al* or *all* in each.

WORD BLENDING Model how to blend the sounds and letters to read the word *fall.* Touch each letter and say its sound. Slide your hand under the letters as you elongate the sounds /ffôôll/. Then say the word naturally—*fall.* Follow a similar procedure with *salt, tall,* and *false.* Then write the words *talk* and *balk* on the board. Point out to students that words with *alk* have the same /ô/ sound, but the *l* is silent. Read *talk* and *balk,* and have students repeat them.

Practice/Apply

APPLY THE SKILL ***Consonant Substitution*** Write the following words on the board, and have students read each aloud. Make the changes necessary to form the words in parentheses. Have a student read aloud each new word.

hall	malt	walk
(call)	(salt)	(talk)
(stall)	(halt)	(stalk)

DICTATION AND WRITING Have students number a sheet of paper 1–8. Dictate the following words, and have students write them. After students write each word, display the correct spelling so students can proofread their work. Have them draw a line through a misspelled word and write the correct spelling beside it.

1. waltz*	2. halt*	3. walrus	4. wall*
5. hall*	6. small*	7. talking*	8. stalk

**Word appears in "The Audition."*

Dictate the following sentence for students to write: *The tall bald man talked while he walked past the walnut tree.*

READ LONGER WORDS ***Review Compound Words*** Write the word *sidewalk* on the board. Tell students that when they see a longer word, they can look to see if it is made up of two shorter words. Cover the word *walk,* and have students read the shorter word *side.* Repeat the procedure and have them read the word *walk.* Have students blend the word parts together to form the longer word *sidewalk.* Repeat the procedure with the words *windfall, baseball, pitfall,* and *basketball.*

REPRODUCIBLE STUDENT ACTIVITY PAGE

INDEPENDENT PRACTICE See the reproducible Student Activity on page 15.

Name ______________________________

The Audition

Read the story. Circle the words with the vowel sound you hear in *salt, hall,* or *stalk*.

Walt is now six feet tall.	He needs to walk to the mall to get longer pants.	He calls Beth to make a plan: "I'll get you a malt if you come with me to the mall."
Then Beth talks. She tells Walt that the baseball game has ended. "I'll meet you at the stone wall next to the lake at three."	Walt hangs up. When he walks outside, the crisp fall breeze makes him smile.	Walt meets Beth at the stone wall at three. He gets her a malt at a shop in the mall. For himself, he gets a frozen treat with walnuts.

Circle and write the word that best completes each sentence.

1. Walt is not _____small_____. **small** **wall** **call**
2. He has to get pants at the _____mall_____. **wall** **mall** **hall**
3. He plans to get there by _____walking_____. **walking** **talking** **balking**
4. He _____calls_____ Beth to see if she'll go. **stalls** **halls** **calls**
5. He tells her he'll get her a _____malt_____. **malt** **salt** **walnut**
6. They _____talk_____ about a plan to meet. **talk** **walk** **stall**
7. Walt likes the _____fall_____ breeze. **fall** **tall** **salt**
8. He asks for a treat with _____walnuts_____. **walnuts** **salt** **stalks**

Harcourt

Introducing Vocabulary

Apply word identification strategies.

LOOK FOR FAMILIAR SPELLING PATTERNS Display the vocabulary words, and ask students to read them silently and identify the ones they know. Remind students that they can sometimes figure out new words by looking for familiar spelling patterns. Point out the double consonants in *flatter*, and remind students that words like this are divided into syllables in between the two consonants. Then call on a volunteer to read the word and tell how he or she was able to figure it out. Help students read the remaining vocabulary words aloud. If necessary, provide clues: able to wait a long time without getting upset (*patient*); related to the word *piano* (*pianist*); large violinlike instrument (*cello*); practiced for a performance (*rehearsed*); careless mistakes (*blunders*). When students misread a word and then self-correct, encourage them by saying, for example, **You read ___ and then changed it to ___. Why? How did you know you needed to do that?**

VOCABULARY DEFINED

blunders careless or clumsy mistakes

cello a musical instrument similar to a violin, but much larger and with a lower, deeper tone

flatter to tell someone he or she is more attractive or talented than is actually the case

patient (adj.) able to endure delays without complaints or anger

pianist a person who is skilled at playing the piano

rehearsed practiced to get ready for a performance

Discuss the meanings of the vocabulary words. Then ask students to invent a story using each of the vocabulary words. Have each student add a sentence to build the story. (You may want to begin the story with this sentence: *The orchestra <u>rehearsed</u> every night before the concert.*) Continue until all the vocabulary words have been used at least once and each student has had an opportunity to respond.

Check understanding.

Ask students to write the vocabulary words on a sheet of paper. Have them name the word that answers each of the following riddles and circle that word on their papers.

- **You can use this word to describe a person who can wait in a very long line without getting upset.** *(patient)*
- **I mean "to tell people they have more talent than they really have."** *(flatter)*
- **I am what the musicians did before they gave a concert.** *(rehearsed)*
- **I play a musical instrument that has many black keys and many white keys.** *(pianist)*
- **I am a musical instrument that is like a huge violin.** *(cello)*
- **You might feel foolish after making these.** *(blunders)*

REPRODUCIBLE STUDENT ACTIVITY PAGE

INDEPENDENT PRACTICE See the reproducible Student Activity on page 17.

NOTE: The following vocabulary words from "Yang the Third and Her Impossible Family" are reinforced in "The Audition." If students are unfamiliar with these words, you may wish to point them out as you encounter them during reading: *audition* (p. 22); *accompanist, simultaneously, sonata, grimaced, accompaniment* (p. 25).

Name ______________________________

The Audition

Read the story. Then fill in the web. Use all the words in dark type in your answers.

Jean plays the **cello**. She hopes to get into the band. She has **rehearsed** her waltz over and over. Now at the hall, she gets set to play. Jean looks at all the kids who hope to get into the band. Chad has his trumpet in hand. Jan is setting up her drums. Then Jean sees Aldo with his cello. This is a problem! The band needs just one cello!

Miss Small, the band's leader, enters the hall at ten. Miss Small asks Aldo to play first. She asks the rest of the kids to sit still and be **patient**. The **pianist** will play with Aldo. Jean will be next to play. She hopes she will not make **blunders**. Still, she will not **flatter** herself that she plays the cello better than Aldo. Aldo and the pianist start to play. The notes of the tune fill the hall.

Whom she saw at the hall

Chad, Jan, Aldo, Miss Small, pianist

What instruments she saw

cello, trumpet, drums

Jean

What she did and needs to do to get into the band

rehearsed; be patient, not make blunders, not flatter herself

How do you think Jean will do when it's time to play the waltz?

Answers will vary.

Harcourt

Directed Reading

Page 22 Ask a volunteer to read the title of the story. Help students identify Jean and the pianist. Have them read page 22 to find out who else is at the audition. (*Chad, Jan, other kids*) Ask: **Why do you think Jean thinks, "Oh no!" when she sees Aldo and his cello?** (Possible response: *Jean also plays the cello, and she is afraid that Aldo might play better than she does.*) CRITICAL: INTERPRET CHARACTERS' MOTIVATIONS

Page 23 Have students read page 23 to find out why Jean is worried about Aldo. Ask: **How many cello players does the band need?** (*one*) LITERAL: NOTE DETAILS **How does Jean feel about her ability to play the cello?** (*She doesn't think that she plays very well, but she still hopes she can win the audition.*) INFERENTIAL: DETERMINE CHARACTERS' EMOTIONS

Pages 24–25 Have students look at the illustration on page 24 and 25. Ask which student they think gets to play first. (*I see Aldo on the stage, so I think Aldo gets to play first.*) Then have students read the page. Ask them what they think happens during Aldo's audition. (Possible response: *It looks as though one of his cello strings is broken, so perhaps Aldo doesn't get to finish his audition.*) INFERENTIAL: MAKE PREDICTIONS/SYNTHESIZE

Page 25 Have students read page 25 to find out what happens during Aldo's audition. Ask: **How do you think Aldo feels when his string breaks?** (Possible responses: *He feels mad, disappointed, and upset.*) INFERENTIAL: DETERMINE CHARACTERS' EMOTIONS **Why?** (Possible response: *I know that I'd be disappointed if I practiced a lot and then my instrument broke on the day of an audition.*) CRITICAL: SUPPORT INTERPRETATIONS

Page 26 After students read page 26, ask: **What happens to Aldo after his string breaks?** (Possible response: *He has to stop playing because he doesn't have a spare string.*) INFERENTIAL: CAUSE-EFFECT **How does Jean feel when she first realizes that Aldo cannot finish his audition?** (Possible response: *She is glad because now she has a better chance of winning the audition.*) INFERENTIAL: DETERMINE CHARACTERS' EMOTIONS **Jean stops to think about what has happened. What does this reaction tell you about her?** (Possible response: *She wants what is best for the band.*) INFERENTIAL: DETERMINE CHARACTERS' TRAITS

Page 27 Have students read page 27 to find out what Jean decides to do next. (*She offers her cello to Aldo so he can finish his audition.*) LITERAL: NOTE DETAILS Ask: **Why do you think Jean feels she has won something, too?** (Possible response: *She knows she has done the right thing by not acting selfishly.*) CRITICAL: INTERPRET CHARACTERS' MOTIVATIONS

SUMMARIZE THE SELECTION Ask students to think about what happened first, next, and last at the audition. Then have them summarize the story.

Page 28

Answers to Think About It Questions

1. A string on his cello has broken. He can't play the sonata. SUMMARY
2. Jean feels she has won the audition because Aldo can't play anymore. At the end, she feels she has won because she has helped Aldo. INTERPRETATION
3. Accept reasonable responses. Compositions should include dialogue in which Aldo thanks Jean for her help. WRITE AN ENDING

Page 29 For instruction on the Focus Skill: Vocabulary in Context, see page 29 in *Timeless Tales*.

Name ______________________

REPRODUCIBLE STUDENT ACTIVITY PAGE

The Audition

Write a sentence in each box below to help you summarize "The Audition." Be sure to write the events in the correct order.

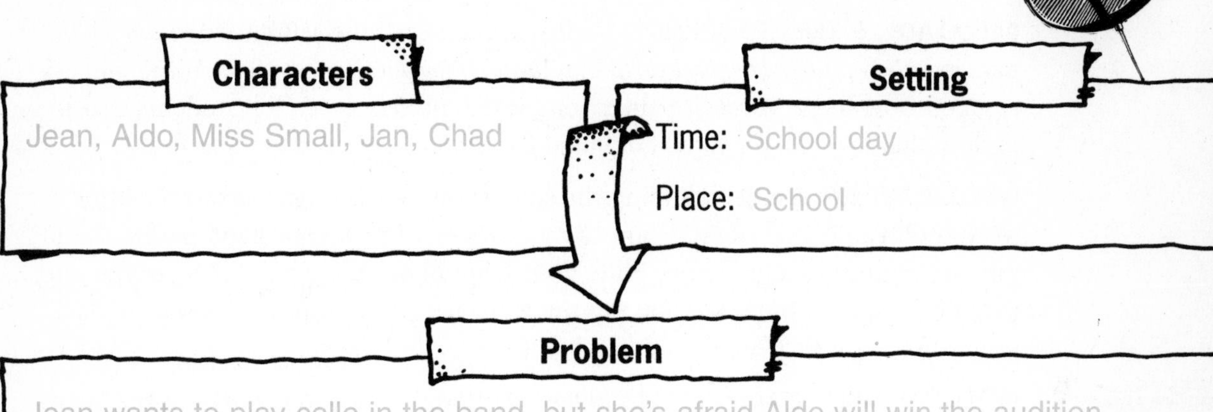

Characters

Jean, Aldo, Miss Small, Jan, Chad

Setting

Time: School day

Place: School

Problem

Jean wants to play cello in the band, but she's afraid Aldo will win the audition.

Important Events

1. Jean waits to audition.
2. Aldo plays his cello first.
3. His string breaks.
4. Jean offers to let him finish with her cello.

Solution

Jean realizes that she did the right thing, even if she doesn't win the audition.

Now write a one-sentence summary of the story.

After Aldo breaks a string on his cello, Jean lets him use her cello to finish the audition, even though it means she may not get a place in the band.

Harcourt

Lessons from Barbara Jordan

by Kana Riley **Use with *Timeless Tales*, pages 30–37.**

Preteaching Skills: *R*-controlled Vowel /är/*ar*

Teach/Model

IDENTIFY THE SOUND Have students repeat the following sentence aloud three times: *You can see the stars sparkle from the dark backyard.* Ask students which words have the /är/ sound. (*stars, sparkle, dark, backyard*)

ASSOCIATE LETTERS TO SOUNDS Write on the board the sentence *You can see the stars sparkle from the dark backyard.* Circle *stars*, *sparkle*, *dark*, and *backyard*, and ask students how these words are alike. (*/är/ sound; the letters* ar) Tell students that in each of these words, the letters *ar* stand for the /är/ sound they hear in *car.*

WORD BLENDING Model blending the sounds of the letters in *stars* to read the word. Point to *s* and say /s/. Point to *t* and say /t/. Draw your hand under *ar* and say /är/. Point to *s* and say /s/. Slide your hand under the entire word as you elongate the sounds /ssttärzz/. Then say the word naturally—*stars.* Follow a similar procedure with *sparkle*, *dark*, and *backyard.*

Practice/Apply

APPLY THE SKILL ***Consonant Substitution*** Write the following words on the board, and have students read each aloud. Make the changes necessary to form the words in parentheses. Have students read each new word aloud. Try to give every student an opportunity to respond.

mat (mark)	can (card)	dash (dart)	standing (starting)
bat (bar)	chat (charm)	past (part)	span (spark)

DICTATION AND WRITING Have students number a paper 1–8. Dictate the following words, and have students write them. After they write each word, display it so students can proofread their work. They should draw a line through a misspelled word and write the correct spelling beside it.

1. charm	2. sharp	3. start*	4. smart*
5. park	6. artist	7. startle	8. varnish

**Word appears in "Lessons from Barbara Jordan."*

Dictate the following sentence: *Farmer Clark drove his car to the barn.*

READ LONGER WORDS ***Introduce Syllables; Introduce Breaking Words with VCCV*** Explain that a *syllable* is a word part that can be said by itself and that every syllable has one vowel sound. Clap your hands once as you say *car.* Explain that this word has one syllable. Then clap your hands twice as you say *carpet.* Explain that this word has two syllables, *car* and *pet.* Say these words: *mar, market, tarnish, tar, star, starling.* Have students clap once after each one-syllable word and twice after each two-syllable word. Then write *carpet* on the board. Have students identify two consonants next to each other. (*r, p*) Draw a line between *r* and *p*, and tell students that two-syllable words that have this pattern are usually divided in between the two consonants that are next to each other. Frame *car* in *carpet*, and ask a volunteer to read it. Repeat with the remaining part *pet.* Then draw your hand under the entire word as students read it.

Follow a similar procedure with the words *market*, *tarnish*, and *starling.* Ask students to read each word and explain how they were able to figure it out.

REPRODUCIBLE STUDENT ACTIVITY PAGE

INDEPENDENT PRACTICE See the reproducible Student Activity on page 21.

Name ______________________

REPRODUCIBLE STUDENT ACTIVITY PAGE

Lessons from Barbara Jordan

Write the word that answers each riddle.

1. I have the *ar* sound you hear in *part*.
   I am driven along streets. What am I? car 
   cart plane car

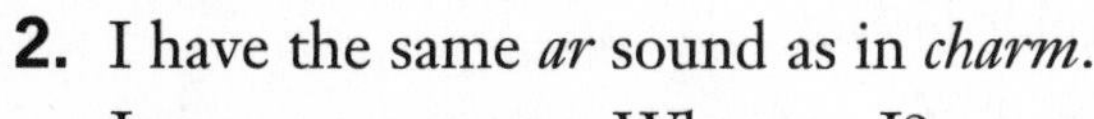

2. I have the same *ar* sound as in *charm*.
   I am a sweet treat. What am I? tart
   tarp tart cake

3. I have the same *ar* sound as in *card*.
   I am a fish. What am I? shark
   shark sharp cod

4. I have the *ar* sound you hear in *harp*.
   I am made of glass and I have a lid. What am I? jar
   glass jar cart

5. I have the same *ar* sound as in *yarn*.
   I shine in the dark. What am I? star
   star mark moon

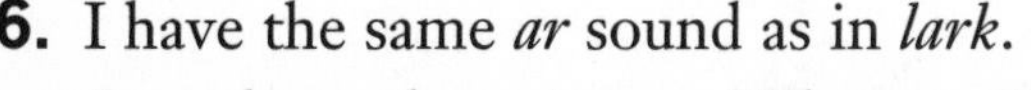

6. I have the same *ar* sound as in *lark*.
   I can keep sheep in me. What am I? barn 
   pen barn bark

7. I have the same *ar* sound as in *tar*.
   I am not close to you. What am I? far
   far mark fast

8. I have the same *ar* sound as in *harm*.
   I am what you do when you stop a car and get out.
   What am I? park
   jump start park

9. I have the same *ar* sound as in *spark*.
   You can toss me at a target. What am I? dart 
   chart dart ball

10. I have the *ar* sound you hear in *smart*.
    You shop for milk and eggs in me. What am I? market
    parsnip market snack

Harcourt

Introducing Vocabulary

Apply word identification strategies.

LOOK FOR FAMILIAR SPELLING PATTERNS Display the vocabulary words, and ask students to identify the ones they know. Remind them that they can sometimes figure out unfamiliar words by looking for familiar spelling patterns. Point out the CVC pattern in the first syllables of *confidence* and *sacrifices.* Call on volunteers to read the words aloud and tell how they were able to figure them out. (*When a vowel is between two consonants, the vowel usually has the short vowel sound.*) Then help students read aloud the other words. If necessary, provide clues: someone's main work during his or her lifetime (*career*); all people (*humanity*); people who are the same age or in the same grade (*peers*); new inventions that help people in some way (*technology*). Sometimes, when students read a word correctly, encourage them by saying, for example, **That's right. Look at the word again. How did you know that was the word?**

VOCABULARY DEFINED

career a person's life work; a profession

confidence trust in oneself and one's abilities

humanity the human race in general; humankind

mail letters or packages from one person to another

peers people who are equals in age, ability, background, or achievements

sacrifices things of value that are given up for a special reason

technology complex inventions that can be used to solve problems

Discuss the meanings of the vocabulary words. Then ask students to use the vocabulary words in sentences describing a job or life work that they find interesting. (Possible response: *I am interested in a <u>career</u> working with animals.*) Continue until all the vocabulary words have been used at least once.

Check understanding.

Ask students to write the vocabulary words on a sheet of paper. Then ask each of the following questions. Have students name the word that best answers the question and circle that word on their papers.

- **Which word describes what you make when you give up or go without things?** *(sacrifices)*
- **Which word can be used to describe all humans?** *(humanity)*
- **Which word has to do with inventions?** *(technology)*
- **Which word names a person's life work?** *(career)*
- **Who are the people who are equal to you in some way?** *(peers)*
- **Which word names a quality that can help you succeed?** *(confidence)*
- **Which word can be used to describe greeting cards sent from one person to another?** *(mail)*

REPRODUCIBLE STUDENT ACTIVITY PAGE

INDEPENDENT PRACTICE See the reproducible Student Activity on page 23.

NOTE: The following vocabulary words from "Dear Mrs. Parks" are reinforced in "Lessons from Barbara Jordan." If students are unfamiliar with these words, point them out as you encounter them during reading: *dignity, correspondence* (p. 31); *ridiculed, counseled* (p. 33); *mentor, inspire, potential* (p. 35).

Name ______________________________

REPRODUCIBLE STUDENT ACTIVITY PAGE

Lessons from Barbara Jordan

You are about to read a story titled "Lessons from Barbara Jordan." Read the story fact sheet.

Who is in the story:
a girl named Jane Barr;
Jane's grandma,
Wilma Downs

How the story is told:
in electronic **mail** sent between Jane and her grandma

What the story is about:
Jane has to tell her class about Barbara Jordan. Jane's grandma met Barbara Jordan one time. Jane's grandma uses **technology** to send Jane facts about Barbara Jordan's life. These are some of the facts that Jane finds out:

Barbara Jordan had a **career** in the U.S. Congress and in teaching.
Barbara Jordan was smart and had a lot of **confidence**.
Her **peers** admired her.
She called for all to make small **sacrifices** that could help **humanity**.

Now answer these questions. Use each word in dark type one time.

1. How do Jane and her grandma send each other notes about Barbara Jordan? They use technology and electronic mail to send the notes.

2. What did Barbara Jordan do with her life? She had a career in the U.S. Congress and in teaching.

3. Who admired Barbara Jordan? Her peers admired her.

4. What was Barbara Jordan like? She was smart and had a lot of confidence.

5. What did Barbara Jordan want all of us to do? She called for all of us to make sacrifices to help humanity.

6. Do you think Jane's class will like her speech about Barbara Jordan? Why?
Answers will vary.

Harcourt

Directed Reading

Page 30 Ask a volunteer to read the title of the story. Explain that the illustration shows Jane Barr using a laptop computer to write an e-mail message. Make sure students understand that the words on the page are the message that Jane has written. Have them read page 30. Ask: **What does Jane ask for?** (*She asks her grandma what Barbara Jordan was like.*) LITERAL: NOTE DETAILS **Why would Jane's grandma know anything about Barbara Jordan?** (*She met her once.*) INFERENTIAL: CAUSE-EFFECT

Page 31 Have students read page 31 to find out what Grandma says in her reply to Jane's message. Ask: **Why was Grandma inspired by meeting Barbara Jordan?** (*Barbara Jordan was a smart woman with a lot of dignity and confidence.*) INFERENTIAL: MAIN IDEA

Page 32 Have students look at the picture on page 32. Ask who they think the picture is of. (*Barbara Jordan*) Have them read page 32 to find out what Jane's mother tells her about Barbara Jordan. (*She sat in Congress.*) INFERENTIAL: IMPORTANT DETAILS

Page 33 Have students read page 33 to find out how Barbara Jordan got her start. Ask: **Why was it unusual for Barbara Jordan to be in the Texas Senate?** (*At the time, it was rare for African Americans to be in Texas's state senate.*) CRITICAL: INTERPRET STORY EVENTS **How did Barbara Jordan's life change after she was elected to the U.S. Congress for the third time?** (Possible responses: *She got sick, moved back to Texas, and went into teaching.*) INFERENTIAL: SEQUENCE/SUMMARIZE

Page 34 After students read page 34, ask: **Was Jane successful in gathering information about Barbara Jordan by using technology? Why or why not?** (Possible response: *She was very successful because she got facts in e-mails from her grandma and she found pictures and other facts by using the Web.*) CRITICAL: INTERPRET STORY EVENTS

Page 35 Have students read page 35 to find out how Grandma feels about Barbara Jordan's life and why she feels that way. (*She admires Barbara Jordan's life because Barbara Jordan inspired people to tell the truth, keep their promises, and help others.*) INFERENTIAL: SUMMARIZE/DETERMINE CHARACTERS' EMOTIONS Ask: **What does Grandma hope Jane will do?** (*be like Barbara Jordan and make small sacrifices to help humanity*) INFERENTIAL: DETERMINE THEME

Page 36 Have students read page 36 to find out whether Jane's talk was a success. Ask: **Was Jane's talk a success? How do you know?** (*It was a success because the essay shows an A+, and she tells Grandma that the class liked the talk.*) METACOGNITIVE: MAKE JUDGMENTS

SUMMARIZE THE SELECTION Have students write two sentences to summarize *how* Jane learned about Barbara Jordan.

Page 37

Answers to Think About It Questions

1. Jane's grandma once met Barbara Jordan, so she can tell Jane what Jordan was like. Jane needs more facts about Jordan's life, so she looks up Jordan on the Web. SUMMARY
2. Possible response: Barbara Jordan was smart, confident, and inspiring. INTERPRETATION
3. E-mails should follow the format used in the selection; they should express thanks and describe the interested responses of other students. WRITE AN E-MAIL

Name ____________________

REPRODUCIBLE STUDENT ACTIVITY PAGE

Lessons from Barbara Jordan

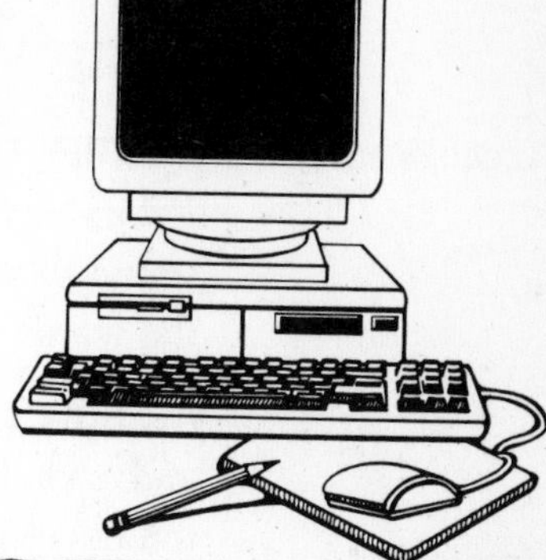

Write one sentence in each box below to summarize the ideas presented on those pages about Barbara Jordan.

Pages 30–31

Main Idea: Possible response: Jane writes to Grandma and asks her about Barbara Jordan.

Pages 32–33

Main Idea: Possible response: Jane finds out that Barbara Jordan started her career in the Texas Senate, was elected to Congress three times, and was a teacher.

Pages 34–35

Main Idea: Jane's grandma encourages her to follow Barbara Jordan's example.

Harcourt

Now write a one-sentence summary of the selection.

Possible response: Jane learns about Barbara Jordan.

That Day Last Week

by Lisa Eisenberg **Use with *Timeless Tales*, pages 38–45.**

Preteaching Skills: Short Vowel /a/*a*; Long Vowel /ā/*ai, ay*

Teach/Model

IDENTIFY THE SOUND Have students repeat the following sentence aloud three times: *Pat wishes to catch the midday train.* Ask them to identify the words that have the /a/ sound they hear in *map.* (*Pat, catch*) Then have students repeat the sentence and name the words with the /ā/ sound they hear in *made.* (*midday, train*)

ASSOCIATE LETTERS TO SOUNDS Write on the board the sentence above. Circle *Pat* and *catch.* Remind students that words that have this pattern of letters, a single vowel in between consonants, usually have a short vowel sound. Have students read each word aloud. Then underline *ay* in *midday.* Point out that in this word, the letters *ay* stand for the /ā/ sound. Underline *ai* in *train,* and tell students that the letters *ai* also can stand for the long *a* sound. Circle *wants,* and tell students that when *a* follows *w,* it usually has the /ô/ sound heard in *wants.* Write *water* and *swan* on the board, read them aloud, and have students repeat them.

WORD BLENDING Write *train* on the board, and then model how to blend and read it. Touch *t* and say /t/. Touch *r* and say /r/. Draw your hand under *ai* and say /ā/. Touch *n* and say /n/. Slide your hand under the whole word as you elongate all the sounds /ttrrāānn/. Then read the word naturally—*train.* Follow a similar procedure with *snail, stay,* and *grab.*

Practice/Apply

APPLY THE SKILL ***Letter Substitution*** Write the following words on the board, and have students read each aloud. Make the changes necessary to form the words in parentheses. Have students read each new word aloud.

hay (hat)	bran (brain)	clay (clap)	stay (stand)
man (main)	pal (pail)	tray (trap)	clam (claim)

DICTATION AND WRITING Have students number a sheet of paper 1–8. Dictate words 1–2, and have students write them. After students write each word, display it so students can proofread their work. Then write *stay* on the board and tell students that in the next three words you will say, the letters *ay* stand for the long *a* sound. Dictate words 3–5, and have students proofread as before. After that, write *pain* on the board and tell students that in the next three words you will say, the letters *ai* stand for the long *a* sound. Dictate words 6–8 and have students proofread as before.

1. last*	2. crash*	3. day*	4. okay*
5. way*	6. strain	7. waited*	8. brain*

**Word appears in "That Day Last Week."*

READ LONGER WORDS ***Review Breaking Words with VCCV*** Write the word *cascade* on the board. Have students identify two consonants next to each other. (*s, c*) Remind students that two-syllable words that have this pattern are usually divided in between the two consonants that are next to each other. Frame *cas* and ask a student to read it. Frame *cade* and ask a student to read it. Then slide your hand under the entire word as students say it aloud. Follow a similar procedure with the words *maintain, payday, happen,* and *mailbag.*

REPRODUCIBLE STUDENT ACTIVITY PAGE

INDEPENDENT PRACTICE See the reproducible Student Activity on page 27.

Name ______________________________

REPRODUCIBLE STUDENT ACTIVITY PAGE

That Day Last Week

Read the story. Then choose the best answer for each question. Mark the letter for that answer.

Clayton looked down the tracks for the midday train. It was always late. As he waited, he started daydreaming about Spain. He was traveling there next week with his wife, Gail.

"Please," said a man who had a little kid with him, interrupting his daydream, "where can we catch the train to Main Street?"

"You can stay here with me. I'm catching that train, too," Clayton responded.

"Good," said the man. Then the man spoke to the kid in Spanish.

Clayton said, "Excuse me for asking, but are you from Spain?"

"Yes, I am!" the man said. He looked puzzled.

"Let me explain," said Clayton. "My wife and I are visiting Spain next week. We are very pleased to be going. The trip is always on my brain!"

The man smiled. "Spain is hot this time of year," he said. "What are your travel plans?"

"We hope to visit some of the historical landmarks, go sailing on the sea, and play in the sun. It will be fantastic!"

1 What was Clayton looking for?
- **A** the midday bus
- **B** a cab on Main Street
- **C** the evening train
- **D** the midday train

2 What did he do while he waited?
- **F** He daydreamed about his trip.
- **G** He clapped his hands.
- **H** He played a game.
- **J** He filed his nails.

3 What are Clayton and Gail going to do?
- **A** wait for rain
- **B** travel to Spain
- **C** sail to Paris
- **D** pay for pancakes

4 The man from Spain
- **F** started daydreaming, too.
- **G** asked Clayton about the mail.
- **H** spoke in Spanish.
- **J** was afraid of cats.

5 What was the man looking for?
- **A** a cab to Main Street
- **B** a bag of grain
- **C** the train Clayton was waiting for
- **D** a needle in a haystack

6 Why did Clayton ask the man if he was from Spain?
- **F** He wanted to explain why the train was late.
- **G** The man spoke in Spanish.
- **H** He wanted to say a joke.
- **J** The man had paid for his Spanish lessons.

Harcourt

Introducing Vocabulary

Apply word identification strategies.

LOOK FOR FAMILIAR SPELLING PATTERNS Display the vocabulary words, and ask students to identify the ones they know. Remind students that they can sometimes figure out a new word by looking for familiar spelling patterns. Point out the CVC pattern in the first syllable of *helmet.* Call on volunteers to read that word aloud and tell how they were able to figure it out. (*A vowel between two consonants usually has the short sound.*) Help students read the remaining vocabulary words aloud, providing clues as necessary: a regular set of actions (*routine*); a return to good health (*recovery*); things remembered (*memories*); ability to make choices and decisions (*judgment*); means "a lack of belief" (*disbelief*). When students self-correct, encourage them by saying, **You read ____ and then changed it to ____. How did you know which word was right?**

VOCABULARY DEFINED

disbelief unwillingness to believe

helmet a protective head covering

judgment the ability to make decisions

memories thoughts about the past

recovery the process of a sick or injured person becoming well again

routine a set of actions done regularly

Discuss the meanings of the vocabulary words. Then ask students to create sentences containing one or more of those words. (Possible response: *I use my judgment to make good decisions.*) Continue until all the vocabulary words have been used at least once and each student has had an opportunity to respond.

Check understanding.

Tell students to write the vocabulary words on a sheet of paper. Ask them to name the word that answers each of the following questions and to circle that word on their papers.

- **Which word best completes this sentence? *I wish you a speedy ____ from the flu.*** *(recovery)*
- **Which word names what you feel when you don't believe something?** *(disbelief)*
- **Which word describes things you do every day?** *(routine)*
- **Which word names what you use when you make decisions?** *(judgment)*
- **Which word names something you wear to protect your head?** *(helmet)*
- **Which word is related to the word *remember*?** *(memories)*

REPRODUCIBLE STUDENT ACTIVITY PAGE

INDEPENDENT PRACTICE See the reproducible Student Activity on page 29.

NOTE: The following vocabulary words from "Mick Harte Was Here" are reinforced in "That Day Last Week." If students are unfamiliar with these words, point them out as you encounter them during reading: *impact, reaction* (p. 41); *anticipation, perspective* (p. 43); *sponsor, podium* (p. 44).

Name ______________________________

That Day Last Week

These sentences are about "That Day Last Week." Write the word from the box that makes sense in each sentence.

helmet	judgment	memories	recovery	routine	disbelief

1. I put on my ____helmet____ to ride over to Mike's home.

2. When I ride my bike, putting on a helmet is always a part of my ____routine____.

3. When Mike looked at my helmet, he asked me in ____disbelief____ if I planned to keep it on.

4. If I had used better ____judgment____, I could have said, "I'm not riding with you unless you put on a helmet, too."

5. I didn't want to have bad ____memories____ of that day.

6. The ____recovery____ from a bonk on the brain can be long and painful.

Answer these questions to tell what you think might happen in "That Day Last Week."

7. What do you think will happen when Andy and Mike go bike riding?

Responses will vary.

8. How do you think Andy will feel if Mike crashes with no helmet on?

Responses will vary.

9. What do you think Mike will find out about staying safe on a bike?

Responses will vary.

Harcourt

Directed Reading

Pages 38–39 Ask a volunteer to read the story title. Help students identify Andy (*wearing a helmet*) and Mike. Read page 39 aloud to students. Have them listen to find out what Mike and Andy say to each other. Ask: **Why is Andy wearing a bike helmet?** (*He doesn't want to scramble his brain if he falls.*) INFERENTIAL: CAUSE-EFFECT **Does Mike think wearing a helmet is important? How do you know?** (Possible response: *No; he looks at Andy's helmet in disbelief and asks him if he's going to keep it on all day.*) METACOGNITIVE: DRAW CONCLUSIONS

Pages 40–41 Ask students to describe what is happening in the illustration. Then have them read page 41 to find out what happens next. Ask: **What two things did Andy hear?** (*He heard Mike yell, and then he heard a crash.*) INFERENTIAL: IMPORTANT DETAILS **What happened to Mike?** (*He crashed his bike.*) INFERENTIAL: DRAW CONCLUSIONS **What caused the crash?** (*Mike rode out in front of a car, and the driver didn't see him.*) INFERENTIAL: CAUSE-EFFECT **Do you think Mike is badly injured? How do you know?** (Possible response: *Yes; he is lying flat on his back, and the woman said he landed with a hard impact.*) METACOGNITIVE: DRAW CONCLUSIONS

Pages 42–43 Help students identify Andy's mom in the illustration. Then have them read page 43 to find out what Andy is doing. (*He is waiting for news about Mike.*) INFERENTIAL: IMPORTANT DETAILS Ask: **How does Andy feel? How do you know?** (Possible response: *Andy is worried. He looks worried, and he jumps every time the phone rings.*) INFERENTIAL: DETERMINE CHARACTERS' EMOTIONS **Who does Andy's mom think is responsible for the accident? How do you know?** (*Mike; she tells Andy that he couldn't make Mike wear a helmet and that Mike's judgment was bad.*) INFERENTIAL: DRAW CONCLUSIONS **How does Mike feel about helmets now?** (Possible response: *He thinks it is important to wear one.*) INFERENTIAL: SYNTHESIZE

Page 44 Have students read page 44 to find out how the story ends. Ask: **What else does Mike tell Andy about?** (*that he and Mr. Gray are starting a bike club and that Mike will be telling other kids about his accident*) LITERAL: SUMMARIZE **Why do you think Mr. Gray wants Mike to tell his story?** (Possible response: *to convince other kids to wear a helmet, too*) CRITICAL: INTERPRET CHARACTERS' MOTIVATIONS

SUMMARIZE THE SELECTION Ask students to think about what happened before, during, and after Mike's accident. Then have them summarize the story in two or three sentences.

Page 45

Answers to Think About It Questions

1. Possible response: When Mike crashed his bike, he wouldn't have been hurt as badly. SUMMARY
2. Possible response: Andy doesn't want his pal to get mad at him or make fun of him. INTERPRETATION
3. Speeches should briefly recount Mike's bike accident from his point of view and stress the importance of wearing a helmet while biking. WRITE A SPEECH

Name ______________________

REPRODUCIBLE STUDENT ACTIVITY PAGE

That Day Last Week

Complete the sequence chart about "That Day Last Week." Write a sentence in each box.

Event 1:

Andy puts on a helmet to go bike riding with Mike.

Event 2:

Possible response: Mike doesn't put on a helmet.

Event 3:

Possible response: Mike crashes his bike into a car and gets hurt.

Event 4:

Possible response: Andy wishes he had made Mike put on a helmet.

Event 5:

Possible response: Andy's mom tells him that he couldn't make Mike put on his helmet.

Event 6:

Possible response: Mike decides he will wear a helmet and tell other kids about what happened.

Now use the information from the boxes to write a one-sentence summary of the selection.

Possible response: Mike learns that he should wear a helmet after he crashes his bike into a car and almost gets killed.

Harcourt

The Pirate Hero

by David Lopez **Use with *Timeless Tales*, pages 46–53.**

Preteaching Skills: Long Vowel /ō/*oa*

Teach/Model

IDENTIFY THE SOUND Have students repeat the following sentence aloud twice: *Bob could not get his boat to float.* Have them identify the words with the /o/ sound they hear in *flock.* (*Bob, not*) Then have them identify the words that have the /ō/ sound they hear in *goat.* (*boat, float*)

ASSOCIATE LETTERS TO SOUNDS Write on the board the sentence above. Underline the *o* in *not*, and remind students that words that have this pattern usually have a short vowel sound. Ask students to identify another word in the sentence that has this pattern. (*Bob*) Next, underline the letters *oa* in *boat.* Tell students that the letters *oa* stand for the long *o* sound. Remind students that when two vowels come together in between consonants, they usually stand for a long vowel sound. Read the entire sentence aloud as you point to each word.

WORD BLENDING Model how to blend and read the word *croak.* Point to *c* and say /k/. Touch *r* and say /r/. Touch *oa* and say /ō/. Touch *k* and say /k/. Slide your hand under all the letters as you elongate the sounds /ccrrōōkk/. Then read the word naturally—*croak.* Repeat the procedure with *coach* and *throat.*

Practice/Apply

APPLY THE SKILL ***Letter Substitution*** Write the following words on the board, and have students read each aloud. Make the changes necessary to form the word in parentheses. Have a student read each new word aloud. Try to give each student an opportunity to respond.

bond (boat)	got (goat)	boss (boast)	rot (roam)
sock (soak)	top (toad)	clock (cloak)	toss (toast)

DICTATION AND WRITING Have students number a sheet of paper 1–8. Tell them that in every word you will say that has the long *o* sound, the vowel sound is spelled *oa.* Then dictate the following words, and have students write them. After they write each word, display the correct spelling so students can proofread their work. Have them draw a line through a misspelled word and write the correct spelling beside it.

1. boat	2. boast*	3. toasted	4. roam
5. throat	6. groan	7. moaning	8. coal

**Word appears in "The Pirate Hero."*

Dictate the following sentence for students to write: *We made toast over hot coals.*

READ LONGER WORDS ***Review Compound Words*** Write the word *tugboat* on the board. Remind students that when they see a longer word, they can look to see if it is made up of two shorter words. Ask students which part of the word sounds like /tug/ and which part sounds like /boat/. Have students blend the word parts together to form the longer word *tugboat.* Repeat the procedure with *boatneck, coachman,* and *roadside.*

REPRODUCIBLE STUDENT ACTIVITY PAGE

INDEPENDENT PRACTICE See the reproducible Student Activity on page 33.

Name ___________________________

REPRODUCIBLE STUDENT ACTIVITY PAGE

The Pirate Hero

Read the story. Circle all the words that have the short *o* sound. Draw a line under all the words that have the long *o* sound.

Rob, Kim, and Joan went camping near a lake. Joan steered the boat into the bank with confidence. Rob jumped out and tugged the boat up onto the rocks. "What a float !" Joan said as she got out. Wind had whipped up the waves on the lake. Her pant legs were wet. Her socks were soaked.

"Let's unload this stuff," Kim said. Rob grabbed the sleeping bags and pitched them up onto the bank. Then he grabbed his rod and reel.

"I'll catch a fine fish!" he boasted. "We can roast it on some coals." Then off he went. Kim moaned. She did not care much for ordinary lake fish. But Joan had said that one must make sacrifices when camping.

"Well, fish it is," Kim said. "I'll put my coat on and get some sticks." Joan helped her. They made a hot blaze. Rob came back in a bit. He held a line of gleaming fish. They roasted the fish on a grate on the coals. They made hot toast to have with it. Then they ate. Kim said with surprise, "This is the best fish I've ever had, Rob! Thanks!"

Now write the long *o* word or the short *o* word that best completes each sentence.

1. Joan said that one must make sacrifices when camping.
2. Joan, Rob, and Kim got to the camping spot in a boat.
3. Joan's pants and socks got wet on the trip.
4. Wind-whipped waves had soaked her.
5. Rob grabbed his fishing rod when they got to the site.
6. He boasted that he'd catch some fine fish.
7. Kim groaned at the prospect of eating lake fish.
8. They roasted the fish.

Harcourt

Introducing Vocabulary

Apply word identification strategies.

LOOK FOR FAMILIAR SPELLING PATTERNS Display the vocabulary words, and ask students to identify the ones they know. Point out the CVC pattern in the first syllable of *promise*. Frame the first syllable, and have students read it aloud. Then uncover the rest of the word, and have students try pronouncing the second syllable with both the long *i* and the short *i* sound to find out which pronunciation results in a word they know.

Then have students identify the two smaller words within the compound word *billboard*. Help them read aloud the other words. Use clues as necessary: something you wear (*uniform*); rhymes with *steeple* (*people*); you can make this out of marble (*statue*); someone you admire (*hero*). As students read a word correctly, encourage them by saying, **That's right. Look at the word again. How did you figure out that was the word?** Discuss the meanings of the vocabulary words. Then ask students to make up riddles that have the vocabulary words as answers.

VOCABULARY DEFINED

billboard a large sign in a public place

hero a person who wins the respect of others through good deeds or great achievements

people more than one person

promise a guarantee made to oneself or others

statue a three-dimensional likeness of a person, place, thing, or animal

uniform an outfit that identifies the wearer as a member of a team or profession

Check understanding.

Ask students to write the vocabulary words on a sheet of paper. Then ask the following questions. Have students name the word that best answers each question and circle it on their papers.

- **What might you see advertising a product next to a highway?** *(billboard)*
- **What might a sculptor make?** *(statue)*
- **Which word names more than one person?** *(people)*
- **What do most police officers wear?** *(uniform)*
- **Which word names a person who has won respect for his or her achievements?** *(hero)*
- **Which word means "a pledge to do something"?** *(promise)*

Provide vocabulary support.

Students may have difficulty with names such as Roberto Clemente, Pittsburgh Pirates, and Baltimore Orioles (p. 46). Introduce the names by writing them on the board and pronouncing each one. As students come across these names in the selection, offer assistance as needed.

REPRODUCIBLE STUDENT ACTIVITY PAGE

INDEPENDENT PRACTICE See the reproducible Student Activity on page 35.

NOTE: The following vocabulary words from "We'll Never Forget You, Roberto Clemente" are reinforced in "The Pirate Hero." If students are unfamiliar with these words, point them out as you encounter them during reading: *ace*, *lineup*, *error* (p. 47); *artificial* (p. 50); *control tower*, *dedicated* (p. 51).

Name ______________________

REPRODUCIBLE STUDENT ACTIVITY PAGE

The Pirate Hero

Read each sentence. Write the word from the box that makes sense in the sentence.

people	billboard	hero	promise	statue	uniform

Roberto Clemente was a baseball star. He was also a fine man. His baseball career and the sacrifices he made for people made Clemente a hero.	Clemente made a promise to his fans. He said he'd play as hard and as well as he could.	In 1971 Clemente led the Pittsburgh Pirates to a top spot in baseball. Some people had said that the Pirates could not beat the Orioles.
Games 1 and 2 were in Baltimore. The billboard at the baseball park said "Home of the Orioles." The Pirates lost games 1 and 2.	The next two games were played back in Pittsburgh. The Pirates did win games 3 and 4. The team was led by Clemente, the man with the number 21 on his uniform.	Clemente's life ended in a sad and sudden way. Today there is a statue of him in Pittsburgh. People will not forget him.

Answer these questions to tell what you think you might find out as you read "The Pirate Hero."

1. How do you think Roberto Clemente helped people when he was not playing baseball?

Answers will vary.

2. What facts do you think you will find out about Clemente as you read?

Answers will vary.

Harcourt

Directed Reading

Page 46 Read aloud the title of the story. Then have students view the illustration on page 46. Ask them to identify the setting (*a baseball game*) and point out Roberto Clemente. Explain that Roberto Clemente was a real baseball player. Have students read page 46 to find out what is important about the baseball game shown in the illustration. (*The team that wins this set of games will be the best team in baseball.*) Ask: **What is Roberto Clemente's vow?** (*He promises himself that he will play hard for the Pirates.*) LITERAL: MAIN IDEA

Page 47 Have students read page 47 to find out if the Pirates win the first two games. (*no*) Ask: **How would you describe Roberto Clemente? Why?** (Possible response: *He is confident. He believes his team will win even though others say it cannot.*) INFERENTIAL: DETERMINE CHARACTERS' TRAITS **At this point, who do you think will win the set of games? Why?** (Possible response: *the Orioles, because they have won all the games so far*) INFERENTIAL: MAKE PREDICTIONS

Pages 48–49 Have students read pages 48–49 to check their predictions. Ask: **How many games did each team win?** (*The Pirates won 4; the Orioles won 3.*) **Did Roberto Clemente play an important role in the Pirates' win? Give examples.** (*Yes. He led the team to victory in games 4 and 5. He hit home runs in games 6 and 7.*) INFERENTIAL: SYNTHESIZE

Page 50 Have students look at the illustration on page 50 and describe the scene. Then have them read page 50. Ask: **How would you describe Roberto Clemente, based on the information on this page? Why?** (Possible response: *He is a fine baseball player. He is also humble. He doesn't boast.*) INFERENTIAL: DETERMINE CHARACTERS' TRAITS **Why was Roberto Clemente considered to be a hero outside of baseball?** (*He liked to help people in need.*) INFERENTIAL: DETERMINE THEME

Page 51 Have students view the illustration on page 51. Ask a volunteer to describe what it shows. (*a statue of Roberto Clemente*) Then have students read page 51 to see who had the statue made. (*the people of Pittsburgh*) Ask: **Why do you think the people of Pittsburgh did this?** (Possible response: *They wanted to honor Clemente and keep his memory alive so others could learn from his life.*) CRITICAL: INTERPRET CHARACTERS' MOTIVATIONS

SUMMARIZE THE SELECTION Ask students to think about what made Roberto Clemente a hero. Then have them summarize the selection.

Page 52

Answers to Think About It Questions

1. He helped the Pirates by playing hard and by hitting a home run in the last game of the series. He helped other people by getting money for someone who needed artificial legs and by taking things to people who needed help. SUMMARY
2. Possible response: Clemente didn't boast because his good baseball playing was his way of keeping his promise to play hard. The fans liked Clemente even more for not boasting. INTERPRETATION
3. Webs and paragraphs should indicate an understanding of Clemente as a hard worker, a good hitter, a man who didn't boast, and a man who helped others. WORD WEB/WRITE A PARAGRAPH

Page 53 For instruction on the Focus Skill: Draw Conclusions/Make Generalizations, see page 53 in *Timeless Tales*.

Name ______________________________

REPRODUCIBLE STUDENT ACTIVITY PAGE

The Pirate Hero

Complete the sequence chart about "The Pirate Hero." Write a sentence in each box.

Event 1:

Possible response: The Pirates lose the first two games to the Orioles.

Event 2:

Possible response: Roberto Clemente helps the Pirates win the third and fourth games.

Event 3:

Possible response: With Roberto Clemente's help, the Pirates win the set of games.

Event 4:

Possible response: In 1972, Roberto Clemente died in a plane crash on his way to help people.

Harcourt

Now use the information from the boxes to write a one-sentence summary of the selection.

Possible response: Roberto Clemente was a hero in and out of baseball.

____

Rookie Robin

by Tomas Castillo **Use with *Timeless Tales*, pages 54–61.**

Preteaching Skills: Long Vowel /ō/*ow*

Teach/Model

IDENTIFY THE SOUND Have students repeat the following sentence aloud twice: *The crow has flown where the wind has blown.* Have them identify the words with the /ō/ sound they hear in *grow.* (*crow, flown, blown*)

ASSOCIATE LETTERS TO SOUNDS Write the sentence *The crow has flown where the wind has blown* on the board. Underline the letters *ow* in *crow.* Tell students that the letters *ow* can stand for the long *o* sound. Ask students to identify the other words in this sentence in which the letters *ow* stand for the long *o* sound. (*flown, blown*) Read the entire sentence aloud as you point to each word.

WORD BLENDING Model how to blend and read the word *blown.* Point to the *b* and say /b/. Point to the *l* and say /l/. Draw your hand under *ow* and say /ō/. Point to *n* and say /n/. Slide your hand under the whole word as you elongate the sounds /bbllōōnn/. Then read the word naturally—*blown.*

Practice/Apply

APPLY THE SKILL ***Letter Substitution*** Write the following words on the board, and have students read each aloud. Make the changes necessary to form the words in parentheses. Have a student read each new word aloud. Try to give each student an opportunity to respond.

top (tow)	moss (mow)	flock (flow)	lot (low)
box (bowl)	on (own)	sock (sow)	throng (throw)

DICTATION AND WRITING Have students number a sheet of paper 1–8. Dictate words 1–8, and have students write them. After they write each word, display it so that students can proofread their work.

1. blow*	2. show	3. blown*	4. fellow
5. towing	6. flow*	7. thrown	8. below

**Word appears in "Rookie Robin."*

Dictate the following sentence, and have students write it: *Let that fellow show us he can throw a fast ball.*

READ LONGER WORDS ***Review Compound Words*** Write the word *slowpoke* on the board. Remind students that when they come to a longer word, they should look to see if it is made up of two smaller words. Ask students which part of the word sounds like *slow* and which part sounds like *poke.* Draw your hand under the entire word as students read it aloud. Then write these words on the board: *blowfish, crow-bar,* and *snowball.* Have students read the words and tell how they figured them out.

REPRODUCIBLE STUDENT ACTIVITY PAGE

INDEPENDENT PRACTICE See the reproducible Student Activity on page 39.

Name ____________________

Rookie Robin

Do what the sentences tell you.

1. Find three cats in a row. Add a cat to the row.
2. Make a bowl for the cats.
3. Make a tree growing next to the pond.
4. Put a crow up in the tree.
5. Make a leaf blowing away from the tree.
6. Put a dog in the shade below the tree.
7. Put an X on the rowboat next to the pond.
8. A boy named Rob owns the boat. Show who Rob is by making an *R* on his hat.
9. Oh, no, it's snowing! Make some snow falling.
10. Make a pile of six snowballs in Rob's boat.
11. Make Rob hold a paddle to row the boat with.
12. Find the fish. Then make an arrow that shows Rob the way to the fishing hole.
13. Show some of the bubbles the fish are blowing.
14. Find one cat that's not in a row of cats. Make a small bowl for it to eat out of.

Now circle the words that have the long *o* sound spelled *ow*.

Harcourt

Introducing Vocabulary

Apply word identification strategies.

LOOK FOR FAMILIAR SPELLING PATTERNS Display the vocabulary words, and ask students to read them silently. Remind students that they can sometimes figure out a new word by looking for spelling patterns they know. Point out the *ar* in the first syllable of *bargain*. Have students read the syllable *bar*, and point out that the second syllable has the same spelling as the second syllable in *again*. Have them read the whole word aloud. Help students read the remaining vocabulary words aloud, using clues as necessary: something you may get if your team wins a championship (*trophy*); what your friend does when he yells, "Go, team!" (*roots*); bats, balls, and gloves are examples of this (*equipment*); announced a person's name (*introduced*); means "huge" (*gigantic*). If students misread a word and then self-correct, encourage them by saying, for example, **You read ___ and then changed it to ___. Why? How did you know to do that?**

VOCABULARY DEFINED

bargain a good deal

equipment things needed for a certain activity

gigantic giant-sized

introduced presented a person by name for the purpose of making someone else acquainted with him or her

roots cheers for a team or player

trophy a prize received for winning a contest or game

Discuss the meanings of the vocabulary words. Then ask students to create a sentence using two or more of the vocabulary words. (Possible response: *The team won a gigantic golden trophy.*) Continue until all the vocabulary words have been used at least once and each student has had an opportunity to respond.

Check understanding.

Ask students to write the vocabulary words on a sheet of paper. Have them name the word that answers each of the following riddles and circle that word on their papers.

- **Hammers, chisels, and saws are examples of me.** *(equipment)*
- **I am the proof that someone is a winner.** *(trophy)*
- **I describe what happened when a player's name got announced for the first time.** *(introduced)*
- **I describe what the crowd does when it cheers for its favorite team.** *(roots)*
- **I describe an elephant and a blue whale.** *(gigantic)*
- **If something usually costs a dollar but you buy it for 50 cents, I describe the deal you got.** *(bargain)*

REPRODUCIBLE STUDENT ACTIVITY PAGE

INDEPENDENT PRACTICE See the reproducible Student Activity on page 41.

NOTE: The following vocabulary words from "The Boonsville Bombers" are reinforced in "Rookie Robin." If students are unfamiliar with these words, point them out as you encounter them during reading: *rookie(s)*, *stadium*, *fielded*, *murmur* (p. 54); *deflected* (p. 57).

Name ______________________________

REPRODUCIBLE STUDENT ACTIVITY PAGE

Rookie Robin

Read the ad.

Meet Jeff Gates: Up-and-Coming Baseball Star

Jeff Gates hopes to make the Robins ball team.
He is one of five rookies in training this season.
The last training game of the season is today.
He has to play his best to make the team.
The game is a **bargain** for the fans—it's free!
Jeff catches a ball, and the team **roots** for him.
At bat, he hits hard at the ball with a **gigantic** swing but strikes out.
He likes hearing his name over the mike and being **introduced** as a Robin.
He gets a walk in the fifth inning and strikes out in the seventh inning.
Later, he trots to the **equipment** box to pick out a different bat.
If he can get a hit, maybe the team will win a **trophy.**
Will Jeff make a big play, help win the game, and make the team?
Read the tale to find out what happens.

Write a word from the ad to complete each sentence. Choose from the words in dark type.

1. The team ___roots___ for Jeff when he gets a ball in the beginning of the game.
2. Jeff takes a ___gigantic___ swing at the ball but makes an out.
3. The game is free to the fans, so it is a real ___bargain___.
4. Jeff is ___introduced___ to the fans by a man at the mike.
5. Jeff picks out a different bat from the ___equipment___ box.
6. If Jeff plays well, he could make the team, and the team could win a ___trophy___.

What do you think will happen in "Rookie Robin"? Will Jeff make the team?

Responses will vary. Accept reasonable responses.

Harcourt

Directed Reading

Page 54 Ask a volunteer to read aloud the title of the story. Have students predict what the story will probably be about by looking at the illustration on pages 54 and 55. Help them identify Jeff Gates and the team name, "Robins," on his jersey in the illustration. Have them read page 54 to find out what Jeff is trying to accomplish. Ask: **Why is this game a big test for Jeff?** (Possible response: *He has to do very well in this game in order to make the team.*) INFERENTIAL: CAUSE-EFFECT

Page 55 Have students read page 55 to find out how Jeff plays in the second inning of the game. **How well does Jeff play in the second inning?** (Possible response: *He hits the ball but it was an out.*) INFERENTIAL: SUMMARIZE **How do you think Jeff feels after getting an out? Why?** (Possible responses: *He feels bad because he didn't get on base. He's worried about not making the team.*) INFERENTIAL: DETERMINE CHARACTERS' EMOTIONS

Page 57 Have students read page 57 to find out what happens next. (*Jeff gets on base by getting hit by the ball.*) Discuss with students how they think Jeff is doing. **Do you think using a new bat will help Jeff? Why or why not?** (Responses will vary; accept reasonable responses.) CRITICAL: MAKE JUDGMENTS

Page 58 Have a volunteer read page 58 aloud. Ask students to listen to find out what happens next. Ask: **What do you think the coach will say to Jeff?** (Possible response: *that Jeff should take a walk*) INFERENTAL: MAKE PREDICTIONS

Page 59 Guide students to view the illustration on pages 58 and 59. Help them identify Jeff, the umpire, the catcher on the opposing team, and the Robins' coach. Then ask them to read page 59. Ask: **Why does Jeff argue with the coach?** (Possible response: *He thinks that if he walks, he will lose his last chance to show how well he can hit the ball.*) CRITICAL: INTERPRET CHARACTERS' MOTIVATIONS **Do you think Jeff will make the team? Why or why not?** (Possible responses: *I don't think he will make the team; he hasn't gotten a big hit.*) INFERENTIAL: MAKE PREDICTIONS

Page 60 Have students read page 60 to see if Jeff makes the team. **Why does the team get a trophy?** (*for team play*) LITERAL: NOTE DETAILS

SUMMARIZE THE SELECTION Ask students to think about how well Jeff played during the Robins' training game, as well as about what happened after the game. Then have students write three sentences to summarize the events of the story.

Page 61

Answers to Think About It Questions

1. Jeff does what the coach asks and lets the last pitch go. That shows that Jeff would play for the team, not just for himself. SUMMARY
2. Possible responses: In the last inning, Jeff wants to get a big hit. He feels upset when the coach asks him to take a walk. After the game, he finds out that he did what was best for the team. INTERPRETATION
3. You may want to review the style for writing friendly letters. The letter should be written from Jeff's point of view and should express his excitement about being chosen as a Robin. WRITE A LETTER

Name ______________________________

REPRODUCIBLE STUDENT ACTIVITY PAGE

Rookie Robin

Write a sentence or two in each box below to summarize the selection. Be sure to write the events in correct order.

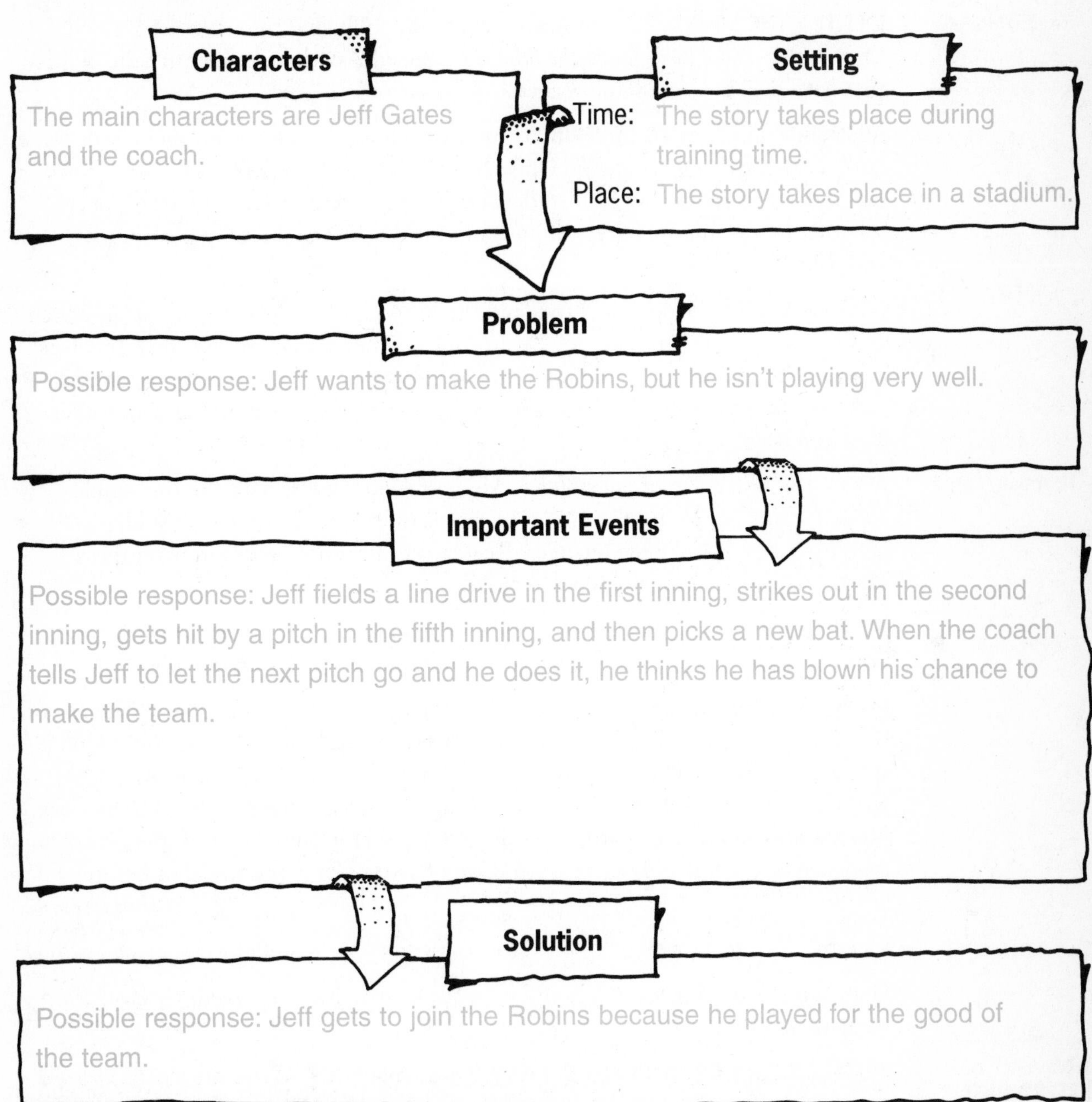

Characters

The main characters are Jeff Gates and the coach.

Setting

Time: The story takes place during training time.

Place: The story takes place in a stadium.

Problem

Possible response: Jeff wants to make the Robins, but he isn't playing very well.

Important Events

Possible response: Jeff fields a line drive in the first inning, strikes out in the second inning, gets hit by a pitch in the fifth inning, and then picks a new bat. When the coach tells Jeff to let the next pitch go and he does it, he thinks he has blown his chance to make the team.

Solution

Possible response: Jeff gets to join the Robins because he played for the good of the team.

Now write a one-sentence summary of the story.

Jeff doesn't think he is playing very well, but he finds out later that he has made the Robins because he showed he could be a team player.

Harcourt

Race for Life on the Iditarod Trail

by Caren B. Stelson **Use with *Timeless Tales*, pages 62–69.**

Preteaching Skills: *R*-controlled Vowel /ôr/*or, oor*

Teach/Model

IDENTIFY THE SOUND Have students repeat the following tongue twister aloud three times: *Did a torch scorch the floor of the porch?* Ask them to identify the words that have the /ôr/ sound. (*torch, scorch, floor, porch*)

ASSOCIATE LETTERS TO SOUNDS Write the following sentence on the board: *Did a torch scorch the floor of the porch?* Underline the letters *or* in *torch*, *scorch*, and *porch*, and the letters *oor* in *floor*. Tell students that when these groups of letters appear together in a word, the letters often stand for the /ôr/ sound they hear in *scorch* and *floor*.

WORD BLENDING Model how to blend the letters and sounds to read *scorch.* Touch *s* and say /s/. Touch *c* and say /k/. Draw your hand under *or* and say /ôr/. Touch *ch* and say /ch/. Slide your hand under the whole word as you elongate the sounds /sskkôôrrch/. Then read the word naturally—*scorch.* Follow a similar process for *torch* and *floor*.

Practice/Apply

APPLY THE SKILL ***Letter Substitution*** Model making words with the /ôr/ sound spelled *or* and *oor*. Write the following words on the board, and have students read each aloud. Make the changes necessary to form the words in parentheses. Have students read each new word aloud.

hot (horn)	flock (floor)	bond (born)	tots (torn)
boxer (border)	dock (door)	pot (pork)	spot (sport)

DICTATION AND WRITING Have students number a sheet of paper 1–8. Write *fort* on the board, and tell students that in the first seven words you say, the /ôr/ sound is spelled *or* as in *fort.* Dictate words 1–7, and have students write them. After they write each word, display the correct spelling so students can proofread their work. Next, write *door* on the board, and tell students that in the last word, the /ôr/ sound is spelled *oor* as in *door*. Dictate word 8, and have students proofread as before.

1. nor	2. corks	3. snowstorm*	4. forest
5. torn	6. morning*	7. transporting*	8. floor

**Word appears in "Race for Life on the Iditarod Trail."*

Dictate the following sentence, and have students write it: *We closed the doors when the storm hit.*

READ LONGER WORDS ***Review Breaking Words with VCCV*** Write the words *forward*, *transporting*, *forgetful*, and *doorstop* on the board. Ask students to identify two consonants that are next to each other in the middle of the word *forward*. (*r, w*) Remind students that words that have this pattern are usually divided into syllables between the two consonants. Frame *for* and have students read it. Next, frame *ward* and ask students to read it. Then ask them to read the whole word aloud. Repeat the process for the remaining words.

REPRODUCIBLE STUDENT ACTIVITY PAGE

INDEPENDENT PRACTICE See the reproducible Student Activity on page 45.

Name ____________________

Race for Life on the Iditarod Trail

Circle and write the word that makes sense in the sentence.

1. Dogsledding is a hard and demanding ___sport___.
   spot **sport** **spoke**

2. Sled drivers, called mushers, must travel in bad ___storms___.
   storms **stoves** **stomps**

3. Huskies are ___born___ to the job of pulling sleds.
   barn **born** **bond**

4. On the trail, sled dogs sleep in ___forts___ made of snow.
   farms **forests** **forts**

5. Thick coats help the dogs sleep well on a ___floor___ made of snow.
   floor **flute** **flock**

6. A lot of sled dog breeders make their homes in the far ___north___.
   north **nor** **not**

7. The musher must keep ___order___ within the team of dogs.
   odder **order** **orchard**

8. A musher must have a job ___for___ each dog and must teach the dog to do it well.
   fort **far** **for**

9. A mush team's day often starts early in the ___morning___.
   moon **mound** **morning**

10. But sled dogs do an ___important___ job, and they like the job they do.
    important **impostor** **immortal**

11. The people of Nome, Alaska, will never ___forget___ how dogsled teams saved lives one winter.
    forget **forlorn** **forts**

Harcourt

Introducing Vocabulary

Apply word identification strategies.

LOOK FOR FAMILIAR SPELLING PATTERNS Display the vocabulary words, and ask students to read them silently. Remind students that they can sometimes figure out a new word by looking for spelling patterns they know. Point out the consonant-vowel-consonant pattern in the first syllable of *champions* and *huskies.* Call on volunteers to read those words aloud and tell how they were able to figure them out. (*A vowel between two consonants usually has the short sound.*) Help students read the remaining vocabulary words aloud, using clues as necessary. When students read each word correctly, encourage them by saying, for example, **That's right. How did you figure out that was the word?**

Discuss the meanings of the vocabulary words. Then ask students to order the words so that they could be used to tell a round-robin story. Have students take turns building the story by making up sentences using the vocabulary words.

VOCABULARY DEFINED

champions people who have beaten others to win first place in a competition

emergency a sudden and unexpected event that requires immediate action

huskies dogs with thick, furry coats; these dogs are often used to pull dogsleds

medicine a drug used to treat, cure, and prevent disease

musher the driver of a dog team

obstacles things that stand in the way of progress

route a path traveled from one place to another

unknots untangles or removes the knots from

Check understanding.

Have students write the vocabulary words on a sheet of paper. Ask them to name the word that answers each of the following questions and to circle that word on their papers.

- **Which word names big, furry dogs that might pull a sled?** *(huskies)*
- **Which word describes a time when danger is near?** *(emergency)*
- **What are things that stand in the way of your reaching a goal?** *(obstacles)*
- **What could you call first-place winners?** *(champions)*
- **What does a comb do for hair?** *(unknots)*
- **Which word has to do with maps or roads for traveling?** *(route)*

Provide vocabulary support.

Students may have trouble with words and names such as *diphtheria, Anchorage* (p. 62); *Iditarod* (p. 65). Introduce the words by writing them on the board and pronouncing each. As students come across these words in the selection, offer assistance as needed.

REPRODUCIBLE STUDENT ACTIVITY PAGE

INDEPENDENT PRACTICE See the reproducible Student Activity on page 47.

NOTE: The following vocabulary words from "Iditarod Dream" are reinforced in "Race for Life on the Iditarod Trail." If students are unfamiliar with these words, point them out as you encounter them during reading: *headquarters* (p. 65); *pace, positions, tangle, handlers* (p. 66).

Name ____________________

Race for Life on the Iditarod Trail

Read the story.

The dogsled drivers drove sleds along the Iditarod Trail in Alaska in the 1920s. They were **champions**.

One day in 1925, Nome, Alaska, had an **emergency. Medicine** was needed fast. The winter conditions made travel by boat or plane impossible. The **route** that had to be taken was the mail route, the Iditarod Trail.

The medicine was 1,000 miles away. A train could bring it to Nenana, 674 miles from Nome. From there, only **huskies** and **mushers** could finish the job.

More than 20 mushers made parts of the trip to Nome. Each traveled nonstop. The mushers had to overcome **obstacles** along the way. Then a snowstorm hit. The huskies got mixed up in the lines. The mushers had to **unknot** the lines with freezing hands.

Write a story word to complete each sentence. Choose from the words in dark type.

1. Dogsleds took the Iditarod Trail to deliver ___medicine___ to Nome, Alaska.
2. They had to travel quickly because Nome had an ___emergency___.
3. The ___route___ to Nome was more than 1,000 miles long.
4. The ___mushers___ and their ___huskies___ had to work together as a team.
5. The dogsled drivers were ___champions___, and they drove the trail fast.
6. The dogs and sled drivers faced ___obstacles___ along the Iditarod Trail.
7. When the dogs' lines tangled, the mushers had to ___unknot___ them.

Do you think the dogs will get to Nome in time? Why do you think this?

Responses will vary.

____

Harcourt

Directed Reading

Pages 62–63 Read aloud the title of the story. Help students identify Dr. Welch, the children who are ill, and the wintry surroundings in the illustration. Explain that the story tells about an event that really happened in 1925, in the small town of Nome, Alaska, very far from other towns. Have them read page 62 to find out what is happening. Ask: **What is Dr. Welch worried about?** (Possible response: *He is worried that the children will die from diphtheria.)* INFERENTIAL: IMPORTANT DETAILS **What problem must be solved in this story?** (Possible response: *Medicine must travel quickly more than 1,000 miles in stormy winter weather.*) INFERENTIAL: IMPORTANT DETAILS

Page 65 Ask students to read page 65 to find out what plans were made to save the town of Nome. (*Twenty dogsled champions would follow the mail route, the Iditarod Trail, to bring the medicine to Nome.*) LITERAL: NOTE DETAILS Ask: **How long does it take to travel the Iditarod Trail?** (Possible response: *It can take up to two weeks, but champion mushers plan to do it in less than a week by sledding nonstop.*) INFERENTIAL: DRAW CONCLUSIONS Ask: **How does the medicine travel during the first part of its journey?** (Possible response: *It travels by train as far as Nenana.*) INFERENTIAL: SEQUENCE

Page 66 Have students read page 66 to find out what obstacles the mushers encounter. Ask: **What are some of the obstacles that the mushers must overcome on the trail?** (Possible responses: *They must untangle knotted dog lines and travel alone without extra dog handlers; snowstorms make the going more difficult.*) INFERENTIAL: IMPORTANT DETAILS Have students predict whether the medicine will reach Nome in time to save the town. INFERENTIAL: MAKE PREDICTIONS Then have them read to see whether they predicted correctly. Ask: **Was the story problem solved? How do you know?** (Possible response: *The problem was solved because the medicine arrived at Nome in time to save the people.*) METACOGNITIVE: DETERMINE STORY RESOLUTION

SUMMARIZE THE SELECTION Ask students to think about the story problem and how it was solved. Then have students write three sentences to summarize the beginning, middle, and end of the story.

Page 68

Answers to Think About It Questions

1. The medicine was needed quickly to stop the illness diphtheria and save lives. There was too much wind and snow for boats and planes to make the trip. SUMMARY
2. Possible response: They wanted to help the people of Nome, and they wanted to show that their dogs could do a good job. INTERPRETATION
3. Accept reasonable responses. Compositions should be written in the first person and should describe the hardships Gunnar Kaasen overcame, as well as his accomplishments. WRITE A COMPOSITION

Name ______________________________

Race for Life on the Iditarod Trail

Complete the sequence chart about "Race for Life on the Iditarod Trail." Write a sentence in each box.

Event 1:

People in Nome, Alaska, get sick with diphtheria and need medicine fast.

Event 2:

Possible response: Dr. Welch explains the emergency, and twenty dogsled champions agree to bring the medicine on the Iditarod Trail.

Event 3:

Possible response: A train takes the medicine to Nenana, and from there the mushers and their teams of huskies take over.

Event 4:

Possible response: A big storm hits, but the dog teams keep on going, and they get to Nome just in time.

Now use the information from the boxes to write a one-sentence summary of the entire selection.

Possible response: The people of Nome are saved from diphtheria when dogsled teams travel the Iditarod Trail to bring them medicine.

Harcourt

Fishing for Four

by Celeste Albright **Use with *Timeless Tales*, pages 70–77.**

Preteaching Skills: *R*-controlled Vowel /ôr/*ore*, *oar*, *our*

Teach/Model

IDENTIFY THE SOUND Have students repeat the following question aloud three times: *Do you sell oars at your store?* Have students identify the words that have the /ôr/ sound. *(oars, your, store)*

ASSOCIATE LETTERS TO SOUNDS Write this question on the board: *Do you sell oars at your store?* Underline the letters *oar, our,* and *ore* in the words in which they appear. Tell students that when these groups of letters appear together in a word, the letters usually stand for the /ôr/ sound in *store*.

WORD BLENDING Write *shore, court,* and *board* on the board. Model blending letters and sounds to read *shore*. Touch *sh* and say /sh/. Draw your hand under *ore* and say /ôr/. Slide your hand under the whole word as you elongate the sounds /shôôrr/. Then read the word naturally—*shore*. Follow a similar process for the words *court* and *board*.

Practice/Apply

APPLY THE SKILL ***Letter Substitution*** Model making words with the /ôr/ sound. Write the following words on the board, and have students read each aloud. Make the changes necessary to form the words in parentheses. Have students read each new word aloud. Try to give each student an opportunity to respond.

ignite (ignore)	pot (pour)	rob (roar)	top (tore)
hot (hoard)	cob (core)	bond (boar)	got (gourd)

DICTATION AND WRITING Have students number a sheet of paper 1–8. Write *core* on the board, and tell students that in the first four words you will say, the /ôr/ sound is spelled *ore* as in *core*. Dictate words 1–4, and have students write them. After they write each one, display the correct spelling so students can proofread their work. Continue with this procedure by writing *soar* or *four* on the board before dictating the numbered words below that have the matching spelling of /ôr/.

1. bore*	2. chore*	3. more*	4. adore*
5. board*	6. oars*	7. tour	8. poured*

**Word appears in "Fishing for Four."*

Dictate the following sentence: *There are four more oars in the shed.*

READ LONGER WORDS ***Introduce Dropping e Before Adding -ing; Review Breaking Words with VCCV*** Write *bore* on the board, and have a volunteer read it aloud. Then write *boring* below it. Tell students that when the ending *-ing* is added to a word with the *ore* pattern, the final *e* is dropped. Follow a similar procedure with *snore/snoring* and *store/storing*. Write *score* and *adore* on the board, and have students add the *-ing* ending to each word, dropping the *e*. Then write the word *ignore* on the board. Ask students which two consonants are surrounded by vowels. *(g, n)* Remind students that words with this pattern are usually broken into syllables between the two consonants. Ask a volunteer to frame the letters */ig/* and then the letters */nôr/*. Follow a similar procedure with the words *oarlock* and *fourteen*.

REPRODUCIBLE STUDENT ACTIVITY PAGE

INDEPENDENT PRACTICE See the reproducible Student Activity on page 51.

Name ______________________________

Fishing for Four

Read the story. Circle all the words that have the vowel sound heard in *more*.

Norm had lots of chores to do. He had to feed his pet boar. He had to cut some boards to fix the boar's pen. He had to stack the oars in the shed. Then there were ripe gourds to pick and store in the attic. "I'm bored with this routine," Norm complained. "What will it matter if I skip the chores just one time?" Norm went up to his bed. He started to snore. Meanwhile, the hungry boar had left its pen to explore. When Norm woke up, he stared in disbelief! What a mess! The boar had gobbled up all the gourds. It had run over the oars and smashed them to bits. "What more?" Norm wailed as he ran to the shed. The boar was there, munching on apple cores. There were no more apples in the bin.

Circle and write the word that best completes each sentence.

1. Norm skipped his ___chores___.	**store**	**boar**	**chores**
2. His pet ___boar___ got out of its pen.	**gourd**	**goat**	**boar**
3. Norm's mistake was getting ___bored___.	**bored**	**poured**	**sore**
4. He was supposed to pick the ___gourds___.	**corn**	**gourds**	**cores**
5. He was supposed to stack the ___oars___.	**cores**	**gourds**	**oars**
6. He was supposed to cut the ___boards___.	**more**	**boards**	**corn**
7. It was not smart of Norm to ___snore___ all day.	**snore**	**core**	**soar**
8. Now he has a bigger job than he had ___before___.	**implore**	**before**	**ignore**

Harcourt

Introducing Vocabulary

Apply word identification strategies.

LOOK FOR FAMILIAR SPELLING PATTERNS

Display the vocabulary words, and ask students to read them silently. Remind students that they can sometimes figure out a new word by looking for spelling patterns they know. Point out the consonant-vowel-consonant pattern in the first syllable of *gratified* and the consonant-vowel-consonant-*e* pattern in the second syllable of *compete*. Ask volunteers to read those words aloud and tell how they were able to figure them out. Help students read the remaining vocabulary words aloud, offering clues as necessary: the beat in music *(rhythm)*; trusting and honest *(innocent)*; what a car did when it gave off exhaust *(emitted)*; added up carefully *(calculated)*. When students read a word correctly, encourage them by saying, for example, **That's right. Look at the word again. How did you know that was the word?**

VOCABULARY DEFINED

calculated used mathematics to determine an amount

compete to take part in a contest

emitted released, gave off, or sent out

gratified felt thankful or pleased

innocent pure and trusting

rhythm a pattern of sounds or movements that repeats in a regular sequence

Discuss the meanings of the vocabulary words. Then ask each student to create a sentence containing at least two of the words. (Possible response: *We listened as the alarm emitted a beeping signal in a regular rhythm.*) Continue until all the vocabulary words have been used at least once and each student has had an opportunity to respond.

Check understanding.

Have students list the vocabulary words on a sheet of paper. Then ask the following questions. Ask students to name the word that best answers each question and to circle it on their papers.

- **Which word describes the trusting and good-hearted nature of a little child?** *(innocent)*
- **Which word describes something you did using mathematics?** *(calculated)*
- **You clap your hands to a song. Which word describes what you are keeping?** *(rhythm)*
- **Which word could be used to describe what an object did when sounds or signals came out of it?** *(emitted)*
- **Which word is related to the word *gratitude*, which means "thankfulness"?** *(gratified)*
- **You will try to win a game against other players. Which word describes what you will do?** *(compete)*

REPRODUCIBLE STUDENT ACTIVITY PAGE

INDEPENDENT PRACTICE See the reproducible Student Activity on page 53.

NOTE: The following vocabulary words from "Woodsong" are reinforced in "Fishing for Four." If students are unfamiliar with these words, point them out as you encounter them during reading: *harness, bulk, disengaged, snort* (p. 72); *retired, resembled* (p. 74).

Name ____________________

REPRODUCIBLE STUDENT ACTIVITY PAGE

Fishing for Four

Read the story. Then fill in the web. Use all the words in dark type in your answers.

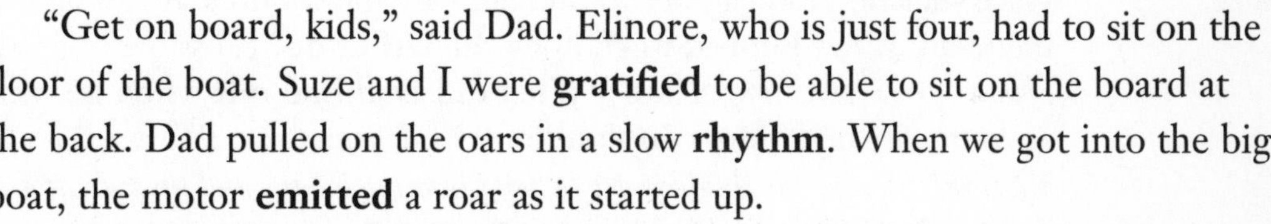

"Get on board, kids," said Dad. Elinore, who is just four, had to sit on the floor of the boat. Suze and I were **gratified** to be able to sit on the board at the back. Dad pulled on the oars in a slow **rhythm**. When we got into the big boat, the motor **emitted** a roar as it started up.

We were helping our dad catch some fish to use as crab bait. We like going fishing with him.

"I'm going to catch more fish than you," said Suze. She and I like to **compete**.

Dad **calculated**. "If we can fill four bushel baskets, that will do it," he said.

Elinore is an **innocent** little kid. She didn't know that Suze and I were having a contest. She ignored her fishing line.

Fishing with Dad

Describe what made the boats move.

Dad pulled the oars of the rowboat in a slow **rhythm**. The big boat's motor **emitted** a roar.

What is little Elinore like?

She is **innocent**.

What do the bigger kids like to do?

They like to **compete**.

How much bait do they need?

Dad **calculated** that four bushel baskets would be enough.

How do they feel about getting to sit on a board in the boat?

They feel **gratified** to be able to sit there.

Who do you think will win the fishing contest? Why? Responses will vary.

Harcourt

Directed Reading

Page 70 Ask a volunteer to read aloud the title. Have students look at the illustration on page 70, and help them identify the four people in the boat: Dad, Elinore (aged 4), Suze, and the speaker. Ask students to predict what they think the story will be about. (Responses will vary.) Read page 70 to students. Ask: **Where are the people going in the little rowboat?** (Possible response: *They are going to their big boat.*) LITERAL: IMPORTANT DETAILS **Why do you think they are going out to a bigger boat?** (*Maybe they need a bigger boat to go farther out to sea.*) INFERENTIAL: SPECULATE

Page 71 Have students read page 71 to find out why the children are going fishing with their dad. **What kind of work does the father do?** (Possible response: *He fishes for crabs.*) LITERAL: IMPORTANT DETAILS **What did Dad find out when he went to the store to get bait? How do you know?** (*He found that the store was out of bait. I know this because the children are helping him catch bait, and the narrator says that they do this when the store is out of bait.*) METACOGNITIVE: DRAW CONCLUSIONS

Page 72 Ask a volunteer to read page 72 aloud while students listen to find out where the family goes in the big boat. **Where does Dad take the boat?** (Possible response: *He steers the boat far offshore.*) LITERAL: IMPORTANT DETAILS

Page 73 Have students read page 73 to find out how much bait they need to catch today. **How many fish does Dad want them to catch?** (Possible response: *He estimates that they need to catch enough fish to fill four bushel baskets, or one basket each.*) LITERAL: NOTE DETAILS

Page 74 Have students read page 74. Ask: **What does the speaker mean by saying that the fish had "retired from swimming"?** (Possible response: *It means that because it was caught, the fish wouldn't be swimming any more.*) CRITICAL: AUTHOR'S CRAFT/APPRECIATE LANGUAGE

Page 75 Have volunteers read aloud the dialogue on page 75 while students listen to find out who appears to be winning the contest. Ask: **Who do you think is winning at this point?** (Responses will vary.) CRITICAL: MAKE JUDGMENTS

Page 76 Have students read page 76 to find out who wins the contest. Ask: **What is the surprise at the end of the story, and why is it so surprising?** (Possible response: *Elinore catches the most fish; it is surprising because she is the youngest and wasn't even competing.*) CRITICAL: INTERPRET STORY EVENTS

SUMMARIZE THE SELECTION Ask students to think about what took place first, next, and last in the story. Then have students summarize the story in three sentences.

Page 77

Answers to Think About It Questions

1. Possible response: They go fishing to catch crab bait. The three girls like fishing a lot. SUMMARY
2. Possible response: The other kids are surprised and happy that Elinore got the most fish. I think so because they weren't mad when they saw how many fish she had. INTERPRETATION
3. Accept reasonable responses. Conversations should indicate friendly competition among all three sisters and perhaps include some joking about the time Elinore caught more fish than her older sisters. WRITE A CONVERSATION

Name ______________________________________

Fishing for Four

Complete the sequence chart about "Fishing for Four."
Write a sentence or two in each box. The first one is done for you.

Event 1 (Pages 70–71)

Dad rows the three kids out to the big boat for a day of fishing for crab bait. The two older kids will compete to see how many fish they can catch.

Event 2 (Pages 72–73)

Dad steers the big boat far offshore, and the kids start to catch fish.

Event 3 (Pages 74–75)

The two older kids catch fish after fish as Suze keeps score, and soon it's time to go home.

Event 4 (Page 76)

The older kids find that Elinore got the most fish without even trying.

Now use the information from the boxes to write a one-sentence summary of the story.

Possible response: On a fishing trip for crab bait, Elinore surprises everyone by catching the most fish without even trying.

Harcourt

Raindrop in the Sun

by Deborah Akers **Use with *Timeless Tales*, pages 78–85.**

Preteaching Skills: *R*-controlled Vowel /ûr/*ear, ur, ir*

Teach/Model

IDENTIFY THE SOUND Have students repeat the following sentence three times: *If I twirl around, it seems as if the Earth is turning beneath my feet.* Ask students to identify the words that have the same vowel sound as in *curl.* (*twirl, Earth, turning*)

ASSOCIATE LETTERS TO SOUNDS Write the sentence from above on the board. Underline the letters that stand for the /ûr/ sound: tw<u>ir</u>l, <u>Ear</u>th, t<u>ur</u>ning. Tell students that the underlined letters can all stand for the /ûr/ sound they hear in *burn.*

WORD BLENDING Model how to blend and read *pearl.* Point to *p* and say /p/. Slide your hand under the letters *ear* and say /ûr/. Touch *l* and say /l/. Slide your hand under the whole word as you read it aloud, elongating the sounds. Then say the word naturally—*pearl.*

Practice/Apply

APPLY THE SKILL ***Letter Substitution*** Write the following words on the board, and have students read each aloud. Make the changes necessary to form the words in parentheses. Have students read each new word aloud. Try to give all students an opportunity to respond.

peas (pearl)	still (stir)	lean (learn)	lunch (lurch)
bark (bird)	blunt (blur)	swing (swirl)	each (earl)

DICTATION AND WRITING Have students number a sheet of paper 1–10. Write the word *dirt* on the board and tell students that in the first four words you will say, the /ûr/ sound is spelled *ir* as in *dirt.* Dictate words 1–4, and have students write them. After they write each word, write it on the board so students can proofread their work. Next, write the word *burn* on the board and tell students that in the next three words, the /ûr/ sound is spelled *ur* as in *burn.* Dictate words 5–7, and have students write and proofread them as before. Then write *earn* on the board and tell students that in the last three words, the /ûr/ sound is spelled *ear* as in *earn.* Dictate words 8–10, and have students write and proofread them.

1. girl*	2. bird	3. shirt	4. firm	5. fur*
6. turned*	7. hurdle	8. learn	9. pearl*	10. early

**Word appears in "Raindrop in the Sun."*

READ LONGER WORDS ***Introduce Breaking Words with R-controlled Vowels into Syllables*** Write the word *turnip* on the board. Ask students to identify the letters that stand for the /ûr/ sound. (*ur*) Tell students that in words in which the letters *ur, ear,* or *ir* stand for the /ûr/ sound, these combinations of letters usually stay together when the word is divided into syllables. Frame the word part *tur,* and have students read it aloud. Do the same for *nip.* Then draw your hand under the entire word as students read it aloud. Follow a similar procedure for the words *earnest* and *stirrup.*

REPRODUCIBLE STUDENT ACTIVITY PAGE

INDEPENDENT PRACTICE See the reproducible Student Activity on page 57.

Name ______________________

REPRODUCIBLE STUDENT ACTIVITY PAGE

Raindrop in the Sun

Write the word that answers each riddle.

1. I have the same vowel sound and spelling as in *pearl.*

I am a planet. What am I? Earth

Earth **earn** **Saturn**

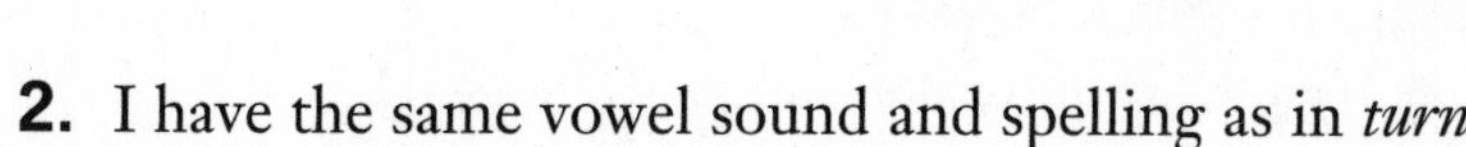

2. I have the same vowel sound and spelling as in *turn.*

I am a color. What am I? purple

purse **purple** **teal**

3. I have the same vowel sound and spelling as in *bird.*

Girls dress up in me. What am I? skirt

twirl **dress** **skirt**

4. I have the same vowel sound and spelling as in *learn.*

I am white and you find me in the sea. What am I? pearl

pearl **search** **whale**

5. I have the same vowel sound and spelling as in *stir.*

I appear at the beginning. What am I? first

firm **start** **first**

6. I have the same sound and spelling as in the first syllable of *early.*

I mean "to have an earnest desire." What am I? yearn

yearn **hope** **learn**

Harcourt

7. I end with the same vowel sound and spelling as in *burn.*

I mean "silly or senseless." What am I? absurd

turned **absurd** **odd**

8. I have the same vowel sound and spelling as in *dirt.*

I am a kind of tree. What am I? birch

birch **maple** **shirt**

Introducing Vocabulary

Apply word identification strategies.

LOOK FOR FAMILIAR SPELLING PATTERNS Display the vocabulary words, and ask students to identify words they know. Remind students that they can sometimes figure out new words by looking for familiar spelling patterns. Point out the CVC*e* pattern in *strode.* Call on volunteers to use what they know about this pattern to read the word aloud. Then help students read aloud the other words, providing these clues as necessary: a small boat used for river travel (*canoe*); the opposite of an exit (*entrance*); rhymes with *pierce* (*fierce*); means "came together" (*gathered*); what a house, a tent, and a hut provide (*shelter*). If students misread a word, encourage them to try again by saying, **Look at the word again. Does it look as though that could be the word?**

VOCABULARY DEFINED

canoe a narrow boat with pointed ends, usually controlled with a paddle

entrance a place to go in

fierce very angry; raging

gathered collected; came together

shelter a place that protects from weather or danger

strode walked with long steps

Discuss the meanings of the vocabulary words. Then have students make up riddles that have vocabulary words as answers. For example: *I am a light boat with pointed ends and no motor. My second syllable rhymes with* shoe. (*canoe*) Continue until all the vocabulary words have been used at least once and each student has had an opportunity to respond.

Check understanding.

Ask students to copy the vocabulary words on a sheet of paper. Have them name the word that best answers each of the following questions and circle it on their papers.

- **Which word names something you can paddle on a lake?** *(canoe)*
- **Which word might you see on a sign over a doorway?** *(entrance)*
- **Which word tells what you did if you put all your books together in one pile?** *(gathered)*
- **Which word describes a storm with thunder, lightning, and strong winds?** *(fierce)*
- **Which word describes a way of walking?** *(strode)*
- **If a storm was coming, what might you look for?** *(shelter)*

REPRODUCIBLE STUDENT ACTIVITY PAGE

INDEPENDENT PRACTICE See the reproducible Student Activity on page 59.

NOTE: The following vocabulary words from "Island of the Blue Dolphins" are reinforced in "Raindrop in the Sun." If students are unfamiliar with these words, point them out as you encounter them during reading: *abalones* (p. 78); *forlorn* (p. 79); *lair, gorged, vainer* (p. 81); *pitched* (p. 83); *overcome* (p. 84).

Name ________________________________

REPRODUCIBLE STUDENT ACTIVITY PAGE

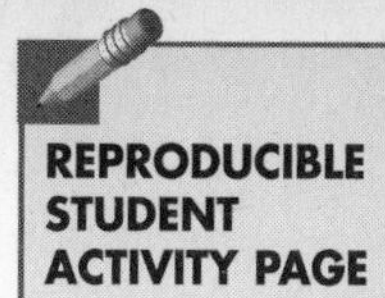

Raindrop in the Sun

You are about to read a story titled "Raindrop in the Sun." Read the story fact sheet.

Who is in the story:
a girl named Lani
a man named Moro
Lani's brother, Kalo
Lani's mom

Story setting:
on the shore
on the sea

What the story is about:
Lani wanted to gather shellfish with the men, but Moro did not let her go. Kalo said, "Meet me over at the **entrance** to the cove. I will hide you." She **strode** over to the cove and got in his **canoe**. The two of them paddled into a rock **shelter**. There, they **gathered** lots of shellfish. But on the way back, a **fierce** storm came up.

Now answer these questions. Use each word in dark type one time.

1. What did Kalo tell Lani? He said to meet him by the entrance to the cove.

2. What did Lani do next? She strode over to the cove and got in Kalo's canoe.

3. What did Lani and Kalo paddle into? They paddled into a rock shelter.

4. What did they do there? They gathered shellfish.

5. What happened on the way back to shore? A fierce storm came up.

6. What do you think Kalo and Lani will do when the storm hits?

Answers will vary.

Harcourt

Directed Reading

Page 78 Read aloud the title of the story. Have students look at the picture on pages 78 and 79 and then read page 78 to find out what the man is telling the girl that makes her angry. (*He is telling her that girls can't gather abalones with the men.*) **What reason does Moro give for not letting girls gather abalones?** (*They aren't strong enough.*) LITERAL: NOTE DETAILS **What words would you use to describe Lani?** (Possible responses: *confident, has strong feelings and opinions)* INFERENTIAL: DETERMINE CHARACTERS' TRAITS

Page 79 Read aloud page 79. Ask: **Why does Kalo say he'll hide Lani in his canoe?** (Possible responses: *He believes she could help bring home more abalones; he thinks the rule against letting girls go is unfair.*) INFERENTIAL: CAUSE-EFFECT

Page 80 Have students read page 80 to find out if Lani hides in Kalo's canoe. Ask: **Why do you think Lani's mother lets her go?** (Possible response: *She disagrees with the rule also.*) CRITICAL: INTERPRET CHARACTERS' MOTIVATIONS

Page 81 After students read page 81, ask: **What animals do Lani and Kalo see on the rocks?** (*seals*) LITERAL: NOTE DETAILS **Why do you think Kalo and Lani smile at each other?** (Possible response: *It's fun to watch the seals.*) INFERENTIAL: SPECULATE

Page 82 Have students read page 82 to find out if Kalo and Lani are successful at gathering abalones. Ask: **What makes Kalo and Lani a good team?** (Possible responses: *They help each other; they are both quick workers.*) INFERENTIAL: DRAW CONCLUSIONS

Page 83 Have students read page 83 to find out what happens to Kalo, Lani, and the men in canoes. (*Kalo and Lani help the others get back to shore safely.*) **Why does Kalo tell Lani to throw the abalones overboard?** (Possible response: *to make the boat lighter and faster, so they can get to the others quickly)* INFERENTIAL: IMPORTANT DETAILS

Page 84 Have students read page 84 to find out what happens to Kalo and Lani once the group returns to shore. Ask: **Why does Moro give the pearl to Lani as a trophy?** (Possible responses: *The pearl is special, and Lani has shown unusual bravery and strength in helping rescue the men.*) CRITICAL: INTERPRET CHARACTERS' MOTIVATIONS

SUMMARIZE THE SELECTION Ask students to tell whether they think "Raindrop in the Sun" is a good title for this story, and why or why not. Then help them summarize the selection in three sentences.

Page 85

Answers to Think About It Questions

1. Possible responses: Moro says that a girl can't paddle a canoe and can't be strong enough to gather abalones; Lani's brother hides her in his canoe. SUMMARY
2. Possible responses: Kalo takes his sister because he agrees that she is big enough and can help him. When the storm comes up, he may be wishing she were safe at home. INTERPRETATION
3. Conversations should show that some men are still reluctant to take girls along and that Lani and her friends present her help on the last trip as evidence that girls are strong enough and quick enough to go along. WRITE DIALOGUE

Name ______________________________

Raindrop in the Sun

Complete the chart to retell the story.

Cause	Effect
Moro told Lani she was too weak to paddle a canoe. **raft canoe rowboat**	Kalo told Lani to meet him by the cave's entrance. He hid her in his boat. **entrance side back**
Kalo and Lani worked well as a team. **worked played hid**	Kalo and Lani gathered a lot of abalones. **cleaned ate gathered**
A fierce storm came up. Lani and Kalo saved the men. **soft fierce winter**	Moro strode up and gave a speech. He called Lani a hero. **drove flew strode**

Now write a sentence that summarizes the story.

Possible response: Lani is told she is not strong enough to help gather abalones, but she later proves to be a valuable member of her tribe.

Harcourt

A Shaky Surprise

by Susan M. Fischer **Use with *Timeless Tales*, pages 86–93.**

Preteaching Skills: Long Vowels /ā/a; /ē/e, y; /ī/i, y; /ō/o; /o͞o/u

Teach/Model

IDENTIFY THE SOUND Ask students to repeat the following sentence aloud twice: *This baby tuna will be a giant fish by October.* Ask students to identify a word other than *a* that has the /ā/ sound. (*baby*) Then have them identify the two words that have the /ē/ sound they hear in *even.* (*be, baby*) Ask students which words have the /ī/ sound. (*giant, by*) Then ask students to identify a word that has the /ō/ sound (*October*) and a word that has the /o͞o/ sound. (*tuna*)

ASSOCIATE LETTERS TO SOUNDS Write on the board the sentence above. Underline the letters that stand for the long vowel sounds other than *a*, as follows: baby, tuna, be, giant, by, October. Tell students that in some words, a single vowel can stand for a long vowel sound. Read aloud each word and have students repeat the word. Then ask: **Which word has the long *o* sound you hear in *hello*?** (*October*) **Which words have the long *e* sound you hear in *we*?** (*be, baby*) **Which word has the long *u* sound heard in *tuba*?** (*tuna*) **Which word has the long *a* sound heard in *label*?** (*baby*) **What long vowel sounds can the letter *y* stand for?** (*long* i, *long* e)

WORD BLENDING Write the word *volcano* on the board. Model how to blend and read the word *volcano.* Slide your hand under the first syllable as you say the sounds /vvooll/. Slide your hand under the second syllable as you elongate the sounds /kkāā/. Repeat this process for the sounds in the third syllable /nnōō/. Then slide your hand under the whole word as you read it naturally—*volcano.*

Practice/Apply

APPLY THE SKILL ***Letter Substitution*** Write the following words on the board, and have students read each aloud. Make the changes necessary to form the words in parentheses. Have students read aloud each new word.

red (regal) jelly (rely) toy (try) hot (host)

DICTATION AND WRITING Have students number a sheet of paper 1–8. Dictate the following words, and have students write them. After they write each word, display it so students can proofread their work.

1. table*	2. she*	3. hurry*	4. fry
5. crying*	6. over*	7. moment*	8. tuba

**Word appears in "A Shaky Surprise."*

Dictate the following sentences: *Omar was carrying the gigantic tuba. That's probably why he bumped into the table.*

REPRODUCIBLE STUDENT ACTIVITY PAGE

INDEPENDENT PRACTICE See the reproducible Student Activity on page 63.

READ LONGER WORDS ***Introduce Open Syllables*** Tell students that in some words with more than one syllable, a vowel in between two consonants can have the long vowel sound. Explain that when students come across such a word, they should try breaking it before the second consonant. Write the word *flavor* on the board. Frame the word part *fla*, and have students repeat it after you. Do the same for the word part *vor.* Then draw your hand under the entire word as students read it aloud. Follow a similar procedure with *premade, labeled,* and *chosen.*

Name ______________________________

REPRODUCIBLE STUDENT ACTIVITY PAGE

A Shaky Surprise

Mark the answer in front of the sentence that tells

1 **A** Willy pets the lion.
 (**B**) Willy stands behind the zebra.
 C Willy fixes the arbor.
 D Willy rolls under the zebra.

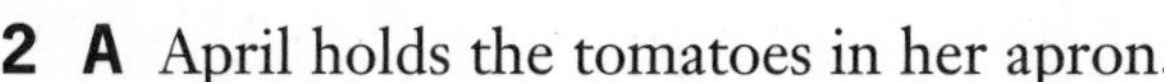

2 **A** April holds the tomatoes in her apron.
 B April holds the tomatoes with a ladle.
 (**C**) April sold the tomatoes in the crate.
 D April sold the tomatoes from her home.

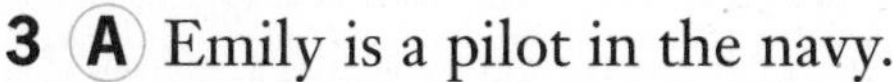

3 (**A**) Emily is a pilot in the navy.
 B Emily cares for lions at the wildlife park.
 C Emily explores volcanoes.
 D Emily has a program on the radio.

4 **A** Ruby's baby sister finds a tiny radio.
 B Ruby's baby sister rides an old bike.
 (**C**) Ruby's baby sister winds the funny clock.
 D Ruby's baby sister finds an acorn.

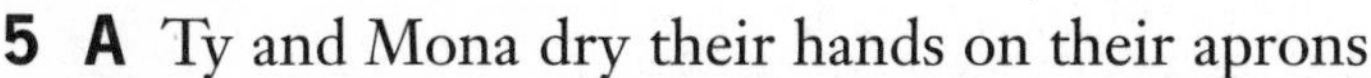

5 **A** Ty and Mona dry their hands on their aprons.
 B Ty and Mona don't like the flavor of tuna.
 (**C**) Ty and Mona try to keep dry in the rain.
 D Ty and Mona think the lake is cold.

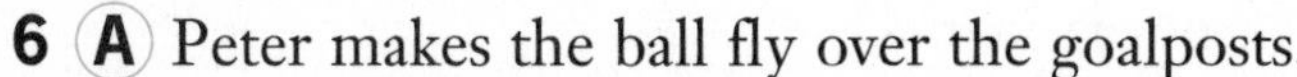

6 (**A**) Peter makes the ball fly over the goalposts.
 B Peter finds a spider behind the piano.
 C Peter grinds the corn with a stone.
 D Peter strolls by the cargo door.

Harcourt

Introducing Vocabulary

Apply word identification strategies.

LOOK FOR FAMILIAR SPELLING PATTERNS Display the vocabulary words, and ask students to read them silently and identify those they know. Remind students that they can sometimes figure out new words by looking for familiar spelling patterns. Frame each syllable in the word *frantic*, pointing out the familiar CVC pattern. Do the same for the first syllable in *staggered.* Then call on volunteers to read the words aloud and tell how they were able to figure them out. (*When a vowel is between two consonants, the vowel usually has the short vowel sound.*) Then frame the first syllable in *lurched*, pointing out the *ur.* Have a volunteer read the word aloud and tell how he or she was able to figure it out. Help students read the remaining vocabulary words aloud. If necessary, provide clues: when the ground shakes (*earthquake*); when there is no sound (*silence*); pushed into a very small space (*wedged*). If students misread a word and then correct themselves, encourage them by saying, for example, **You read ___ and then changed it to ___. How did you know to do that?**

VOCABULARY DEFINED

earthquake a shaking or rolling movement of the ground caused by volcanic activity or shifts in the earth's crust

frantic acting with great fear or worry

lurched moved or rolled suddenly forward or sideways

silence the absence of sound

staggered walked unsteadily

wedged forced into a small space

Discuss the meanings of the vocabulary words. Then ask students to invent a story using the vocabulary words, with each student adding a sentence to build the story. You may want to begin the story with this sentence: *The <u>earthquake</u> hit early in the morning.*

Check understanding.

Ask students to copy the vocabulary words on a sheet of paper. Have students name the word that best answers each question and circle it on their papers.

- **Which word describes someone who is acting very worried or fearful?** *(frantic)*
- **Which word describes what passengers did when the car came to a sudden halt?** *(lurched)*
- **Which word describes a ball that is stuck tightly between the branches of a tree?** *(wedged)*
- **Which word means "walked unsteadily"?** *(staggered)*
- **Which word names what happens when the ground shakes?** *(earthquake)*
- **Which word describes a condition when you hear no sounds?** *(silence)*

REPRODUCIBLE STUDENT ACTIVITY PAGE

INDEPENDENT PRACTICE See the reproducible Student Activity on page 65.

NOTE: The following vocabulary words from "Earthquake Terror" are reinforced in "A Shaky Surprise." If students are unfamiliar with these words, point them out as you encounter them during reading: *engrossed* (p. 86); *ominous* (p. 87); *bolt, susceptible, undulating, heaved* (p. 88); *evaporating* (p. 91).

Name ______________________________

REPRODUCIBLE STUDENT ACTIVITY PAGE

A Shaky Surprise

These sentences are about "A Shaky Surprise." Write the word from the box that makes sense in each sentence. Use each word only once.

silence	staggered	lurched	earthquake	wedged	frantic

1. Dave, Kate, and her brother worked in silence while stacking cards and blocks.
2. Then an earthquake began to shake the floor! The stacks began to shake.
3. The boys staggered as they went to a safe spot.
4. The table lurched to one side as the floor kept on shaking.
5. Some blocks got wedged between the table and the wall.
6. Kate was frantic when she went to get her blocks.

Answer these questions to tell what you think might happen in "A Shaky Surprise."

1. What do you think Kate will do next? Possible response: She will get her blocks and then find her mother, her brother, and Dave.

2. What do you think will happen after the shaking stops? Possible response: Kate's mother and brother will take care of Kate; Kate, her brother, and Dave will pick up the cards and blocks.

Harcourt

Directed Reading

Page 86 Ask a volunteer to read the title of the story. Help students identify Kate, her brother, their mother, and Dave. Have students read page 86 to find out what Kate's brother and Dave hope to do with the cards. Ask: **Why do you think this story is called "A Shaky Surprise"?** (Possible response: *Kate will surprise her brother and Dave by knocking over the stack of cards.*) INFERENTIAL: MAKE PREDICTIONS

Page 87 Have students read page 87. Ask: **What does the author compare to the sound of a big truck?** (*the earthquake's rumble*) INFERENTIAL: UNDERSTAND FIGURATIVE LANGUAGE **What do you think the children will do now?** (Possible response: *They will hide under the table.*) INFERENTIAL: MAKE PREDICTIONS

Page 88 Have students read page 88 to confirm their predictions. Ask: **How do you think an earthquake is like a bolt of lightning?** (Possible response: *It can happen quickly. You never know exactly where it will strike.*) CRITICAL: INTERPRET IMAGERY **Why do you think Kate staggered after the blocks?** (Possible response: *She had never been in an earthquake before and was confused.*) CRITICAL: INTERPRET CHARACTERS' MOTIVES

Page 89 Have students read page 89 to find out what happens to Kate. Ask: **How does Kate's brother help her through the earthquake?** (*He goes to her, takes her hand, says, "It's okay," and brings her to the doorway.*) INFERENTIAL: IMPORTANT DETAILS/SUMMARIZE **Why is a doorway a good place to be in an earthquake?** (*because it is the strongest part of the wall*) INFERENTIAL: CAUSE-EFFECT

Page 90 After students read page 90, ask: **How do you know that Kate has never been in an earthquake before?** (*She asks what the big shake was, and her mom tells her it was her first earthquake.*) METACOGNITIVE: CAUSE-EFFECT **How can you tell Kate's brother is kind?** (*He offers to help her make a new stack with her blocks.*) INFERENTIAL: DETERMINE CHARACTERS' TRAITS

Page 91 Have students read page 91 to find out what happens after the earthquake. **How do you know the children are no longer scared?** (Possible responses: *They begin to play again; they smile.*) METACOGNITIVE: DRAW CONCLUSIONS **What is the "shaky surprise"?** (Possible responses: *the earthquake that began without warning; the big cake that said "Happy Earthquake!" in shaky frosting letters*) CRITICAL: INTERPRET THEME

SUMMARIZE THE SELECTION Have students think about what happened before, during, and after the earthquake in "A Shaky Surprise." Then help them summarize the selection in three sentences.

Page 92

Answers to Think About It Questions

1. The stacks of cards and blocks fall down, and the earth undulates. Mom and the children go to the doorway to stay safe. SUMMARY
2. Possible response: They know from the start that the rumbling sound and the shaking are being made by an earthquake. INTERPRETATION
3. Accept reasonable responses. News stories should be written objectively and should focus on general effects of the earthquake. WRITE A NEWS STORY

Page 93 For instruction on the Focus Skill: Cause and Effect, see page 93 in *Timeless Tales*.

Name ________________________________

REPRODUCIBLE STUDENT ACTIVITY PAGE

A Shaky Surprise

Write one sentence in each box below to tell the main points of "A Shaky Surprise."

Pages 86–87

Main Idea: Dave, Kate, and Kate's brother are building stacks of cards and blocks when they feel the rumble of an earthquake.

Pages 88–89

Main Idea: Kate's mom tells everyone to stand under a doorway until the earthquake stops.

Pages 90–91

Main Idea: The boys build Kate a castle with her blocks after the earthquake.

Harcourt

Now write a one-sentence summary statement about the story. Use the information in the boxes above.

An earthquake interrupts Dave, Kate, and Kate's brother as they build stacks of cards and blocks.

Flowers After the Flames

by Kana Riley **Use with *Timeless Tales*, pages 94–101.**

Preteaching Skills: Vowel Diphthongs /ou/*ou, ow*

Teach/Model

IDENTIFY THE SOUND Have students repeat the following sentence aloud three times: *We heard the hound howl all around town.* Have students identify the words that have the /ou/ sound. (*hound, howl, around, town*)

ASSOCIATE LETTERS TO SOUNDS Write on the board the sentence above. Underline the letters *ou* in *hound* and *around.* Tell students that the vowel combination *ou* usually stands for the /ou/ sound in *sound.* Then underline the letters *ow* in *howl* and *town.* Point out that the letters *ow* also can stand for the /ou/ sound.

WORD BLENDING Model how to blend and read the word *shout.* Point to each letter and say its sound. Slide your hand under the whole word as you elongate the sounds /shout/. Then say the word naturally—*shout.* Follow a similar procedure with *cloud, growl,* and *clown.*

Practice/Apply

APPLY THE SKILL ***Letter Substitution*** Write the following words on the board, and have students read each aloud. Make the changes necessary to form the words in parentheses. Ask a volunteer to read each new word.

toll (towel) choke (chow) pond (pound) run (round)

DICTATION AND WRITING Have students number a sheet of paper 1–8. Dictate the following words, and have students write them. After they write each word, display it so students can proofread their work. They should draw a line through a misspelled word and write the correct spelling beside it.

1. out*	2. ground*	3. sprout*	4. sounds*
5. brown*	6. now*	7. flowers*	8. however*

**Word appears in "Flowers After the Flames."*

Dictate the following sentences for students to write: *I dug the weeds out of the ground with my trowel. Now I can plant these flowers.*

READ LONGER WORDS ***Introduce Breaking Words with Vowel Diphthongs; Review Breaking Words with VCCV*** Write the following words on the board: *power, outdoors.* Have volunteers identify the letters that stand for the /ou/ sound in *power.* (*ow*) Tell students that when they read a longer word with the letters *ow* or *ou*, these letter combinations usually stay together when the word is broken into syllables. Ask: **Which part of the first word sounds like /pou/? Which part sounds like /ər/?** Draw your hand under the entire word while students read it. Then have students identify the two consonants that are next to each other in *outdoors.* (*t, d*) Draw a line between *t* and *d*, and remind students that words that have this pattern are usually divided into syllables between the two consonants. Frame *out* and have students read it. Frame *doors* and have students read it. Ask students to read the whole word. Repeat the procedure with *cloudburst, cowhand, outside,* and *plowshare.*

REPRODUCIBLE STUDENT ACTIVITY PAGE

INDEPENDENT PRACTICE See the reproducible Student Activity on page 69.

Name ______________________________

REPRODUCIBLE STUDENT ACTIVITY PAGE

Flowers After the Flames

Read the story, and circle all the words with the same vowel sound as in *pound* and *now*.

Last summer a traveling carnival came to town. For several days, we heard the pounding of hammers and the humming of drills.

A big crowd came to it the first day. Inside the grounds the visitors found lots of rides and games. There was a Ferris wheel that went around and around. There was a winding slide connected to a big tower.

Every hour a parade would wind its way around the grounds. It was led by a grouchy clown mounted on a purple cow. The clown's lips were painted into a big red frown and she wore a funny gown. Just behind her strolled a big round sow. Behind the sow was a growling hound. In the middle of the parade, the hound bounded past the sow. He jumped and landed on the clown, making her fall off the cow. The clown groaned out loud. Everyone in the crowd clapped and cheered.

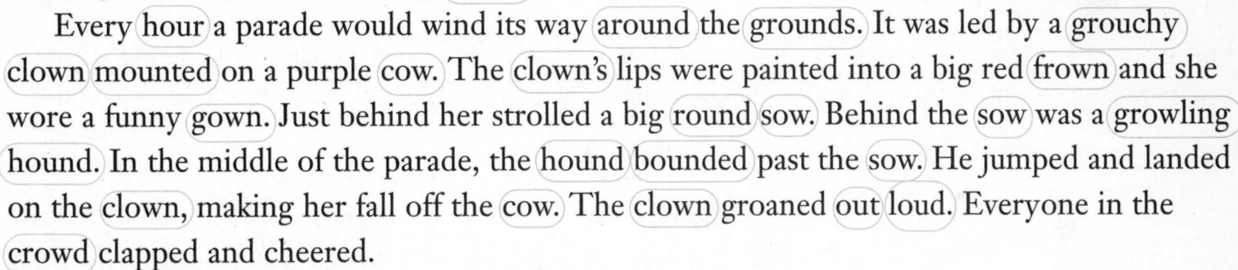

Now write the word with the same vowel sound as in *pound* and *now* that best completes each sentence.

1. The carnival came to ___town___ last summer.
2. The slide was connected to a ___tower___.
3. The first day a big ___crowd___ attended the carnival.
4. Every hour a parade wound its way ___around___ the grounds.
5. A ___grouchy___ clown led the parade.
6. The clown wore a funny gown and had a big red ___frown___.
7. A sow and a ___hound___ were behind her.
8. The hound made the clown fall off a purple ___cow___.

Harcourt

Introducing Vocabulary

Apply word identification strategies.

LOOK FOR FAMILIAR SPELLING PATTERNS Display the vocabulary words, and ask students to identify the ones they know. Remind students that they can sometimes figure out a new word by looking for familiar spelling patterns. Help students divide the word *forecast* into syllables (fore•cast). Point out the patterns in each syllable: a vowel surrounded by consonants followed by an *e* in the first syllable, a vowel surrounded by consonants in the second syllable. Call on volunteers to read this word aloud and tell how they were able to figure it out. Help students read the remaining vocabulary words aloud, using clues as necessary: an area of land (*region*); faced with danger (*threatened*); plots of land equal to 43,560 square feet (*acres*); substances with special properties (*chemicals*); to protect (*defend*). When students read a word correctly, encourage them by saying, for example, **Look at the word again. How did you figure out that was the word?**

VOCABULARY DEFINED

acres areas of land, each equal to 43,560 square feet

chemicals substances with special properties

defend to guard against harm; to protect

forecast a prediction of future weather conditions

region an area of land

threatened put in danger

Discuss the meanings of the vocabulary words. Then ask students to make up sentences that include at least two of those words. (Possible response: *The entire <u>region</u> was <u>threatened</u> by a large forest fire.*) Have students continue making up sentences until all the words have been used.

Check understanding.

Ask students to write the vocabulary words on a sheet of paper. Then have them name the word that matches each of the following clues and circle that word on their papers.

- **Two of us are equal to 87,120 square feet. What are we?** *(acres)*
- **You might use us in a science experiment. What are we?** *(chemicals)*
- **I'm what soccer goalies do for their teams. What am I?** *(defend)*
- **I'm an area you might live in or visit. What am I?** *(region)*
- **You might feel this way if a fire was nearby.** *(threatened)*
- **Sometimes I say it will rain tomorrow. What am I?** *(forecast)*

Provide vocabulary support.

Students may have trouble with words such as *Yellowstone* (p. 94), *renewed* (p. 97), and *charred* (p. 99). Introduce the words by writing them on the board and pronouncing each. As students come across these words in the selection, offer assistance as needed.

REPRODUCIBLE STUDENT ACTIVITY PAGE

INDEPENDENT PRACTICE See the reproducible Student Activity on page 71.

NOTE: The following vocabulary words from "Summer of Fire" are reinforced in "Flowers After the Flames." If students are unfamiliar with these words, point them out as you encounter them during reading: *geysers, tinder, policy* (p. 94); *veer, canopy, embers* (p. 95); *dwindled* (p. 96).

Name ______________________________

REPRODUCIBLE STUDENT ACTIVITY PAGE

Flowers After the Flames

Read each sentence. Write the word from the box that makes sense in the sentence.

forecast	threatened	chemicals	region	acres	defend

In the spring of 1988, very little rain fell in the region around Yellowstone National Park.

As the summer went by, the forecast said there would be no more rain.

Several fires broke out in June. Before long, the entire park was threatened.

Many firefighters came to defend the park against the fires.

They dropped water and chemicals on the flames, but it was too late.

Many acres of forest were blackened.

Answer these questions to tell what you think will happen in the story.

1. How do you think the 1988 Yellowstone National Park fires were put out at last?

Possible response: I think rain finally arrived in late summer and put the fires out.

2. How do you think plants and trees in the park were different right after the fires?

Possible response: The fires destroyed many plants and left the forest blackened.

Harcourt

Directed Reading

Page 94 Ask a volunteer to read the title of the story. Have students read page 94 to find out what happened in Yellowstone National Park in June 1988. (*Fires broke out.*) INFERENTIAL: MAIN IDEA Ask: **Why did people let the fires burn?** (Possible response: *It was park policy to let fires burn.*) INFERENTIAL: CAUSE-EFFECT

Page 95 Have students look at the illustration on page 95. Then ask them to read the page to find out what happened to the fires. Ask: **How did the winds make the fires worse?** (Possible responses: *The winds made the fires veer this way and that; they carried hot embers, which fell to the ground and started more fires.*) INFERENTIAL: CAUSE-EFFECT

Page 96 Have students read page 96 to find out what happened to the fires and the park. Ask: **What caused the fires to finally go out?** (*snow and rain*) INFERENTIAL: CAUSE-EFFECT **Why do you think the geysers and hot springs were not harmed by the fires?** (Possible response: *The fires never reached these areas.*) CRITICAL: SPECULATE

Page 97 Have students read page 97 to find out how animals adapted to the blackened forest. Ask: **How did elk adapt to the blackened forest?** (*They licked the ash for minerals and then ate the grasses that sprang up.*) INFERENTIAL: IMPORTANT DETAILS **How did the fires help to feed birds and small animals?** (*They made the pinecones pop open and spill seeds on the ground, which small animals could eat.*) INFERENTIAL: CAUSE-EFFECT

Page 98 After students read page 98, ask: **What had to happen before seeds hidden under the scorched ground could sprout?** (*The sun had to melt the snow. Then the water from the snow had to trickle underground, soaking the seeds.*) INFERENTIAL: SEQUENCE **Do you think the fact that bison and brown bears returned to the area was a good or bad sign? Explain why.** (Possible response: *good, because it probably meant there was enough food for them to survive*) CRITICAL: MAKE OBSERVATIONS

Page 99 Have students think about the changes that the forest has undergone as they read page 99. Ask: **How does the author help you create a mental picture of the forest?** (*The author describes what the flowers looked like and tells about the sounds of birds singing and woodpeckers pounding holes in charred trees.*) CRITICAL: AUTHOR'S CRAFT/APPRECIATE LANGUAGE

Page 100 Have students read page 100. Ask: **Do you think the policy to let the fires burn was a good one? Explain.** (Responses will vary.) CRITICAL: MAKE JUDGMENTS/EXPRESS OPINIONS

SUMMARIZE THE SELECTION Ask students to think about what happened before, during, and after the fires. Then have them summarize the selection.

Page 101

Answers to Think About It Questions

1. The forest fires made way for renewed life at Yellowstone. The heat of the fires popped open pinecones, spilling seeds for the animals to eat. The fires made way for more sunshine, so that more flowers and little trees could grow. SUMMARY
2. Possible response: In the summer of 1988, people probably felt afraid of the fires. The next summer, people probably felt glad that the fires had made way for renewed life. INTERPRETATION
3. Postcard messages should describe the scenery and plant and animal life and should express personal reactions to the park. WRITE A POSTCARD

Name ______________________

REPRODUCIBLE STUDENT ACTIVITY PAGE

Flowers After the Flames

Write one sentence in each box below to summarize the ideas presented on those pages about the Yellowstone forest fires.

Pages 94–95

Main Idea: In the summer of 1988, dry conditions caused fires at Yellowstone National Park to spread out of control.

Pages 96–97

Main Idea: When snow and rain finally put out the fires, the plants and animals found new ways to survive.

Pages 98–99

Main Idea: Throughout the spring season new life returned to Yellowstone.

Now write a one-sentence summary of "Flowers After the Flames."

Possible response: Forest fires at Yellowstone National Park made way for new life.

Harcourt

The Krakatoa Wave

by Lee Chang **Use with *Timeless Tales*, pages 102–109.**

Preteaching Skills: Long Vowel /ī/*igh, ie*

Teach/Model

IDENTIFY THE SOUND Have students repeat the following sentence twice: *They lie under the bright light of summer skies.* Ask students to identify the words that have the /ī/ sound. (*lie, bright, light, skies*)

ASSOCIATE LETTERS TO SOUNDS Write on the board the sentence above. Underline the letters *igh* in the words *bright* and *light.* Tell students that the letter combination *igh* stands for the /ī/ sound. Point out that the letters *gh* are silent. Then underline the letters *ie* in *lie* and *skies.* Explain that the letters *ie* often stand for the /ī/ sound heard in *lie* and *skies.* Remind students that they have learned many other patterns of letters that also stand for the long *i* sound. Write this sentence on the board: *Mike flies a kite right behind the twins.* Ask volunteers to underline the letter or letters that stand for the /ī/ sound in each word. (Mike flies a kite right behind the twins.)

WORD BLENDING Model how to blend and read the word *skies.* Point to the initial *s* and say /s/. Point to *k* and say /k/. Slide your hand under *ie* and say /ī/. Point to the final *s* and say /z/. Slide your hand under the whole word as you elongate the sounds /sskkīīzz/. Then say the word naturally—*skies.* Repeat the procedure with *light.*

Practice/Apply

APPLY THE SKILL ***Letter Substitution*** Write each of the following words on the board, and have students read it aloud. Make the changes necessary to form the words in parentheses. Have a volunteer read aloud each new word.

fit (fight)	mitt (might)	frill (fright)	trip (tried)
pit (pie)	sit (sight)	spin (spies)	slit (slight)

DICTATION AND WRITING Have students number a sheet of paper 1–8. Write the word *light* on the board, and tell students that in the first four words you will say, the /ī/ sound is spelled *igh.* Dictate words 1–4, and have students write them. After they write each word, display the correct spelling so students can proofread their work. Then write the word *pie* on the board, and tell students that in the last four words you will say, the /ī/ sound is spelled *ie.* Dictate words 5–8, and have students proofread as before.

1. high*	2. night*	3. flight	4. brighter*
5. tie	6. cried	7. tries	8. denies

**Word appears in "The Krakatoa Wave."*

Dictate the following sentence for students to write: *She tied a bright light on her bike for a night ride.*

REPRODUCIBLE STUDENT ACTIVITY PAGE

INDEPENDENT PRACTICE See the reproducible Student Activity on page 75.

READ LONGER WORDS ***Review Compound Words*** Write the word *nightfall* on the board. Remind students that when they come to a longer word, they can check to see if it is made up of two shorter words. Ask students which part of the word sounds like /night/ and which part sounds like /fall/. Ask what the words *night* and *fall* together sound like. Have students blend the word parts to read the longer word *nightfall.* Follow a similar procedure with *oversight, limelight,* and *sightseeing.*

Name ______________________________

REPRODUCIBLE STUDENT ACTIVITY PAGE

The Krakatoa Wave

Do what the sentences tell you.

1. Outside, there is not much daylight. Put dark clouds in the skies.
2. Inside, Dwight tries to fix his bike seat. Add a seat to his bike.
3. Dwight's sight is not good. Give him glasses so he can see his work.
4. Dwight must put a bright reflector on the seat of his bike. Put the round reflector in his hand.
5. Dwight has put the bike light on backward. Cross out the light and sketch it the right way.
6. It is not very bright in here. Add a new lightbulb.
7. Mom tries to reach a box, but it is too high. Make a ladder for her.
8. She will need a flashlight to see inside the box. Give her one.
9. Dad has pried open a sealed box. Sketch what is inside.
10. Dad's bow tie is missing. Put a bow tie around his collar.
11. Flick, the dog, cries for a bone. Make a bone for Flick.
12. Flick is missing his spots! Add spots on his thighs and back.
13. Flick likes to lie on rugs. Make a rug for Flick to lie on.
14. Flick is frightened by a bee that flies by. Sketch the bee.
15. Someone might trip over the supplies on the floor. Cross them out and put them on the shelf.

Now circle the words that have the /ī/ sound spelled *igh* or *ie*.

Harcourt

Introducing Vocabulary

VOCABULARY DEFINED

coastline a stretch of land along the seashore

explosion the act of blowing up, usually with a loud noise

island a piece of land that is surrounded on all sides by water

ocean an enormous body of salt water

tsunami a huge wave caused by an underwater earthquake

volcano an opening in the earth which can erupt, spewing steam, ashes, and lava

Apply word identification strategies.

LOOK FOR FAMILIAR SPELLING PATTERNS Display the vocabulary words, and ask students to identify the ones they know. Remind them that they can sometimes figure out an unfamiliar word by looking for familiar spelling patterns. Draw students' attention to the word *coastline.* Point to the letters *oa*, and ask what sound these letters usually stand for. (*long* o) Then point out the familiar CVC*e* pattern of the second syllable, and ask students to use what they know about this pattern to read the whole word. Then help students read aloud the other words. (You may need to read the word *tsunami* aloud and explain its meaning.) Use clues as necessary: rhymes with *motion* (*ocean*); a kind of wave (*tsunami*); a growling mountain (*volcano*); a huge bang (*explosion*); a piece of land offshore (*island*). Sometimes when students read a word correctly, encourage them by saying, **That's right. Look at the word again. What made you think that could be the word you said?** Discuss the meanings of the vocabulary words.

Check understanding.

Have students copy the vocabulary words on a sheet of paper. Ask them to name the word that answers each of the following questions and to circle that word on their papers.

- **What does hot lava come out of?** *(volcano)*
- **Which word names a huge, dangerous wave caused by an earthquake?** *(tsunami)*
- **Where do whales live?** *(ocean)*
- **What word names a place where the land meets the sea?** *(coastline)*
- **Construction workers used explosives to take a building down. What did they cause when they lit the fuse?** *(explosion)*
- **What word names a place that is completely surrounded by water?** *(island)*

Provide vocabulary support.

Students may have trouble with names such as Krakatoa (p. 102), Java (p. 103), and Sumatra (p. 103). Introduce the words by writing them on the board and pronouncing each one. As students come across these words in the selection, offer assistance as needed.

REPRODUCIBLE STUDENT ACTIVITY PAGE

INDEPENDENT PRACTICE See the reproducible Student Activity on page 77.

NOTE: The following vocabulary words from "Oceans" are reinforced in "The Krakatoa Wave." If students are unfamiliar with these words, point them out as you encounter them during reading: *inlet*, *generated* (p. 104); *bulge*, *gravitational*, *energy* (p. 105); *shallow* (p. 106).

Name ______________________________

The Krakatoa Wave

Read the ad.

Meet Krakatoa

Krakatoa was a big **volcano**. It was on an **island** in the middle of the **ocean**. It sometimes gave off smoke or made loud sounds. Still, people nearby were not very frightened of it. That was because it had not had a big **explosion** in a long time.

One day, however, it did explode! Smoke and ash shot into the sky. Red-hot melted rock seeped out and glowed in the night. Under the water, there were big earthquakes. The earthquakes made huge waves called **tsunamis**.

What did this mean for the people on the **coastline** of Java and Sumatra? Read "The Krakatoa Wave" and find out.

Write a word from the ad to complete each sentence. Choose from the words in dark type.

1. Krakatoa was a volcano.
2. The volcano was located on an island.
3. One day there was a loud explosion.
4. The blast made earthquakes beneath the ocean.
5. These earthquakes made tsunamis form and make their way to land.
6. These huge waves came ashore at the coastline of Java and Sumatra.

Do you think Krakatoa's wave will do much harm to the towns on the coast? Why or why not?

Possible response: yes, because if they were not expecting Krakatoa to erupt, they may not have been prepared

Harcourt

Directed Reading

Pages 102–103 Read aloud the title of the story. Then point out the volcano in the illustration on page 102 and explain that this volcano is called Krakatoa. Point out the smoke in the illustration and ask students what they think caused it. (*Krakatoa erupted.*) Have them read pages 102–103 to check their predictions. Ask: **Why weren't the people of Java and Sumatra worried when they saw smoke and heard explosions coming from the volcano?** (*They were used to this. For years, the volcano did this without a major eruption.*) INFERENTIAL: DRAW CONCLUSIONS **What do you think happened on August 26, 1883?** (Possible response: *Krakatoa erupted violently.*) METACOGNITIVE: MAKE PREDICTIONS/UNDERSTAND FIGURATIVE LANGUAGE

Page 104 Have students read page 104 to see if they predicted correctly. Ask: **What happened on the day Krakatoa "woke up"?** (*There was a huge explosion of steam, smoke, and hot ash, followed by several earthquakes.*) INFERENTIAL: SUMMARIZE **What caused the gigantic wave?** (*underwater earthquakes*) LITERAL: CAUSE-EFFECT

Page 105 Read page 105 aloud. Ask: **How is a tsunami different from an ordinary high wave?** (*An ordinary high wave is caused by the gravitational pull of the moon. A tsunami is caused by the energy of an earthquake.*) LITERAL: MAKE COMPARISONS **Why did people rush to high ground?** (*They were afraid that the lowlands near the shore would be flooded by the wave.*) INFERENTIAL: CAUSE-EFFECT

Page 106 Have students read page 106 to find out what happened next. (*Huge explosions blew Krakatoa apart. A new tsunami formed and grew to be over 120 feet high.*) To help students visualize how far 2,500 miles is, point out that this is almost the distance from one coast of the United States to the other. Ask: **What do you think was the greater threat to humans, the explosions or the tsunami? Why?** (Possible response: *the tsunami, because its size and force devastated buildings and caused great loss of human life*) CRITICAL: INTERPRET STORY EVENTS

Page 107 Have students read page 107 to find out what happened when the tsunami hit land. (*It wiped out towns and killed thousands of people.*) Ask: **What do you think Krakatoa's wave teaches us about nature?** (Possible response: *Nature is an awesome force that should be respected and, at times, feared.*) CRITICAL: INTERPRET THEME

SUMMARIZE THE SELECTION Have students think about the sequence of events leading up to Krakatoa's wave hitting the coastline. Then ask them to summarize the story in a few sentences by telling about this sequence of events.

Page 108

Answers to Think About It Questions

1. A tsunami is a very high wave made by the energy of an underground explosion. When the tsunami hit, towns were wiped out and people died. SUMMARY
2. Possible response: The wave moved very fast and hit the shores of Java and Sumatra. It killed so many people and frightened so many others that people will always talk and write about what happened. INTERPRETATION
3. Accept reasonable responses. Lists and paragraphs should show an understanding of the island as lush and green before the volcano eruption, and without plant and animal life after the eruption. MAKE A LIST/WRITE A PARAGRAPH

Page 109 For instruction on the Focus Skill: Graphic Sources, see page 109 in *Timeless Tales.*

Name ______________________________

REPRODUCIBLE STUDENT ACTIVITY PAGE

The Krakatoa Wave

Complete the sequence chart about "The Krakatoa Wave." Write a sentence in each box. The first one is done for you.

Event 1:

Krakatoa exploded on August 26, 1883.

Event 2:

Possible response: Underwater earthquakes caused by the explosion started a tsunami.

Event 3:

Possible response: The first tsunami hit the coastlines of Java and Sumatra. People ran for high ground.

Event 4:

Possible response: Another tsunami grew to be over 120 feet tall. It destroyed many lives on these islands.

Now use the information from the boxes to write a one-sentence summary of the selection.

Possible response: Tsunamis caused by the explosion of Krakatoa killed thousands of people on the islands of Java and Sumatra in 1883.

Harcourt

Cindy "Science" Spots the Clues

by Mary Wright **Use with *Timeless Tales*, pages 110–117.**

Preteaching Skills: Consonant /s/c

Teach/Model

IDENTIFY THE SOUND Have students repeat the following sentence aloud three times: *The circus clown rode on a unicycle in the center ring.* Ask students to identify the words that have the /s/ sound. (*circus, unicycle, center*)

ASSOCIATE LETTERS TO SOUNDS Write on the board the sentence above. Underline the *c* with the /s/ sound in *circus, unicycle,* and *center* as you say each word aloud. Explain that in these words the *c* stands for the /s/ sound. Then write the words *cat, corn,* and *cup* on the board, and have a volunteer read them aloud. Point out that in these words the *c* stands for the /k/ sound. Have students read all of the words on the board and form a generalization about which vowels follow /s/ and which follow /k/. (Example: *When* c *is followed by* e, i, *or* y, *it usually stands for the* /s/ *sound; when* c *is followed by* a, o, *or* u, *it usually stands for the* /k/ *sound.*) Remind students that *y* can act as a vowel, as it does in the word *unicycle.*

WORD BLENDING Model how to blend the letters and sounds to read the word *cinder.* Point to each letter and say its sound. Slide your hand under the whole word as you elongate the sounds /ssiinnddder/. Then say the word naturally—*cinder.*

Practice/Apply

APPLY THE SKILL ***Letter Substitution*** Write each of the following words on the board, and have students read it aloud. Make the changes necessary to form the words in parentheses. Ask volunteers to read the new words.

call (cell) canter (center) cave (civil) collar (cellar)

DICTATION AND WRITING Have students number a sheet of paper 1–8. Dictate the following words, and have students write them. After they write each word, display the correct spelling so students can proofread their work. Have them draw a line through a misspelled word and write the correct spelling beside it.

1. trace	2. bicycle*	3. space*	4. slice*
5. lace	6. cells*	7. center*	8. cereal*

**Word appears in "Cindy Science Spots the Clues."*

Dictate the following sentence for students to write: *Cindy decided to ride her bicycle to the concert.*

READ LONGER WORDS ***Review Open Syllables; Introduce Closed Syllables*** Write *celebrate* on the board and read it aloud. Remind students that they have learned that words such as *bicep* and *protest* often have a long vowel sound in the first syllable; such words are divided right after the vowel in the first syllable. Tell them that *celebrate* has the same pattern of letters but that *celebrate* is divided after the *l* and that the first syllable has a short vowel sound. Point to *celebrate.* Ask a volunteer which part of the word sounds like /sel/, which part sounds like /ə/, and which part sounds like /brāt/. Then draw your hand under the entire word as students read it aloud. Repeat the procedure with *precise, civil, pencil, Pacific,* and *icy.*

REPRODUCIBLE STUDENT ACTIVITY PAGE

INDEPENDENT PRACTICE See the reproducible Student Activity on page 81.

Name ______________________________

REPRODUCIBLE STUDENT ACTIVITY PAGE

Cindy "Science" Spots the Clues

Circle and write the best word to complete each sentence.

1. Cathy is teaching Cyrus how to tap ___dance___.
dance (circled) **date** **dark**

2. Cathy has taken tap classes ___since___ she was six.
skill **since** (circled) **silence**

3. Cyrus ___decided___ to learn how to dance
decoded **decided** (circled) **deduced**
after he saw Cathy dance in a talent show.

4. Cathy and Cyrus stand in the ___center___ of the hall. They wait for the music to begin.
center (circled) **circle** **corner**

5. Cathy shows Cyrus a new routine. They spin in ___circles___ as they dance.
collars **processes** **circles** (circled)

6. Cathy hopes to perform with Cyrus at the winter ___concert___.
center **concert** (circled) **crowd**

7. She circles the date in ___pencil___ on her calendar.
pencil (circled) **purple** **puzzle**

8. On the big night, Cyrus and Cathy both wear ___fancy___ costumes.
fancy (circled) **finally** **finicky**

9. When the dancing ___ceases___,
causes **calls** **ceases** (circled)
the people clap wildly.

10. After the concert, Cathy and Cyrus ___celebrate___ their success.
celery **career** **celebrate** (circled)

Harcourt

Introducing Vocabulary

Apply word identification strategies.

LOOK FOR FAMILIAR SPELLING PATTERNS Display the vocabulary words, and ask students to identify the ones they know. Remind them that they can sometimes use familiar spelling patterns to help them figure out unfamiliar words. Point out the *er* spelling pattern in the second syllable of *experts* and the *ear* spelling pattern in the second syllable of *research.* Ask students to use what they know about these patterns to read these words aloud. Also point out the *or* spelling pattern in the first syllable of *orbited* and the CVC pattern in the second syllable of that word. Ask a volunteer to read *orbited* aloud. Then help students read the remaining words aloud. Use clues as necessary: people who fly to the moon (*astronauts*); air around the Earth (*atmosphere*); means "takeoff" (*launch*). If students self-correct after reading a word, encourage them by saying, **You read ___ and then changed it to ___. How did you know to do that?**

VOCABULARY DEFINED

astronauts people trained to pilot spacecraft

atmosphere the lowest layer of air that surrounds Earth

expert a person with a great deal of knowledge about a subject

launch the takeoff of a spacecraft

orbited revolved around

research the careful study of a subject

Discuss the meanings of the vocabulary words. Then ask students to make up riddles that have vocabulary words as answers. (Possible response: *We wear helmets and space suits. We train for many years to learn how to fly spacecraft. Who are we?* <u>*astronauts*</u>) Continue until all the vocabulary words have been used at least once and each student has had an opportunity to respond.

Check understanding.

Ask students to write the vocabulary words on a sheet of paper. Then ask the following questions, and have students circle the word that answers each one.

- **Which word names people who visit outer space?** *(astronauts)*
- **Which word names the layer of air that surrounds planet Earth?** *(atmosphere)*
- **Whom would you ask if you wanted information on a subject?** *(expert)*
- **Which word means the opposite of *landing*?** *(launch)*
- **Which word tells what the spacecraft did when it circled the planet?** *(orbited)*
- **Which word names something you can do to learn about a topic?** *(research)*

REPRODUCIBLE STUDENT ACTIVITY PAGE

INDEPENDENT PRACTICE See the reproducible Student Activity on page 83.

NOTE: The following vocabulary words from "The Case of the Shining Blue Planet" are reinforced in "Cindy Science Spots the Clues." If students are unfamiliar with these words, point them out as you encounter them during reading: *cosmonaut* (p. 111); *breakthrough, enrolls* (p. 112); *disregarded, formulas* (p. 113); *altimeter, satellite* (p. 114); *dejectedly* (p. 115).

Name ______________________________

REPRODUCIBLE STUDENT ACTIVITY PAGE

Cindy "Science" Spots the Clues

Read the story.

Cindy "Science" Vincent uses her new computer to do **research** on outer space. She can't wait to tell Cyrus what she's learned. When she gets to his house, she meets Professor Durak. He claims to have **orbited** planets in space. Professor Durak tells Cindy that he helped with a space **launch.** Professor Durak claims he helped the **astronauts** solve a big problem. He describes the sights beyond Earth's **atmosphere**. Cindy thinks that Professor Durak can't be trusted. Cindy is an **expert** on space science. She spots mistakes in what Professor Durak says.

Write a story word to complete each sentence. Choose from the words in dark type.

1. Professor Durak claims to have ___orbited___ planets in space.
2. Professor Durak said he has helped ___astronauts___ solve big problems.
3. He also claims to have seen amazing sights beyond Earth's ___atmosphere___.
4. One time the professor helped with a space ___launch___ that went badly.
5. Cindy "Science" Vincent enjoys doing ___research___ on her computer.
6. Cindy can spot the professor's mistakes since she is an ___expert___ on space science.

Do you think Professor Durak is a real astronaut. Why, or why not?

Answers will vary.

____

Harcourt

Directed Reading

Page 110 Ask a volunteer to read the title aloud. Ask students what kind of story they think this will be, and why. (*A mystery; the main character "spots the clues."*) INFERENTIAL: DRAW CONCLUSIONS Have students read page 110, ask: **Why is this character nicknamed Cindy "Science"?** (Possible response: *She's interested in science, especially space research.*) INFERENTIAL: DRAW CONCLUSIONS

Page 111 Have students read page 111 to find out what Cyrus tells Cindy about the visitor at his house. (*He is a cosmonaut; he orbited the sun.*) LITERAL: NOTE DETAILS **How can you tell that Cindy knows more about science than Cyrus does?** (*She corrects him when he says the man had orbited the sun.*) INFERENTIAL: DRAW CONCLUSIONS

Page 112 Have students read page 112 to find out who the visitor is. (Possible response: *His name is Professor Durak; he says he's a space scientist.*) INFERENTIAL: IMPORTANT DETAILS Ask: **What important thing does Professor Durak say he did?** (*made a break-through for space science in 1969*) INFERENTIAL: IMPORTANT DETAILS

Page 113 After students read page 113, ask: **Why, according to Professor Durak, were the astronauts on the 1969 launch grateful to him?** (*He helped them fix a problem.*) INFERENTIAL: CAUSE-EFFECT **What does the professor say they did for him to show their gratitude?** (*They signed the shirt he is wearing.*) INFERENTIAL: IMPORTANT DETAILS

Page 114 Have students read page 114 to find out what Professor Durak claims to have seen in space. (*Mars; Jupiter with its ring; Venus with its Great Red Spot*) INFERENTIAL: IMPORTANT DETAILS **What do you think will happen next?** (Responses will vary.) INFERENTIAL: MAKE PREDICTIONS

Page 115 After students read page 115, ask: **Why does Cindy take Cyrus into the kitchen?** (*to tell him privately that Professor Durak is a fake*) CRITICAL: INTERPRET CHARACTERS' MOTIVATIONS **Do you think Cyrus was right to believe her? Why or why not?** (Possible responses: *yes, because she knows a lot about science; no, because she's a child, not a trained expert*) CRITICAL: MAKE JUDGMENTS

Page 116 Have students read page 116 to find out what clues Cindy spotted. **Why does the date on his shirt help show that Professor Durak is a fake?** (*The date on his shirt is 1999; he said the astronauts signed it in 1969.*) INFERENTIAL: IMPORTANT DETAILS **Why does Cindy tell Cyrus to "read about Jupiter"?** (*Because the information Professor Durak gave about the planets is wrong; Jupiter, not Venus, has the Great Red Spot.*) INFERENTIAL: IMPORTANT DETAILS

SUMMARIZE THE SELECTION Have students each share one fact they know about the planets in our solar system. Then help them summarize the selection.

Page 117

Answers to Think About It Questions

1. Cindy can tell that Professor Durak is a fake. The date he gave for his space flight was not correct. SUMMARY
2. Possible response: At first, he probably doesn't think much about meeting Cindy. To him, she is just a girl. Later, he must wish he had never met Cindy, because she proves that he is a fake. INTERPRETATION
3. Accept reasonable responses. Webs and paragraphs should show an understanding of Cindy as knowledgeable about science. WORD WEB/WRITE A PARAGRAPH

Name ____________________

REPRODUCIBLE STUDENT ACTIVITY PAGE

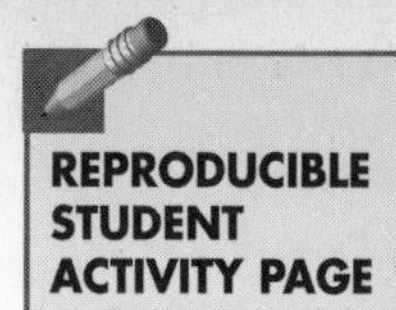

Cindy "Science" Spots the Clues

Write a sentence in each box below to help you summarize "Cindy 'Science' Spots the Clues." Be sure to write the events in the correct order.

Characters

Cindy, Cyrus, Cyrus's dad, Professor Durak

Setting

Time: winter

Place: Cyrus's house

Problem

Cindy suspects that Professor Durak is lying about his experiences in space.

Important Events

1. Cyrus tells Cindy that Professor Durak orbited the sun.
2. Cindy meets Professor Durak.
3. Professor Durak tells all about his adventures in space.
4. Cindy drags Cyrus into the kitchen.

Solution

Cindy proves to Cyrus that Professor Durak is a fake by pointing out the mistakes in his story.

Harcourt

Write a one-sentence summary of the selection.

Possible response: Cindy uses what she knows about space to prove that Professor Durak isn't telling the truth.

Gardens of the Sea: Coral Reefs

by Caren B. Stelson **Use with *Timeless Tales*, pages 118–125.**

Preteaching Skills: Consonant /j/g, dge

Teach/Model

IDENTIFY THE SOUND Have students repeat the following sentence aloud three times: *The giant engine uses steam energy to pull the huge train over the bridge.* Have students identify the words that have the /j/ sound. (*giant, engine, energy, huge, bridge*)

ASSOCIATE THE LETTER TO ITS SOUND Write the sentence *The giant engine uses steam energy to pull the huge train over the bridge* on the board. Underline g in *giant, engine,* and *energy,* g in *huge,* and *dge* in *bridge.* Explain that in these words, the letters *g,* and *dge* stand for the /j/ sound. Then write the words *gate, goal,* and *gulp* on the board and have a volunteer read them aloud. Point out that in these words the g stands for the /g/ sound. Next, write *gold, giraffe, change, garden, mangy,* and *gutter* on the board. Ask students to read each one aloud chorally and then form a generalization about the vowels that follow the /j/ sound or the /g/ sound. (Example: *When* g *is followed by an* e, i, *or* y, *it often stands for the /j/ sound. When* g *is followed by* a, o, *or* u, *it usually stands for the /g/ sound.*)

WORD BLENDING Write the words *giant, general, ledge, stage,* and *stingy* on the board. Model how to blend and read the word *giant.* Point to *g* and say /j/. Point to *i* and say /ī/. Slide your hand under the letters *ant* as you say /ənt/. Next, slide your hand under the whole word as you elongate the sounds /jjīī•ənt/. Then say the word naturally—*giant.* Follow a similar procedure for the remaining words.

Practice/Apply

APPLY THE SKILL ***Letter Substitution*** Write the following words on the board, and have students read each aloud. Then make the changes necessary to form the words in parentheses. Have a volunteer read each new word aloud.

gong (ginger)	wag (wage)	bag (badge)	lag (large)
gum (gem)	rag (rage)	rig (ridge)	gap (gypsy)

DICTATION AND WRITING Have students number a sheet of paper 1–8. Then dictate the following words, and have students write them. After students write each word, display it so they can proofread their work.

1. change	2. gently*	3. giant	4. largest*
5. fringe*	6. gems	7. ridges*	8. edge*

**Word appears in "Gardens of the Sea: Coral Reefs."*

READ LONGER WORDS ***Review Breaking Words with VCCV*** Write the words *gentleman* and *gyrating* on the board. Remind students that when they come across a word in which two consonants come together between two vowels, they usually should break the word into syllables in between the consonants. Point to *gentleman* and ask students which part of the word sounds like /jen/, which part sounds like /təl/, and which part sounds like /man/. Follow the same procedure with *gyrating.*

REPRODUCIBLE STUDENT ACTIVITY PAGE

INDEPENDENT PRACTICE See the reproducible Student Activity on page 87.

Name ______________________________

REPRODUCIBLE STUDENT ACTIVITY PAGE

Gardens of the Sea: Coral Reefs

Read the story. Circle all the words that have the sound the letter *g* stands for in the word *general*.

The giant giraffe wanted to drink some water. She walked slowly to the edge of the lake.

At the same time, a villager crossed the bridge. He wanted to fill his large bucket with water for his vegetables.

Neither the giraffe nor the villager saw the danger lurking in the hedges. Then a strange sound made them both look up.

A huge cat came flying out of the hedge. It was the largest beast the villager had ever seen.

The villager flew like a gymnast into a tree. The giraffe turned and ran over the ridge.

Luckily, wildlife biologists also heard the sound. They trapped the cat in a cage. Then they drove it far away from the village and the lake.

Circle and write the word that best completes each sentence.

1. The giant ____giraffe____ was thirsty.
   giraffe **gerbil** **hedgehog**

2. A villager needed water for his ____vegetables____.
   vegetables **pages** **fringe**

3. A huge cat was hiding behind the ____hedge____.
   hedge **sludge** **ginger**

4. Neither the giraffe nor the man saw the ____danger____.
   gem **engine** **danger**

5. Some wildlife ____biologists____ trapped the cat in a cage.
   geologists **biologists** **badges**

Harcourt

Introducing Vocabulary

Apply word identification strategies.

LOOK FOR FAMILIAR SPELLING PATTERNS Display the vocabulary words, and ask students to read them silently and identify those they know. Remind students that they can sometimes figure out a new word by looking for spelling patterns they know. Point out the consonant and long vowel pattern in *globe* and in the first syllable of *craters.* Call on volunteers to read those words aloud and to tell how they were able to figure them out. (*When a vowel is between two consonants and the second consonant is followed by* e, *it often has the long vowel sound.*) Help students read the remaining vocabulary words aloud. If necessary, provide clues: flows out of a volcano (*lava*); very, very old (*ancient*); a tiny ocean animal (*coral*); dangerous chemicals or trash in the air or water or on land (*pollution*). When students self-correct, encourage them by saying, for example, **You read ____ and then changed it to ____. Why? How did you know ____ was the correct word?**

VOCABULARY DEFINED

ancient very old

coral a tiny sea animal whose skeleton forms a hard, stony mass

craters bowl-shaped pits formed at the openings of volcanoes

globe a sphere-shaped model of the Earth

lava molten rock that flows from a volcano

pollution waste or other harmful substances in the air, land, or water

Discuss the meanings of the vocabulary words. Then ask students to use the vocabulary words in sentences that describe islands. (Possible responses: *Some islands are formed from <u>ancient</u> volcanoes. Some islands are surrounded by <u>coral</u> reefs.*) Continue until all the vocabulary words have been used at least once and each student has had an opportunity to respond.

Check understanding.

Ask students to write the vocabulary words on a sheet of paper. Have them name the word that answers each of the following riddles and circle that word on their papers.

- **I am round. You can find any place in the world on me.** *(globe)*
- **Without me, air and water are clean and pure.** *(pollution)*
- **I am very hot when I flow out of a volcano.** *(lava)*
- **I am from a past age.** *(ancient)*
- **I live in the sea.** *(coral)*
- **We are formed when meteors hit the ground.** *(craters)*

REPRODUCIBLE STUDENT ACTIVITY PAGE

INDEPENDENT PRACTICE See the reproducible Student Activity on page 89.

NOTE: The following vocabulary words from "Seeing Earth from Space" are reinforced in "Gardens of the Sea: Coral Reefs." If students are unfamiliar with these words, point them out as you encounter them during reading: *reef, sensors* (p. 118); *lagoon, atoll* (p. 121); *meander* (p. 122), *barren* (p. 124).

Name ____

REPRODUCIBLE STUDENT ACTIVITY PAGE

Gardens of the Sea: Coral Reefs

Read the story. Then fill in the web. Use all the words in dark type in your answers.

If you look at a **globe**, you can see that more than two-thirds of the Earth's surface is underwater. Many sea animals make their homes in this water. Some of the smallest sea animals help form **coral** reefs. Coral reefs are formed by tiny tubelike animals that are less than 1/2 inch across. As each tiny coral animal dies, its skeleton gets left behind. Other coral animals attach themselves to these skeletons. In this way, over time, the reefs can grow as tall as cliffs. Some people call coral reefs the gardens of the sea.

Coral reefs grow in warm ocean waters. Some coral reefs began growing around the edges of **ancient** islands formed from volcanoes. Hot **lava** may no longer flow from the **craters** of the volcanoes, but the coral reefs keep growing. Many other sea animals live among the coral reefs. Coral reefs need warm water and sunlight to keep growing. **Pollution** can harm the reefs. People must take care to keep the oceans clean.

Coral

How reefs are formed

coral reefs are formed from skeletons of small sea animals

Where coral reefs grow

found in warm oceans around the globe

around edges of ancient islands formed as hot lava flowed from craters of volcanoes

What other animals live near a coral reef

fish, turtles, sea stars, clams, sea horses

What can harm coral

pollution

Why do you think coral reefs might be called gardens of the sea?

Responses will vary; accept reasonable responses.

Harcourt

Directed Reading

Page 118 Have students read aloud the story title and preview the story by looking at the illustrations and photos and reading the captions. Have them predict what the selection is about. Then ask students to read page 118 to find out whether their predictions are correct. Ask: **In what kind of water are coral reefs found?** (*warm, shallow, clean, clear water*) LITERAL: NOTE DETAILS **How do corals get food?** (Possible response: *Tentacles around the mouth catch tiny sea animals that float by in the water.*) INFERENTIAL: MAIN IDEA

Page 120 Read page 120 aloud to students, asking them to listen to find out how a coral reef is formed. Then provide the following prompt: **In one sentence, summarize how coral reefs are formed.** (Possible response: *Corals grow on top of the skeletons of dead corals; over time a reef builds up.*) INFERENTIAL: SUMMARIZE

Page 121 Have students study the diagram on page 121 and read the page silently to find out how a coral atoll forms. Ask: **How does a coral atoll form in three stages?** (Possible response: *First, a fringing reef grows around the edge of a volcanic island. Next, the island sinks, forming a barrier reef and a lagoon. Then, as the island disappears, only the ring-shaped reef is left—an atoll.*) LITERAL: SEQUENCE **Does the diagram make the text on this page easier to understand? In what way?** (Possible response: *Yes, the three stages are easy to see in the diagram.*) CRITICAL: INTERPRET TEXT STRUCTURE

Page 122 Ask students to study the map on page 122, and help them locate the Great Barrier Reef. Then have them read page 122 to find out about the Great Barrier Reef. Ask: **Why is the Great Barrier Reef so important?** (Possible response: *It's the largest coral reef on Earth and the richest in sea life.*) INFERENTIAL: DRAW CONCLUSIONS

Page 123 Ask volunteers to read the captions for each picture on page 123. Ask: **What animals live along the Great Barrier Reef?** (Possible responses: *sea horses, green sea turtles, crown-of-thorns sea stars, giant clams, butterfly fish*) INFERENTIAL: IMPORTANT DETAILS **What facts from this page did you find the most interesting or unusual? Why?** (Answers will vary.) CRITICAL: EXPRESS PERSONAL OPINIONS

Page 124 Read page 124 aloud to students and have them listen to find out what could harm or kill the world's coral reefs. Ask: **Why are the living coral reefs in danger of dying?** (Possible response: *Corals need clean water, and ocean pollution kills the corals.*) INFERENTIAL: CAUSE-EFFECT **How can the world's coral reefs be saved?** (Possible response: *Stop pollution of the oceans.*) INFERENTIAL: DRAW CONCLUSIONS

SUMMARIZE THE SELECTION Ask students to think about where coral reefs grow, how they are formed, why they are important, and how they are in danger. Then have students write four sentences to summarize the selection.

Page 125

Answers to Think About It Questions

1. Coral reefs grow in oceans around the world, but only where the water is warm, shallow, clean, and clear. SUMMARY
2. Possible responses: A coral reef is like a garden because it grows in one place. It's different from a garden of plants because the growing things are animals. INTERPRETATION
3. Remind students to present specific reasons for choosing that animal. WRITE A PARAGRAPH

Name ____________________

REPRODUCIBLE STUDENT ACTIVITY PAGE

Gardens of the Sea: Coral Reefs

Write one or two sentences in each box below to show what you learned about coral reefs in "Gardens of the Sea: Coral Reefs."

Pages 118–120

Main Ideas: Possible response: Coral reefs are found in the warmest oceans all around the world. They are formed by the skeletons of small sea animals.

Pages 121–122

Main Ideas: Possible response: There are three kinds of reefs: fringing reefs, barrier reefs, and coral atolls. The Great Barrier Reef is the largest reef on Earth.

Pages 123–124

Main Ideas: Possible responses: Sea horses, sea turtles, sea stars, giant clams, and colorful fish live in and around reefs. We must prevent pollution from destroying the reefs.

Write a one-sentence summary statement about the selection.

Possible response: Coral reefs are beautiful undersea gardens full of life that we must care for and preserve.

Harcourt

Peppermint-Peanut-Butter Fudge

by Pam Zollman **Use with *Timeless Tales*, pages 126–133.**

Preteaching Skills: Vowel Diphthong /oi/*oi, oy*

Teach/Model

IDENTIFY THE SOUND Have students say the following sentence three times: *Roy annoys Joy with his loud noises.* Have students identify the words that have the /oi/ sound. (*Roy, annoys, Joy, noises*)

ASSOCIATE LETTERS TO SOUNDS Write the sentence *Roy annoys Joy with his loud noises* on the board. Underline the letters *oy* or *oi* in each word. Remind students that they have learned that when two vowels come together between consonants, they usually stand for a long vowel sound. Give *coat* and *grain* as examples. Tell students that the vowel combinations *oi* and *oy* do not follow this rule; these letter combinations usually stand for the /oi/ sound in *Roy* and *noises.*

WORD BLENDING Write *coil, oyster, royal,* and *moist* on the board. Model how to blend and read the word *coil.* Point to *c* and say /k/. Slide your hand under *o* and *i* and say /oi/. Point to *l* and say /l/. Draw your hand under the whole word as you elongate the sounds: /kkoill/. Then say the word naturally—*coil.* Repeat the procedure with the remaining words.

Practice/Apply

APPLY THE SKILL ***Letter Substitution*** Write each of the following words on the board, and have students read it aloud. Then make the changes necessary to form the words in parentheses. Ask a volunteer to read each new word aloud.

jay (joy)	fowl (foil)	nose (noise)	later (loiter)
mist (moist)	pint (point)	Jon (join)	decay (decoy)

DICTATION AND WRITING Have students number a sheet of paper 1–8. Write *oil* on the board, and tell students that in the first four words you will say, the /oi/ sound is spelled *oi.* Dictate words 1–4, and have students write them. After students write each word, display it so they can proofread their work. Then write the word *boy* on the board.

1. foil 2. annoyed 3. enjoying 4. spoiled

Dictate the following sentences and have students write them: *We had our choice of oysters or broiled fish. The boys pointed to the oysters.*

READ LONGER WORDS ***Review Breaking Words with Vowel Diphthongs*** Write these words on the board: *employment, asteroid.* Have a volunteer identify the two letters that together stand for the /oi/ sound in *employment.* (*oy*) Then point to *asteroid* and ask students which letters stand for the /oi/. (*oi*) Underline the letters *oy* and *oi,* and tell students that these letter combinations stay together when a word is broken into syllables. Help students identify the syllables in *employment* by asking: **Which letters stand for /em/? Which letters stand for /ploi/? Which letters stand for /ment/?** Then draw your hand under the entire word while students read it. Repeat this procedure for the words *overjoyed* and *disappoint.*

REPRODUCIBLE STUDENT ACTIVITY PAGE

INDEPENDENT PRACTICE See the reproducible Student Activity on page 93.

Name ______________________

REPRODUCIBLE STUDENT ACTIVITY PAGE

Peppermint-Peanut-Butter Fudge

Write the word that answers each riddle.

1. I have the same vowel sound as in *boy*.

You put me in a car's motor. What am I? oil

oil **gas** **owl**

2. I have the same vowel sound as in *toy*.

I live in the sea. What am I? oyster

flounder **oyster** **employee**

3. I have the same vowel sound as in *joy*.

You can pay for things with me. What am I? coin

coin **dollar** **coil**

4. I have the same vowel sound as in *boil*.

You use me to speak. What am I? voice

choice **voice** **mouth**

5. My second syllable has the same vowel sound as in *loyal*.

I am someone's boss. What am I? employer

enjoying **foreman** **employer**

6. I have the same vowel sound as in *join*.

I can be loud or soft. What am I? noise

sound **noise** **poise**

7. My first syllable has the same vowel sound as in *moist*.

I am a king. What am I? royalty

royalty **loyalty** **ruler**

8. I have the same vowel sound as in *boys*.

You can plant seeds in me. What am I? soil

ground **soil** **foil**

9. My second syllable has the same vowel sound as in *broil*.

I mean "to bother." What word am I? annoy

appoint **annoy** **distract**

Harcourt

Introducing Vocabulary

VOCABULARY DEFINED

brief short

generous large or ample

occasion a special event or celebration

precious valuable; much loved

relatives family members, including parents, brothers, aunts, cousins, grandparents, and others

wondrous wonderful, marvelous, or excellent

Apply word identification strategies.

LOOK FOR FAMILIAR SPELLING PATTERNS Display the vocabulary words, and ask students to identify the ones they know. Remind them that they can sometimes figure out an unfamiliar word by relating it to other words they know. Point out the word *wondrous.* Ask students if they can think of a shorter word that begins the same way. (*wonder*) Guide students to use their knowledge of the word *wonder* to read *wondrous.* Then help students read aloud the other words. Use clues as necessary: rhymes with *thief* (*brief*); a birthday or other special day (*occasion*); diamonds are this (*precious*); people you are related to (*relatives*); the opposite of *skimpy* (*generous*). As students read each word, encourage them by saying, **That's right. Look at the word again and tell me how you figured it out.**

Discuss the meanings of the vocabulary words. Then ask students to make up sentences that use two or more vocabulary words. (Possible response: *The reunion was a wondrous occasion with relatives coming from all over the world.*) Have students continue making up sentences until all the words have been used at least once and each student has had a chance to respond.

Check understanding.

Ask students to write the vocabulary words on a sheet of paper. Then ask each of the following questions. Have students name the word that best answers the question and circle it on their papers.

- **Imagine that you took a trip. If your trip was full of adventure, how might you describe it?** *(wondrous)*
- **If your trip was very short, how might you describe it?** *(brief)*
- **You visited family members on your trip. Whom did you visit?** *(relatives)*
- **You went to a special event on your trip. What is another word for *special event*?** *(occasion)*
- **You bought some expensive items on your trip. How might you describe these items?** *(precious)*
- **You ate at a restaurant that served huge meals. How would you describe the portions there?** *(generous)*

REPRODUCIBLE STUDENT ACTIVITY PAGE

INDEPENDENT PRACTICE See the reproducible Student Activity on page 95.

NOTE: The following vocabulary words from "Hattie's Birthday Box" are reinforced in "Peppermint-Peanut-Butter Fudge." If students are unfamiliar with these words, point them out as you encounter them during reading: *perch, homestead* (p. 126); *despair* (p. 128); *brooded, undeniable* (p. 129); *ration, concocted* (p. 130).

Name ______________________

REPRODUCIBLE STUDENT ACTIVITY PAGE

Peppermint-Peanut-Butter Fudge

You are about to read a story titled "Peppermint-Peanut-Butter Fudge." Read the story fact sheet.

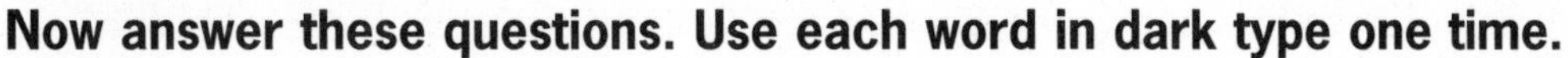

Who is in the story:
a boy named Roy;
Roy's sister, Pearl;
Granny; other **relatives**

When and where the story takes place:
on a homestead during a big **occasion**—Granny's birthday

What happens:
Roy and Pearl want to give Granny a **wondrous** birthday gift—a **generous** batch of fudge. Roy puts peanut butter in it by mistake. A **brief** moment later, he spills peppermints into the mix. Will Granny think the fudge is a **precious** gift or an awful mess? Read the story and find out.

Now answer these questions. Use each word in dark type one time.

1. Who is in the story besides Roy and Pearl? Granny and other relatives are also in the story.

2. Why have Roy, Pearl, Granny, and the other relatives gathered on the homestead? It is a special occasion. They are celebrating Granny's birthday.

3. What do Roy and Pearl want to do? They want to give Granny a wondrous gift.

4. What do Roy and Pearl decide to give Granny? They decide to give her a generous batch of fudge.

5. How does Roy almost spoil the fudge? First he adds peanut butter by mistake. A brief moment later, he spills peppermints into the mix.

6. Do you think Granny will like the fudge? Why or why not? Possible response: She will love the fudge. Grandparents usually appreciate any gift from their precious grandchildren.

Harcourt

Directed Reading

Page 126 Read aloud the title of the story. Ask students what is unusual about the title. (*Peppermint and peanut butter fudge do not normally go together.*) Then have them read page 126. Ask: **Why aren't Roy and Pearl enjoying the occasion?** (*They have no gift for Granny.*) LITERAL: CAUSE-EFFECT

Page 127 Have students read page 127 to find out what Roy and his sister do about a birthday gift for Granny. **What does Roy mean when he says, "You're looking at a boy who can't boil water"?** (*He knows nothing about cooking.*) INFERENTIAL: UNDERSTAND FIGURATIVE LANGUAGE **Why do you think Roy confuses peanut butter and butter?** (*Since he knows nothing about cooking, he assumes that anything with the word* butter *in it must be the same as butter.*) CRITICAL: INTERPRET STORY EVENTS

Page 128 Ask students to read page 128 to find out what happens next with the fudge. (*Roy spills a bowl of peppermints into the mix.*) Ask: **How does Roy feel when he spills the peppermints into the fudge mix? How can you tell?** (*He feels guilty and embarrassed. He nearly cries; he says, "I've spoiled it!"*) METACOGNITIVE: DETERMINE CHARACTERS' EMOTIONS

Page 129 Have students read page 129 to find out how the fudge tastes. (*It is nice and moist, but Roy thinks it is too sweet.*) Ask: **What do Roy and Pearl each think they should do with the fudge?** (*Roy thinks they should throw it away. Pearl thinks they should feed it to the pigs later.*) LITERAL: NOTE DETAILS

Page 130 Ask students to view the illustration on page 130 and describe the scene. Have them read page 130 to find out what happens when Granny tastes the fudge. (*She likes it.*) Ask: **Does Granny make the face Roy expects her to make? Explain.** (*No, Roy expected her to make a disgusted face. Instead, she made a face of enjoyment.*) INFERENTIAL: COMPARE AND CONTRAST

Page 131 Have students read page 131 to see who wins the kitchen contest. (*Pearl and Roy*) **What do Pearl and Roy do with the prize-winning fudge?** (*They give it to Granny as a birthday gift.*) INFERENTIAL: SUMMARIZE

SUMMARIZE THE SELECTION Ask students to think about what Pearl and Roy think will happen with their fudge and what actually happens. Then help them summarize the story in three or four sentences.

Page 132

Answers to Think About It Questions

1. Roy and Pearl don't like the fudge because it's too sweet. Granny likes it because she missed sweets as a child and enjoys very sweet things now. SUMMARY
2. Accept reasonable responses. Possible response: They worry that the other relatives will find out who made the awful fudge. They think everyone will make fun of them. INTERPRETATION
3. Accept reasonable responses. Letters should follow the friendly-letter format. They should express Granny's thanks and her love for her grandchildren. WRITE A LETTER

Page 133 For instruction on the Focus Skill: Narrative Elements: Plot, Character, Setting, see page 133 in *Timeless Tales.*

Name ______________________

REPRODUCIBLE STUDENT ACTIVITY PAGE

Peppermint-Peanut-Butter Fudge

Complete the sequence chart about "Peppermint-Peanut-Butter Fudge." Write a sentence in each box. The first one has been done for you.

Event 1:

Pearl and Roy decide to make fudge to give to Granny for her birthday.

Event 2:

Possible response: Roy puts peanut butter and peppermint in the fudge by mistake.

Event 3:

Possible response: Roy thinks the fudge is spoiled, but he and Pearl still enter it in the kitchen contest.

Event 4:

Possible response: Granny likes the fudge and names Pearl and Roy kitchen champions.

Now use the information from the boxes to write a one-sentence summary of the selection.

Possible response: Pearl and Roy accidentally make peppermint-peanut-butter fudge for Granny's birthday gift, and even though they think the fudge is no good, Granny loves it.

Harcourt

Awesome Ants

by Lisa Eisenberg **Use with *Timeless Tales*, pages 134–141.**

Preteaching Skills: Vowel Variants /ô/*aw, au(gh)*

Teach/Model

IDENTIFY THE SOUND Ask students to repeat the following sentence aloud several times: *Paul taught the hawk to hide its claws.* Have them identify the words that have the /ô/ sound. (*Paul, taught, hawk, claws*)

ASSOCIATE LETTERS TO SOUNDS Write on the board the sentence *Paul taught the hawk to hide its claws.* Have students read the sentence. Underline the letters *au, augh,* or *aw* in each word in which they appear. Tell students that in these words, the letters *au, aw,* and *augh* stand for the /ô/ sound. Then ask students to look for two words that have two vowels together with a consonant on either side. (*Paul, taught*) Remind students that when two vowels come together in a word, the word often has a long vowel sound. Use *float* and *chain* as examples. Explain that the letters *au* are different. Then point to the word *taught,* read it, and underline *augh.* Tell students that the letters *gh* are silent in this word.

WORD BLENDING Model how to blend and read the word *hawk.* Point to *h* and say /h/. Point to *aw* and say /ô/. Point to *k* and say /k/. Slide your hand under the whole word as you elongate the sounds /hhôôkk/. Then say the word naturally—*hawk.* Follow a similar procedure with the words *Paul* and *taught.*

Practice/Apply

APPLY THE SKILL ***Letter Substitution*** Write the following words on the board, and have students read each one aloud. Then make the changes necessary to form the words in parentheses. Have a volunteer read each new word. Try to give each student an opportunity to respond.

sack (saw) claim (claw) lunch (launch) cat (caught)

DICTATION AND WRITING Have students number a sheet of paper 1–8. Write the word *raw* on the board, and tell students that in the first four words you will say, the /ô/ sound is spelled *aw,* as in *raw.* Dictate words 1–4, and have students write them. After they write each word, display the correct spelling so students can proofread their work. Then write *haul* on the board, and tell students that the next two words have the *au* vowel pattern for the /ô/ sound. Dictate words 5 and 6, and have students proofread as before. Finally, write *caught* on the board, and tell students that the last two words have the *augh* pattern for the /ô/ sound. Dictate words 7 and 8, and have students proofread as before.

1. claws* 2. thaw 3. dawn 4. straw*
5. taut 6. launch 7. taught 8. haughty

**Word appears in "Awesome Ants."*

READ LONGER WORDS ***Introduce Breaking Words with Vowel Variants*** Write these words on the board: *author, naughty, clawing, astronaut, strawberry.* Tell students that the letter combinations *au* and *aw* usually stay together when a word is broken into syllables. Point to *author* and ask: **Which part of the word stands for /ô/? Which part stands for /thər/?** Then point to *naughty,* and tell students that the letters *augh* stay together when this word is divided. Have students read this word aloud. Then have them read the remaining words aloud and explain how they figured out each one.

REPRODUCIBLE STUDENT ACTIVITY PAGE

INDEPENDENT PRACTICE See the reproducible Student Activity on page 99.

Name ______________________________

Awesome Ants

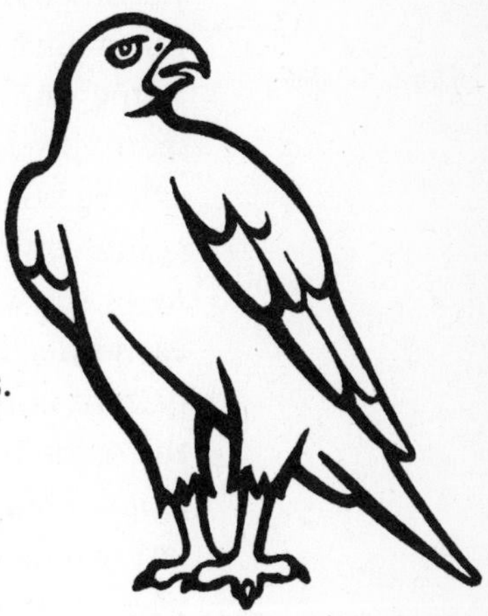

Read the story. Then mark the answer that makes each sentence below tell about the story.

"Let's hurry up and finish lunch. Our show is starting," said Saul. Saul and Dawn wanted to watch the new nature show on TV. It had been launched only two weeks ago. It was a big success.

The first part of today's show was about wild birds. "Is that a hawk?" asked Dawn.

"Yes," Saul said. "It saw a mouse and caught it with its claws. Hawks have to work hard for their lunch."

The second part featured trout. "I didn't know some trout live in the sea," Saul said.

"The narrator said they have to travel to fresh water to spawn," Dawn explained. "It's a long haul upstream to lay their eggs."

The last part was about deer. Saul said, "That fawn is eating plants near a lawn. Now it's yawning. I guess deer feel sleepy after lunch, too. This show has taught me all sorts of things about animals!" he said.

1 The new nature show
- **A** is about lawyers.
- **(B)** was launched two weeks ago.
- **C** started at dawn.
- **D** made Saul yawn.

2 What did the hawk do?
- **F** It saw a rabbit.
- **(G)** It caught some lunch.
- **H** It landed on the lawn.
- **J** It crawled up a tree.

3 Why do trout go upstream?
- **A** to launch a rocket
- **B** to haul a bale of straw
- **C** to cause a stir
- **(D)** to spawn

4 Where was the fawn?
- **F** on a seesaw
- **(G)** near someone's lawn
- **H** in a vault
- **J** in Saul's kitchen

5 What did the fawn do?
- **A** run across the lawn
- **B** draw a picture
- **(C)** yawn after eating
- **D** eat a prawn

6 What has the show done?
- **F** It has taught Saul about autumn.
- **G** It has shown astronauts.
- **H** It has told stories about authors.
- **(J)** It has taught Saul about animals.

Harcourt

Introducing Vocabulary

Apply word identification strategies.

LOOK FOR FAMILIAR SPELLING PATTERNS Display the vocabulary words, and ask students to identify the ones they know. Remind students that they can sometimes figure out a new word by looking for familiar spelling patterns. Frame each syllable in the word *disappointment.* Point out the consonant-vowel-consonant pattern in the first and last syllables. Also point out the letters *oi.* Call on a volunteer to read this word aloud and tell how he or she was able to figure it out. Then frame each syllable in *delay,* pointing out the open vowel pattern in the first syllable and the *ay* pattern in the second. Call on a volunteer to read this word aloud. Help students read the remaining vocabulary words aloud, providing clues as necessary: what an expert in one subject does (*specializes*); in the middle (*average*); is ready to be used (*available*). When students read and then self-correct, encourage them by saying, **You read ___ and then changed it to ___. Why? How did you know which was right?**

VOCABULARY DEFINED

available at hand and ready to be bought or sold

average typical or usual

delay an amount of time that something is put off

disappointment a feeling of unhappiness when something that was expected does not happen

forced made to do something

specializes becomes an expert in a specific line of work or study

Discuss the meanings of the vocabulary words. Then ask each student to create a sentence containing at least two of the words. (Possible response: *I felt <u>disappointment</u> when the book wasn't <u>available</u>.*) Continue until all the vocabulary words have been used at least once and each student has had an opportunity to respond.

Check understanding.

Have students list the vocabulary words on a sheet of paper. Then ask each of the following questions. Have students name the word that best answers the question and circle that word on their papers.

- **Which word names a wait?** *(delay)*
- **Which word best completes this sentence?** ***The ______ temperature in July is 80°.*** *(average)*
- **Which word might describe what you feel when something you wanted badly doesn't work out?** *(disappointment)*
- **Which word tells what an expert does?** *(specializes)*
- **Which word describes something that you don't have to wait for?** *(available)*
- **Which word best completes this sentence?** ***The rain ______ us to cancel the game.*** *(forced)*

REPRODUCIBLE STUDENT ACTIVITY PAGE

INDEPENDENT PRACTICE See the reproducible Student Activity on page 101.

NOTE: The following vocabulary words from "The Empty Box" are reinforced in "Awesome Ants." If students are unfamiliar with these words, point them out as you encounter them during reading: *booming* (p. 135); *distressed, negotiating, distributor, inefficient* (p. 136); *duplicate* (p. 138).

Name ____________________

Awesome Ants

These sentences are about "Awesome Ants." Write the word from the box that makes sense in each sentence.

delay	disappointment	average	forced	specializes	available

1. The students wrote to a company that specializes in ant farms and other products related to animals.
2. The students wanted ants that weren't too big or too small. They ordered ants of average size.
3. The ant company had too many orders for ants. There weren't any more ants available.
4. The ant company wrote a letter explaining that there would be a delay in the shipment.
5. When the students read this letter, they felt disappointment.
6. They were forced to complain when the shipment took too long.

Answer these questions to tell what you think might happen in "Awesome Ants."

7. Do you think the students' complaint letter will make a difference? Why or why not?
Possible response: yes, because businesses want to keep customers happy

8. What do you think the ant company will do? Possible response: The ant company will apologize.

9. Do you think the students will get their ants? Explain. Responses will vary.

Harcourt

Directed Reading

Page 134 Have a volunteer read the story title. Make sure students understand the meaning of *awesome*. Point out that this story is told in the form of letters that the story characters have written. Have students read page 134 to find out who the letter is from, to whom it was written, and why. INFERENTIAL: IMPORTANT DETAILS Ask: **When did the students write this letter?** (*January 14*) LITERAL: IMPORTANT DETAILS

Page 135 Before they read page 135, ask students to predict who the letter is from and what it says. (*the ant company; to say it got the students' letter and to tell them about their ant farm)* INFERENTIAL: MAKE PREDICTIONS After reading, ask: **Why haven't the students gotten their ant farm yet?** (*Many people have ordered ant farms, so there are delays in shipping.*) INFERENTIAL: DRAW CONCLUSIONS

Page 136 Have a volunteer read aloud the top letter only. Ask: **How long have the students been waiting for their ant farm?** (*a month*) LITERAL: IMPORTANT DETAILS Then have another volunteer read the bottom letter. Ask: **What explanation does the company give for the long delay?** (*The old distributor was inefficient.*) INFERENTIAL: SYNTHESIZE

Page 137 Have students read the letter on page 137 to find out if the students got what they ordered. (Possible response: *No, they got giant ants instead of average-sized ants.*) INFERENTIAL: SYNTHESIZE Ask: **Why did the students write this letter?** (*to complain and to ask the company to send the right ants*) INFERENTIAL: SUMMARIZE

Page 138 Have students tell what is happening in the illustration on page 138. (*The giant ants are eating a hat.*) Read the letter aloud, and have students listen to learn what the company is going to do. Make sure they understand that *Dinoponera grandis* is the scientific name for the giant ants. Ask: **Who was supposed to get the giant ants?** (*a lab*) INFERENTIAL: IMPORTANT DETAILS **What will the company do?** (*It will send the students a shipment with the right ants.*) INFERENTIAL: SYNTHESIZE

Page 139 Ask students to read the letter on page 139 and to tell in their own words what happened. (*The students had to buy the principal a new straw hat after the giant ants ate the old one. They sent a bill for the hat to the distributor. They sent the giant ants back to the ant company.*) LITERAL: SUMMARIZE

Page 140 Point out that the letter on page 140 is a memo, a letter that a company sends to its employees. Have students read the memo to learn how the story ends. Ask: **Who sent out the memo?** (*the mailroom*) LITERAL: NOTE DETAILS **Why do you think the memo is unfinished?** (Possible response: *The ants took over the mailroom and chased away the employees.*) CRITICAL: INTERPRET STORY EVENTS

SUMMARIZE THE SELECTION Ask students to think about what happened at the beginning, in the middle, and at the end of the story. Then have them write three sentences to summarize the story.

Page 141

Answers to Think About It Questions

1. First the students complain because the ants they ordered have not arrived. Then they complain because the ants that have been delivered are gigantic rather than average-sized. SUMMARY
2. Possible response: The fifth graders might enjoy knowing that the huge ants were causing problems at Lawton and Company. INTERPRETATION
3. Paragraphs should be based at least in part on story facts. WRITE A PARAGRAPH

Name ______________________________

REPRODUCIBLE STUDENT ACTIVITY PAGE

Awesome Ants

Complete the sequence chart about "Awesome Ants." Write a sentence in each box.

Event 1

The Paulson School fifth graders ordered an ant farm and average-sized ants from Lawton and Company.

Event 2

The ant company told them that there would be a shipping delay.

Event 3

The students complained about the long delay.

Event 4

The students finally got their ant farm, but it came with giant ants.

Event 5

The ants ate the principal's hat, and the students sent them back to the ant company.

Event 6

The giant ants ate their way out of the shipping box and escaped from the mailroom.

Now use the information from the boxes to write a one-sentence summary of the selection.

Possible response: The students of Paulson School returned the ants they received because the company sent them the wrong ones.

Harcourt

My Imaginary World

by Istvan Banyai **Use with *Timeless Tales*, pages 142–149.**

Preteaching Skills: Vowel Variants /o͝o/*oo, ou*

Teach/Model

IDENTIFY THE SOUND Read the following sentence aloud three times: *Tom should take in some wood to make a cooking fire.* Ask students to identify words that have the vowel sound heard in *hood.* (*should, wood, cooking*)

ASSOCIATE LETTERS TO SOUNDS Write the sentence *Tom should take in some wood to make a cooking fire* on the board. Underline the vowels *oo* in *wood* and *cooking.* Remind students that they have learned that when two vowels come together in a word, they often stand for a long vowel sound. Tell students that in these words, the letters *oo* are different because they stand for the /o͝o/ sound heard in *look.* Next, underline the vowels *ou* in *should.* Explain that in this word, the letters *ou* also stand for the /o͝o/ sound. Also explain that the *l* in *should* is silent. Point to each word with the /o͝o/ sound and have students read it aloud.

WORD BLENDING Model how to blend and read the word *should.* Point to *sh* and say /sh/. Point to *ou* and say /o͝o/. Point to *d* and say /d/. Slide your hand under the whole word as you elongate the sounds. Then say the word naturally—*should.* Follow a similar procedure for the word *wood.*

Practice/Apply

APPLY THE SKILL ***Letter Substitution*** Write the following words on the board, and have students read each aloud. Make the changes necessary to form the words in parentheses. Have a volunteer read each new word. Try to give each student an opportunity to respond.

feet (foot)	show (should)	coal (cook)	goal (good)
woke (would)	cold (could)	croak (crook)	shock (shook)

DICTATION AND WRITING Have students number a sheet of paper 1–8. Write *would* on the board. Tell students that in the first two words you will say, the /o͝o/ sound is spelled *ou* as in *would.* Dictate words 1–2, and have students write them. After they write each word, display it so that students can proofread their work. Then write the word *nook* on the board. Tell students that in the next six words you will say, the /o͝o/ sound is spelled *oo* as in *nook.* Dictate words 3–8, and have students proofread as before.

1. would*	2. should	3. book*	4. looking
5. stood	6. cook	7. hooked	8. wooden*

**Word appears in "My Imaginary World."*

Dictate the following sentence, and have students write it: *Would you take a good look at that crooked fence?*

REPRODUCIBLE STUDENT ACTIVITY PAGE

INDEPENDENT PRACTICE See the reproducible Student Activity on page 105.

READ LONGER WORDS ***Review Breaking Words with VCCV*** Write these words on the board: *goodwill, overlook, dogwood.* Point to *goodwill* and read it aloud. Ask: **Which part of the word sounds like /good/? Which part sounds like /will/?** Draw a vertical line between the two consonants. Remind students that when two consonants come together between two vowels in a word, the word is usually divided into syllables between the two consonants. Follow a similar process with *overlook* and *dogwood.*

Name ______________________________

REPRODUCIBLE STUDENT ACTIVITY PAGE

My Imaginary World

Read the story. Circle the words that have the vowel sound you hear in *took* and *would*.

Snook Stops a Crook!

Jenny owns a bookstore. Her cat, Snook, comes with her each day to her job. Snook likes to curl up in a peaceful nook in the back corner. Shoppers at the store will stop to look at the sleeping cat. "Would it be okay to pet him?" they ask Jenny. "Yes!" says Jenny with a smile. "He enjoys that!"

One day Snook helped catch a crook. A man was looking at the cookbooks while Jenny spoke with a customer. The man slid a book under his woolen coat. He would have left without paying for it, but he bumped into the sleeping cat with his foot by mistake. Snook sprang up surprised and

took off running. The crook couldn't stop himself from tripping. He fell. The stolen book slipped out. It landed on the wooden steps.

After the police took the crook away, Jenny hugged Snook. "What a good cat you are!" she said. "You should get a prize!"

Now write the circled word that best completes each sentence.

1. Jenny's cat, ____Snook____, comes to work with her each day.
2. Snook likes to curl up in a quiet ____nook____ and sleep.
3. The cat once helped catch a ____crook____.
4. The man was looking at ____cookbooks____ in the store.
5. When Jenny wasn't looking, he put a book under his ____woolen____ coat.
6. He ____would____ have left without paying for it, but he tripped over the cat!
7. The police ____took____ the man away.
8. Jenny said her cat ____should____ get a prize!

Harcourt

Introducing Vocabulary

Apply word identification strategies.

LOOK FOR FAMILIAR SPELLING PATTERNS Display the vocabulary words, and ask students to identify the ones they know. Remind students that they can sometimes figure out a new word by looking for familiar spelling patterns. Point out the CVC pattern in the first syllable of *sketches.* Ask a volunteer to read that word aloud and tell how he or she was able to figure it out. (*A vowel between two consonants usually has the short sound.*) Also point out the long *i* sound in *style*, and have a student read it aloud. Help students read the remaining vocabulary words aloud, providing clues as necessary: a person who writes books for a living (*author*); the one you like the best (*favorite*); not real (*imaginary*); means "frightening" (*scary*). When students misread a word and then self-correct, encourage them by saying, **You read ___ and then changed it to ___. How did you know to do that?**

VOCABULARY DEFINED

author a writer

favorite the one that is liked the best

imaginary something that exists only in the imagination

scary frightening

sketches quick or simple drawings

style a special way of doing something

Discuss the meanings of the vocabulary words. Then have students make up sentences that each contain two vocabulary words. (Possible responses: *Scary books are my favorite kind. She drew sketches of imaginary creatures.*) Continue until all the vocabulary words have been used at least once.

Check understanding.

Ask students to write the vocabulary words on a sheet of paper. Then ask each of the following questions. Have students name the word that best answers the question and circle that word on their papers.

- **Which word names a person who writes books?** *(author)*
- **Which word describes something you like better than the rest?** *(favorite)*
- **Which word describes something that exists in your mind?** *(imaginary)*
- **Which word describes a story or movie that frightens you?** *(scary)*
- **Which word names pictures you draw in a hurry?** *(sketches)*
- **Which word names the special way an artist paints or draws?** *(style)*

Provide vocabulary support.

Students may have trouble with names such as Istvan Banyai (p. 142), Budapest (p. 142), and Danube (p. 142). Introduce the words by writing them on the board and pronouncing each. As students come across the words in the selection, offer assistance as needed.

REPRODUCIBLE STUDENT ACTIVITY PAGE

INDEPENDENT PRACTICE See the reproducible Student Activity on page 107.

NOTE: The following vocabulary words from "The World of William Joyce Scrapbook" are reinforced in "My Imaginary World." If students are unfamiliar with these words, point them out as you encounter them during reading: *encouraged, charcoal, pastels, series* (p. 145); *illustrating* (p. 146).

Name ______________________

REPRODUCIBLE STUDENT ACTIVITY PAGE

My Imaginary World

Read each sentence. Write the word from the box that makes sense in the sentence.

author	favorite	imaginary	scary	sketches	style

Istvan Banyai is a real person. As a boy, Istvan played alone much of the time. This helped him create a vivid imaginary world.	His favorite toy was his grandmother's slide lantern. He liked the images it made on the wall.	He enjoyed drawing images of his own, too. A teacher told him to keep making his sketches.
Some of the things he liked to draw were scary. Other drawings he made were funny.	Over time, Istvan learned to draw using a style all his own.	Like an author of books, Istvan made up tales to go with his drawings.

Answer these questions to tell what you think will happen in the story.

1. What kind of job do you think Istvan Banyai will have when he grows up?

Responses will vary.

2. Where do you think Istvan gets his ideas for his drawings?

Responses will vary.

3. What facts do you think you will find out about Istvan Banyai as you read?

Responses will vary.

Harcourt

Directed Reading

Page 142 Read aloud the title of the story. Explain that this selection tells about a real person, Istvan Banyai. Ask students what sort of job they think Istvan Banyai might have and why they think this. (Possible response: *He must be a person who makes up things in his imagination, such as a writer or painter, because the story is called "My Imaginary World."*) INFERENTIAL: DRAW CONCLUSIONS Then read aloud page 142. Tell students to listen to confirm their predictions. (*Istvan Banyai is an illustrator.*) **What things helped Istvan develop his imagination during his childhood?** (Possible response: *He didn't have a TV to watch or brothers and sisters to play with. He made up lots of things to do by himself. This made him good at imagining things.*) INFERENTIAL: IMPORTANT DETAILS/ SPECULATE

Page 143 Ask students to read page 143 to find out what Banyai remembers most about living with his grandmother. (Possible response: *that her house was filled with wonderful old things*) INFERENTIAL: MAIN IDEA **What was Istvan's favorite thing at his grandmother's house? Why was it his favorite?** (*her slide lantern, because it made images on the wall*) INFERENTIAL: IMPORTANT DETAILS

Page 145 Read aloud page 145. As students listen, have them pay attention to the kinds of things Istvan drew as a child. (*both scary and funny scenes from his imagination*) INFERENTIAL: IMPORTANT DETAILS **How does Istvan Banyai create his illustrations today?** (*He makes a series of drawings first. Next, he transfers these to clear plastic sheets. Then he paints in the colors on the plastic sheets.*) LITERAL: SEQUENCE

Page 146 Ask a volunteer to read aloud page 146. **What do you think Istvan Banyai means when he says, "I take a shower in ideas"?** (Possible response: *His imagination is active even while he's doing ordinary activities.*) INFERENTIAL: AUTHOR'S CRAFT/DETERMINE IMAGERY

Page 147 Have volunteers take turns reading aloud sentences from page 147. **Why does Istvan describe his books as "windows into (his) imaginary world"?** (Possible response: *His stories and illustrations show what he thinks, feels, and sees inside his mind.*) INFERENTIAL: AUTHOR'S CRAFT/DETERMINE IMAGERY Invite students to read the book titles on page 148.

SUMMARIZE THE SELECTION Have students name the things in Istvan Banyai's childhood that helped him develop his imagination and become an illustrator. Then ask them to summarize the selection in two or three sentences.

Page 148

Answers to Think About It Questions

1. Possible responses: Istvan Banyai had no brothers or sisters, so he often played alone. He played with the old things in his grandmother's house. He spent hours drawing. SUMMARY
2. Possible response: He is very happy about being an illustrator. He seems to enjoy describing the process of illustrating and creating books. INTERPRETATION
3. Possible responses: What do you like about working in pencil? What subjects do you most enjoy drawing, and why? Have you been back to your childhood home? If so, what was it like to go back? WRITE QUESTIONS

Page 149 For instructions on the Focus Skill: Fact and Opinion, see *Timeless Tales*, page 149.

Name ______________________

REPRODUCIBLE STUDENT ACTIVITY PAGE

My Imaginary World

Write one or two sentences in each box to sum up what each part of the story tells you about Istvan.

Pages 142–143

Main Idea: Possible response: Istvan Banyai grew up with his grandmother. He used his imagination to entertain himself when he was a child.

Page 145

Main Idea: Possible response: Istvan drew a lot when he was a child. He studied art and learned different styles, and today Istvan Banyai is an artist.

Pages 146–147

Main Idea: Possible response: Being an artist and author is Istvan Banyai's job, and he gets ideas from many places.

Write a one-sentence summary of the selection.

Possible response: Istvan Banyai has always had a great imagination, and he has used it to become an artist and author.

Harcourt

With Love from Ella

by Susan M. Fischer **Use with *Timeless Tales*, pages 150–157.**

Preteaching Skills: Vowel Variant /o͞o/*oo, ue, ew, ui, u*

Teach/Model

IDENTIFY THE SOUND Have students repeat the following sentence aloud three times: *Ruth wore a new blue swimsuit to the pool party.* Ask students to name the words with the /o͞o/ sound they hear in *soon.* (*Ruth, new, blue, swimsuit, pool*)

ASSOCIATE LETTERS TO SOUNDS Write the sentence above on the board. Explain to students that many combinations of letters can stand for the /o͞o/ sound. Underline the letter *u* in *Ruth,* the letters *ew* in *new,* the letters *ue* in *blue,* the letters *ui* in *swimsuit,* and the letters *oo* in *pool.* Point out that the letters *u, ew, ue, ui,* and *oo* can all stand for the /o͞o/ sound.

WORD BLENDING Write *ruby, drew, clue, bruise,* and *bamboo* on the board. Model how to blend and read the word *ruby.* Point to *r* and say /r/. Draw your hand under *u* and say /o͞o/. Point to *b* and say /b/. Point to *y* and say /ē/. Slide your hand under the whole word as you elongate the sounds /rro͞o′ bbēē/. Then say the word naturally—*ruby.* Follow a similar procedure for the remaining words.

Practice/Apply

APPLY THE SKILL ***Letter Substitution*** Write the following words on the board, and have students read each aloud. Make the changes necessary to form each word in parentheses. Have volunteers read each new word.

club (clue) sled (stew) hop (hoop) trust (truth)

DICTATION AND WRITING Have students number a sheet of paper 1–8. Dicate the following words, and have students write them. After students write each word, display the correct spelling so they can proofread their work. Have them draw a line through a misspelled word and write the correct spelling beside it.

1. stoop*	2. smooth*	3. Drew*	4. brew
5. ruby	6. duty	7. sluice	8. blue*

**Word appears in "With Love, from Ella."*

Dictate the following sentence, and have students write it: *Sue heard a rumor that the new fruit-flavored gum will be in stores soon.*

READ LONGER WORDS ***Review Breaking Words with Vowel Variants; Review Breaking Words with VCCV*** Write these words on the board: *soonest, jewelry, suitcases.* Remind students that when two letters appear together in a word and stand for a single vowel sound, those letters usually stay together when the word is broken into syllables. Point out the *oo* in *soonest,* and read the word aloud. Then cover the suffix *-est,* and have a volunteer read *soon;* cover *soon* and have a volunteer read *est.* Draw your hand under the entire word as students read it aloud. Follow a similar procedure with the two remaining words. Then write *fruitful* on the board. Remind students that when two consonants appear between two vowels, the word usually is broken into syllables between the consonants. Cover the word part *-ful* and have a volunteer read *fruit.* Then cover *fruit* and have a volunteer read *ful.* Draw your hand under the entire word as students read it aloud.

REPRODUCIBLE STUDENT ACTIVITY PAGE

INDEPENDENT PRACTICE See the reproducible Student Activity on page 111.

Name ______________________________________

With Love from Ella

Do what the sentences tell you.

1. There is a ball in the pool. Draw the ball.
2. Give Andrew a hula hoop to play with.
3. Sue is holding a tool. Draw her tool.
4. Ruth has a bowl of stew. Draw her bowl.
5. Give Ruth a spoon, too.
6. Ruth's stool is missing? Draw a stool for her to sit on.
7. Sue has a cup of juice. Draw the cup.
8. Who threw a boot in the pool? Draw a boot in the water.
9. Andrew's swimsuit has stripes on it. Draw the stripes.
10. There are a few flowers blooming in the vase. Draw them there.
11. Andrew blew a big bubble with his gum. Draw the bubble.
12. A bird flew onto the roof. Put a bird there.
13. Draw a broom by the door.
14. The wind blew over a potted plant. Draw the plant coming out of the pot.
15. The plant's leaves are strewn around the pool. Draw a few leaves.

Now circle the words that have the long *oo* sound.

Harcourt

Introducing Vocabulary

Apply word identification strategies.

LOOK FOR FAMILIAR SPELLING PATTERNS

Display the vocabulary words, and call on volunteers to identify the ones they know. Remind students that they can sometimes figure out a new word by looking for familiar spelling patterns. Point out the familiar CVC pattern in *jazz.* Ask students to use what they know about this pattern to read the word aloud. Help students read the other words aloud, using clues as necessary: someone who writes music (*composer*); the opposite of *unfamiliar* (*familiar*); another word for the music business is the music _____ (*industry*); what someone did when she stopped for a short amount of time (*paused*); people in general (*public*). As students read each word, encourage them by saying, **That's right. Look at the word again. What made you think that could be the word?**

VOCABULARY DEFINED

composer a person who writes music

familiar easily recognized; well known

industry a specific group of related businesses

jazz music that comes from the blues and ragtime and is known for having complex rhythms and some amount of improvisation

paused made a temporary stop

public the general population; people

Discuss the meanings of the vocabulary words. Then ask students to create a round-robin story. Have them take turns building the story by adding sentences that contain one or more vocabulary words. (Possible starter sentences: *The composer wrote tunes that are familiar to everyone. When he started his career, the public loved him.*) Continue until all the vocabulary words have been used at least once and each student has had an opportunity to add to the story.

Check understanding.

Have students write the vocabulary words on a sheet of paper. Read aloud the following riddles. Call on students to answer each one, using a vocabulary word. Then have them circle that word on their papers.

- **I mean "made a brief stop," and I rhyme with *caused*. What am I?** *(paused)*
- **I can name a group of businesses, and I begin like *industrial.* What am I?** *(industry)*
- **I am a person who writes music, and I begin like *compare*. What am I?** *(composer)*
- **I describe something that is well known, and I begin like *family*. What am I?** *(familiar)*
- **We are people who buy products and have opinions. What are we?** *(public)*
- **I can be played with saxophones and trumpets, and I begin like *jacket.* What am I?** *(jazz)*

REPRODUCIBLE STUDENT ACTIVITY PAGE

INDEPENDENT PRACTICE See the reproducible Student Activity on page 113.

NOTE: The following vocabulary words from "Satchmo's Blues" are reinforced in "With Love from Ella." If students are unfamiliar with these words, point them out as you encounter them during reading: *pawnshop, produce, gravelly* (p. 151); *errands* (p. 152); *numerous, international* (p. 153).

Name ____________________

REPRODUCIBLE STUDENT ACTIVITY PAGE

With Love from Ella

Read the ad.

Meet Ella Fitzgerald!

Ella Fitzgerald was a popular **jazz** singer.
In this story she writes a letter to a fan.
She tells about singing when she was seventeen.
One night a man in the music **industry** came to hear her sing.
He was a famous **composer** and bandleader named Chick Webb.
He asked her to sing in his band.
Ella and Chick wrote many songs together.
The songs became **familiar** to many jazz fans.
The **public** came to love her music.
Years later, Ella **paused** to think about her singing career.
What do you think she thought about it?
Find out in the story.

Write a word from the ad to complete each sentence. Choose from the words in dark type.

1. Ella Fitzgerald and Chick Webb were in a ___jazz___ band.
2. Chick Webb wrote songs, so he is called a ___composer___.
3. Ella's songs are ___familiar___ to many of her fans.
4. After being in a band for many years, Ella ___paused___ to think about the next step.
5. Chick and Ella were part of the music ___industry___.
6. The ___public___ became big fans of Ella Fitzgerald.

What do you think Ella might tell her fan in the letter she writes?

Responses will vary.

Harcourt

Directed Reading

Page 150 Read aloud the title of the selection. Explain that it tells about a real person, Ella Fitzgerald. The author imagines a letter Ella might have written to a fan and includes real facts about Ella's life in the letter. Read aloud page 150 as students follow along. Ask: **What clues tell you that Ella is probably a musician?** (*the clues "composer," "want to know about my career," "love music"*) INFERENTIAL: DRAW CONCLUSIONS

Page 151 Have students read page 151 to find out what Ella's childhood is like. Remind them to picture story details in their minds. Ask: **How does Ella become a good singer?** (*She sings at church, sings with friends after school, and copies the styles of singers on the radio.*) INFERENTIAL: SUMMARIZE **What do you think will happen next?** (Possible response: *She will try to be a dancer.*) INFERENTIAL: MAKE PREDICTIONS

Page 152 Read page 152 aloud. Ask students to listen to find out what happens when Ella goes on stage. Ask: **What happens when Ella tries to dance on stage?** (*She can't dance, so she sings instead and wins first prize.*) LITERAL: SUMMARIZE

Page 153 Call on volunteers to read each sentence on page 153. Ask: **How does Chick Webb help Ella?** (*She joins his band; he helps her develop her rhythm and style; he introduces her to important people.*) INFERENTIAL: SUMMARIZE **How can you tell that Ella is world famous?** (*the clue "international star"*) METACOGNITIVE: IMPORTANT DETAILS

Page 154 Ask students to read page 154 to find out what other major events shape Ella's life. Ask: **What is one of Ella's best-known songs?** (*"A-Tisket, A-Tasket"*) LITERAL: NOTE DETAILS **How does Ella's life change after Chick Webb dies?** (*She becomes the leader of the band. After three years, she goes solo.*) INFERENTIAL: CAUSE-EFFECT

Page 155 Ask students to read page 155 to find out Ella's message to her fan. Ask: **What is special about "scat" singing?** (*The voice sounds like musical instruments.*) LITERAL: IMPORTANT DETAILS **Why do you think Ella tells Drew to be true to his dreams?** (Possible response: *She was true to her dreams and had a lot of success, so maybe she thinks this is a good motto to live by.*) CRITICAL: SPECULATE

Page 156 Read aloud page 156 as students follow along. Point out that this is the author's note about Ella. Ask: **How can you tell that the author admires Ella Fitzgerald?** (*The author mentions her career highlights, some of her honors, and her famous style of "scat" singing.*) CRITICAL: INTERPRET AUTHOR'S VIEWPOINT **Does this story make you want to hear Ella's "scat" singing? Why or why not?** (Possible response: *Yes; I think it would be fun to hear a voice that sounds like an instrument.*) CRITICAL: EXPRESS PERSONAL OPINIONS

SUMMARIZE THE SELECTION Ask students to discuss the important events in Ella Fitzgerald's life. Then have them summarize the story in three sentences.

Page 157

Answers to Think About It Questions

1. She was surrounded by music from an early age. Even as a child, she enjoyed singing and knew she sang well. SUMMARY
2. She wanted to be a dancer until she tried to dance in a contest. She was too scared to dance, so she sang—and won first prize in the contest. INTERPRETATION
3. Paragraphs should describe Drew's love for music, his interest in becoming a composer, and the letter he received from Ella Fitzgerald. WRITE A LETTER

Name ______________________________

REPRODUCIBLE STUDENT ACTIVITY PAGE

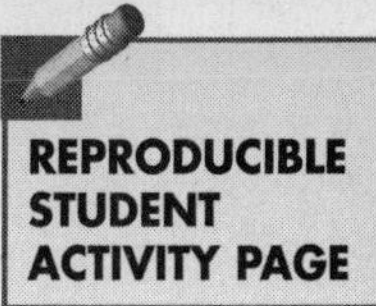

With Love from Ella

Complete the sequence chart about "With Love from Ella." Write a sentence in each box. The first box has been done for you.

Event 1

Sixteen-year-old Ella Fitzgerald wins first prize for her singing in a contest.

Event 2

Possible response: Bandleader Chick Webb hires Ella to sing in his jazz band, and she becomes an international star.

Event 3

Possible response: Years later, Ella goes solo and develops a new style of music called "scat" singing.

Event 4

Possible response: Before she died in 1996, Ella won many honors and became a member of the National Women's Hall of Fame.

Harcourt

Now use the information from the boxes to write a one-sentence summary of the selection.

Possible response: Ella Fitzgerald followed her dream to become one of the world's greatest singers of all time.

Lourdes López: Ballet Star

by Doris Licameli **Use with *Timeless Tales*, pages 158–165.**

Preteaching Skills: Digraphs /n/*kn, gn*; /r/*wr*

Teach/Model

IDENTIFY THE SOUND Have students repeat the following sentence aloud three times: *The gnat flew from Carl's knee to his wrist.* Have students identify the words that begin with the /n/ sound. (*gnat, knee*) Then read the sentence again, and ask students which word begins with the /r/ sound. (*wrist*)

ASSOCIATE LETTERS TO SOUNDS Write on the board the sentence above. Underline the digraphs *gn* in *gnat* and *kn* in *knee*. Tell students that the letters *gn* and *kn* can stand for the /n/ sound; the *k* and the *g* are silent. Next, underline the letters *wr* in *wrist*, and tell students that the letters *wr* stand for the /r/ sound; the *w* in *wr* is silent.

WORD BLENDING Write the words *knot, gnome,* and *wrap* on the board, and model how to blend and read them. Point to each letter and say its sound. Slide your hand under the whole word as you elongate the sounds: /nnoott/. Then say the word naturally—*knot*. Repeat the procedure with *gnome* and *wrap*.

Practice/Apply

APPLY THE SKILL *Consonant Substitution* Write the following words on the board, and have students read each aloud. Make the changes necessary to form the words in parentheses. Have a volunteer read each new word.

fit (knit) stack (wrack) block (knock) flash (gnash)

DICTATION AND WRITING Have students number a piece of paper 1–9. Tell them that in the first three words you will say, the /n/ sound is spelled *kn*. Dictate words 1–3, and have students write them. After students write each word, display the correct spelling so they can proofread their work. They should draw a line through any misspelled word and write the correct spelling beside it. Then tell students that in the next three words you will say, the /n/ sound is spelled *gn*. Dictate words 4–6, and have students proofread as before. Then tell students that in the last three words you will say, the /r/ sound is spelled *wr*. Dictate words 7–8, and have students proofread.

1. knob	2. knew*	3. kneecap	4. gnaw
5. gnat	6. resign	7. wriggled*	8. wrong*

**Word appears in "Lourdes Lopez: Ballet Star."*

Dictate the following sentences for students to write: *Meg laid the blanket in the shade of a gnarled tree. Then she kneeled on it and unwrapped the sandwiches.*

READ LONGER WORDS *Review Breaking Words with VCCV* Write these words on the board:

knapsack wrapper knothole

Remind students that when two or more consonants appear between two vowels, usually the word is broken into syllables between the consonants. Point to the word *knapsack*. Cover the word part *sack*, and have a volunteer read the word *knap*. Then cover *knap*, and ask a volunteer to read *sack*. Draw your hand under the whole word as students read it aloud. Call on volunteers to read the remaining two words and tell how they figured them out.

REPRODUCIBLE STUDENT ACTIVITY PAGE

INDEPENDENT PRACTICE See the reproducible Student Activity on page 117.

Name ______________________________

REPRODUCIBLE STUDENT ACTIVITY PAGE

Lourdes López: Ballet Star

Circle and write the word that best completes each sentence.

1. Luke packed a sandwich, an apple, a soda, and a dog treat in his ____knapsack____.

knuckle **knapsack** **freezer**

2. He ____kneeled____ to put a leash on Racer.

kneeled **kneaded** **begged**

3. Racer was excited because he ____knew____ they were going for a walk!

knocked **knew** **nabbed**

4. They walked up a path that led to a grassy ____knoll____.

knoll **knot** **nest**

5. At the top, Luke sat down and ____unwrapped____ his sandwich.

unplugged **ordered** **unwrapped**

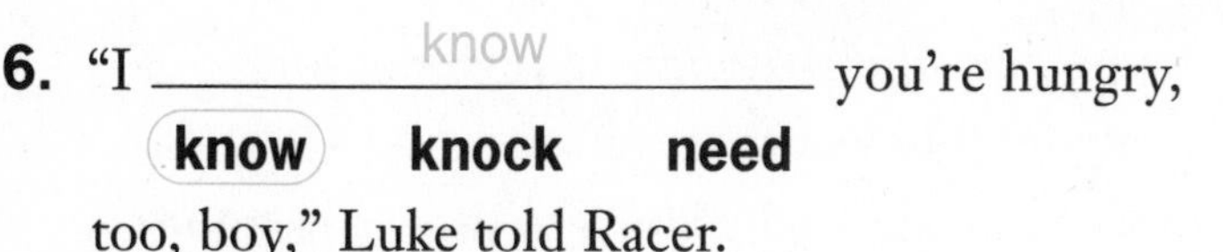

6. "I ____know____ you're hungry,

know **knock** **need**

too, boy," Luke told Racer.

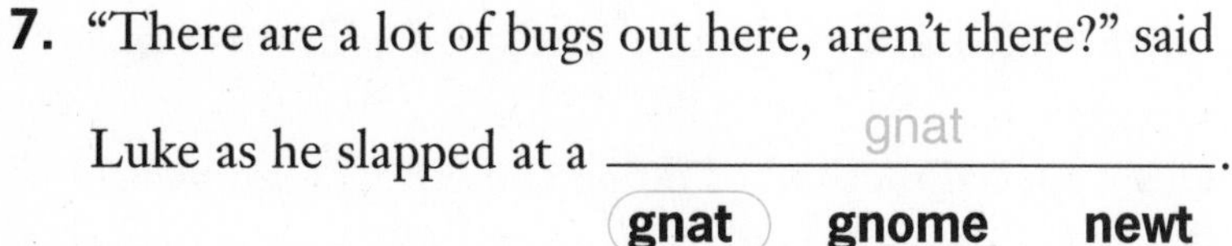

7. "There are a lot of bugs out here, aren't there?" said Luke as he slapped at a ____gnat____.

gnat **gnome** **newt**

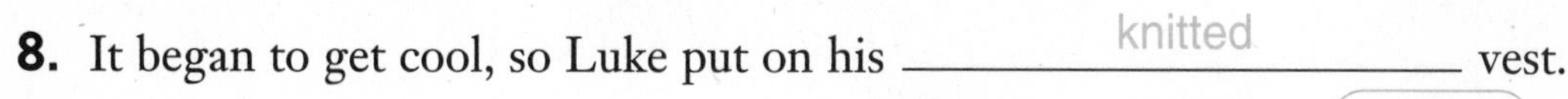

8. It began to get cool, so Luke put on his ____knitted____ vest.

knickers **never** **knitted**

9. As they walked home, Luke spotted a ____wren____ on a tree branch.

wren **wrist** **runt**

10. That night Luke ____wrote____ a letter

wrapped **wrote** **resisted**

to a pal about the nice spot he and Racer had found.

Harcourt

Introducing Vocabulary

Apply word identification strategies.

LOOK FOR FAMILIAR SPELLING PATTERNS Display the vocabulary words, and ask students to identify the ones they know. Remind them that they can sometimes figure out an unfamiliar word by looking for familiar spelling patterns. Point out the /är/ sound in the first syllable in *artistic.* Also point out the CVC pattern in the last syllable. Ask students to use what they know about these patterns to read the word aloud. Then help students read aloud the other words. Use clues as necessary: people who judge art (*critics*); showed how (*demonstrated*); what you have when you're liked by many (*popularity*). Sometimes, as students read a word, encourage them by saying, **That's right. Look at the word again. What made you think that could be the word you said?** Discuss the meanings of the vocabulary words. Then ask students to make up sentences that each contain at least two vocabulary words.

VOCABULARY DEFINED

artistic in a way that is artful or creative

career an occupation

critics people whose job is to give their opinions about artistic works

demonstrated showed

popularity a state of being liked or admired by many people

technique skill; method of doing something

triumph a state of great accomplishment and success

Check understanding.

Ask students to write the vocabulary words on a sheet of paper. Then give the following clues and have students circle the word that answers each one.

- **This word describes you if you are good at painting, dancing, or singing.** *(artistic)*
- **Which word names the people who write movie reviews?** *(critics)*
- **Which word names a person's life work?** *(career)*
- **What did the artist do when he showed us how to draw a cartoon?** *(demonstrated)*
- **This word tells what someone with many friends and admirers has.** *(popularity)*
- **Which word names a special method of doing something?** *(technique)*
- **You might feel this if you scored the winning point in a game.** *(triumph)*

Provide vocabulary support.

Students may have difficulty with names such as Lourdes López (p. 158), Alexander Nigodoff (p. 159), and George Balanchine (p. 161). Introduce the names by writing them on the board and pronouncing each one. As students come across these names in the selection, offer assistance as needed.

REPRODUCIBLE STUDENT ACTIVITY PAGE

INDEPENDENT PRACTICE See the reproducible Student Activity on page 119.

NOTE: The following vocabulary words from "Evelyn Cisneros" are reinforced in "Lourdes López: Ballet Star." If students are unfamiliar with these words, point them out as you encounter them during reading: *devote* (p. 159); *scholarship* (p. 160); *apprentice, timid, thrived, flexibility* (p. 163).

Name ______________________

REPRODUCIBLE STUDENT ACTIVITY PAGE

Lourdes López: Ballet Star

Read the story.

Even as a little girl, Lourdes López **demonstrated** real talent as a dancer. She had a lot of **artistic** skill, but she also trained hard. She learned a lot from her teachers. They helped her master each new dance **technique. Critics** who saw her perform praised her gifts. The more she danced, the more her **popularity** with the public grew. Her goal was to become a ballet star. That, for her, would be a real **triumph**.

Write a story word to complete each sentence. Choose from the words in dark type.

1. Lourdes López had strong artistic talent at an early age.

2. At first she demonstrated her skill at school events.

3. Later she studied with master teachers who trained her in proper ballet technique.

4. Her popularity with fans made her happy and proud.

5. Critics also praised her skill.

6. She hoped to someday feel the triumph of being a ballet star.

Do you think Lourdes López will reach her goal? Why or why not?

Possible response: Yes. She is talented and also works very hard. Talented people can become stars if they are willing to work hard.

Harcourt

Directed Reading

Page 158 Read aloud the title of the story. Tell students that this selection is about a real person, Lourdes López. Then have them read page 158 to find out where Lourdes López's family came from and where Lourdes grew up. (*Cuba; Florida*) Ask: **What problem did young Lourdes have that might have made it hard to become a dancer?** (*She had a problem with her feet.*) INFERENTIAL: SYNTHESIZE

Page 159-160 Have students read page 159 to find out why Lourdes first started taking ballet classes. (*Her doctor said dance lessons would make her legs stronger.*) Ask: **Why do you think Lourdes felt triumphant after her recital?** (*Her friends could finally understand how good she was and why dancing mattered to her so much.*) INFERENTIAL: CAUSE-EFFECT **Where did Lourdes study next?** (*the School of American Ballet in New York City*) Ask: **Who noticed Lourdes's talent at the school?** (*the founder, George Balanchine*) INFERENTIAL: IMPORTANT DETAILS **What do you think this shows about Lourdes?** (Possible response: *It shows that she was an especially good dancer.*) INFERENTIAL: DRAW CONCLUSIONS

Page 163 Have students read page 163 to find out how old Lourdes was when she joined the New York City Ballet. (*fifteen*) Explain to students that an apprentice is someone who is learning a craft, trade, or skill. Ask: **Why do you think Lourdes didn't believe she'd become a ballet star at first?** (Possible response: *It was such a hard goal to achieve that she didn't think she'd ever reach it.*) INFERENTIAL: CAUSE-EFFECT **What abilities and qualities did critics praise in Lourdes?** (*her artistic talent, technique, and flexibility*) INFERENTIAL: IMPORTANT DETAILS

Page 164 After students read page 164, ask: **What happened to threaten Lourdes's career?** (*She hurt her foot.*) INFERENTIAL: IMPORTANT DETAILS **How did this injury affect her career?** (*She got better quickly and made a triumphant comeback.*) INFERENTIAL: IMPORTANT DETAILS **What does Lourdes do now that she has stopped dancing professionally?** (*She teaches ballet to children in New York City.*) INFERENTIAL: IMPORTANT DETAILS

SUMMARIZE THE SELECTION Have students each share a goal they would like to accomplish. Then have them summarize the selection.

Page 165

Answers to Think About It Questions

1. She moved to New York City to study at the School of American Ballet. Before long, she joined the New York City Ballet. There she became a soloist, a ballerina, and finally a ballet star. SUMMARY
2. Possible responses: Yes; she was very drawn to ballet and seemed to have a natural ability. No; her parents probably would not have sent her to ballet classes. INTERPRETATION
3. Accept reasonable responses. Diary entries should be written in the first person from Lourdes López's point of view. They should express the dancer's excitement and pleasure. WRITE A DIARY ENTRY

Name ____________________

Lourdes López: Ballet Star

Complete the sequence chart about "Lourdes López: Ballet Star." Write a sentence in each box

Event 1:

Possible response: Lourdes López was born with a problem with her feet.

Event 2:

Possible response: Her doctor ordered dance lessons to make her legs stronger.

Event 3:

Possible response: Lourdes was talented and won a scholarship to the School of American Ballet.

Event 4:

Possible response: She joined the New York City ballet and became a star.

Now use the information from the boxes to write a one-sentence summary of the selection.

Possible response: Lourdes López overcame foot problems to become a ballet star.

Harcourt

Certain Steps

by Charlene Norman **Use with *Timeless Tales*, pages 166–173.**

Preteaching Skills: Digraphs /f/ph, gh

Teach/Model

IDENTIFY THE SOUND Have students repeat the following sentence aloud three times: *I always laugh at the phony elephants.* Ask them to identify the words with the /f/ sound. (*laugh, phony, elephants*)

ASSOCIATE LETTERS TO SOUNDS Write on the board the sentence *I always laugh at the phony elephants.* Underline the letters *ph* in *phony* and *elephants*. Explain that the letters *ph* in these words stand for the /f/ sound. Next, underline the letters *gh* in *laugh*, and tell students that the letters *gh* stand for the /f/ sound in *laugh*.

WORD BLENDING Model how to blend and read the word *laugh.* Point to *l* and say /l/. Slide your hand under *au* and say /a/. Slide your hand under *gh* and say /f/. Then slide your hand under the whole word as you elongate the sounds: /llaaff/. Then say the word naturally—*laugh.* Follow a similar procedure with the words *phony* and *elephants.*

Practice/Apply

APPLY THE SKILL ***Letter Substitution*** Write the following words on the board, and have students read each aloud. Make the changes necessary to form the words in parentheses. Have a volunteer read each new word aloud. Try to give each student an opportunity to respond.

elegant (elephant) grab (graph) prone (phone)

DICTATION AND WRITING Have students number a sheet of paper 1–8. Tell them that the first word you will read has the /f/ sound spelled *gh.* Then dictate word 1, and have students write it. After they write the word, display the correct spelling so students can proofread their work. Next, write the word *phone* on the board. Explain that in the next seven words you will read, the /f/ sound is spelled *ph.* Dictate the words, and have students write and proofread them as before.

1. laughed*	2. photo*	3. telegraph	4. phrases*
5. asphalt	6. graphic	7. emphasis*	8. geography*

**Word appears in "Certain Steps."*

Dictate the following sentence for students to write: *The photograph made Philip laugh.*

READ LONGER WORDS ***Introduce Breaking Words with Digraphs*** Write *laughter* on the board. Remind students that when two or more consonants appear between vowels, the word usually is broken into syllables between the consonants that stand for different sounds. Point to the word *laughter.* Draw a line between the syllables (laugh´ter). Tell students that in the division of a word in which the letters *gh* or *ph* stand for the /f/ sound, these letters always stay together. As you draw your hand under each syllable, have students read the word aloud. Then ask students to read these words and explain how they figured them out: *alphabet, emphasis.*

REPRODUCIBLE STUDENT ACTIVITY PAGE

INDEPENDENT PRACTICE See the reproducible Student Activity on page 123.

Name ______________________________

REPRODUCIBLE STUDENT ACTIVITY PAGE

Certain Steps

Read the story. Circle all the words with the /f/ sound spelled *gh* or *ph*.

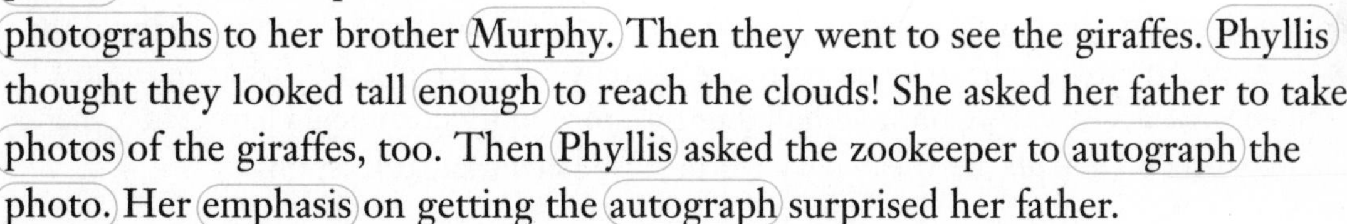

Phyllis and her father went to the zoo in Philadelphia. Phyllis is five years old. This was her first trip to the zoo. First they went to see the African elephants. The baby elephant trumpeted emphatically and made Phyllis laugh. Phyllis asked her father to take photos of it. She hoped to show the photographs to her brother Murphy. Then they went to see the giraffes. Phyllis thought they looked tall enough to reach the clouds! She asked her father to take photos of the giraffes, too. Then Phyllis asked the zookeeper to autograph the photo. Her emphasis on getting the autograph surprised her father.

"Why did you ask the zookeeper to sign the photo?" her father asked.

"That way Murphy will know the photos aren't phony," she said. Her response made the keeper laugh.

Circle and write the word that best completes each sentence.

1. Phyllis and her father visited the zoo in ___Philadelphia___.
   Pennsylvania **Flowerville** **Philadelphia**

2. Their first stop was to see the ___elephants___.
   graphs **elephants** **panthers**

3. Her father took lots of ___photographs___ of the baby elephant.
   photographs **alphabets** **autographs**

4. Phyllis wanted to show them to ___Murphy___.
   Ralph **Murphy** **Philip**

5. She asked the keeper for an ___autograph___.
   alphabet **elephant** **autograph**

6. Phyllis made the keeper ___laugh___.
   talk **laugh** **frown**

Harcourt

Introducing Vocabulary

Apply word identification strategies.

LOOK FOR FAMILIAR SPELLING PATTERNS Display the vocabulary words, and ask students to identify the ones they know. Remind students that they can sometimes figure out a new word by looking for familiar spelling patterns. Point out the *oo* pattern in *mood* and the CVC pattern in the first syllable of *seldom.* Call on volunteers to read those words aloud and tell how they were able to figure them out. (*I remember the sound that* oo *stands for. A vowel between two consonants usually has the short sound.*) Help students read the remaining vocabulary words aloud, using clues as necessary: less than sure (*uncertain*); a person's picture (*portrait*); a vote (*election*); said they were sorry (*apologized*). When students read and self-correct, encourage them by saying, **You read ___ and then changed it to ___. How did you know that the first word was wrong?**

VOCABULARY DEFINED

apologized said "I'm sorry"

election the process of choosing people for office by voting

mood a temporary state of mind or feeling

portrait a picture of someone's face

seldom rarely

uncertain not sure

Discuss the meanings of the vocabulary words. Then ask students to invent a story using all of the vocabulary words, with each student adding a sentence to build the story. You may want to begin with this sentence: *The election for class president was only two weeks away.* Continue building the story until all students have had a chance to respond and all the vocabulary words have been used at least once.

Check understanding.

Ask students to write the vocabulary words on a sheet of paper. Then ask them to name the word that answers each of the following riddles and to circle that word on their papers.

- **I name a process in which people choose other people for office.** *(election)*
- **I mean "not often."** *(seldom)*
- **I describe what you might have done when you were sorry for doing something.** *(apologized)*
- **I am the opposite of *sure*.** *(uncertain)*
- **Your school photo is an example of me.** *(portrait)*
- **I am the word that best completes this sentence: *Sam was in a good ___ after winning the election.*** *(mood)*

REPRODUCIBLE STUDENT ACTIVITY PAGE

INDEPENDENT PRACTICE See the reproducible Student Activity on page 125.

NOTE: The following vocabulary words from "Off and Running" are reinforced in "Certain Steps." If students are unfamiliar with these words, point them out as you encounter them during reading: *campaign* (p. 166); *endorse* (p. 167); *obnoxious, residences, graffiti* (p. 168).

Name ______________________________

REPRODUCIBLE STUDENT ACTIVITY PAGE

Certain Steps

Read the story. Then fill in the web. Use all the words in dark type in your answers.

"Vote for Al! He's a pal!" Al said. Al was running for student council in the school **election**. Murphy was helping him put up some of his posters. Al had his name all over the school. His name was on posters, on T-shirts, and even on pencils. He asked Murphy to help him on the campaign. Murphy asked Al what he planned to do for his fellow students if he got elected. "Cut out all the homework," said Al.

Murphy was **uncertain** about helping Al. He didn't agree that cutting out homework would be useful for students. He looked at a **portrait** of Abraham Lincoln. His uncertain **mood** vanished. He decided to stand up for what was right.

Murphy waited for Al before class. Then he **apologized**, "I'm sorry, Al, but I won't work on a campaign that promises to get rid of homework." Murphy had **seldom** felt so bad.

The School Election

What Al Wanted

Possible responses: to win the **election**; to get Murphy to help him on the campaign

How Murphy Felt, and Why

Possible responses: He was in an **uncertain mood** about helping Al. He did not agree with Al about cutting out homework.

What Helped Murphy Decide

Possible response: a **portrait** of Abraham Lincoln

What Murphy Told Al, and How Murphy Felt Afterward

Possible responses: Murphy waited for Al before class. He **apologized** to Al and said he couldn't work on his campaign. He had **seldom** felt so bad.

What do you think will happen when it's time for the election?

Responses will vary. Accept reasonable responses.

____

Harcourt

Directed Reading

Page 166 Have a volunteer read the story title. Help students identify Al and Murphy in the illustration. Then read page 166 aloud to students. Ask: **What does Al want Murphy to do?** (*help him on his campaign*) INFERENTIAL: IMPORTANT DETAILS

Page 167 Ask students to read page 167 to find out more about Al's campaign. Ask: **What does Al say his campaign platform is?** (*to cut out all homework*) LITERAL: NOTE DETAILS **Do you think Al is serious when he says this? Why?** (Possible response: *No, he laughs after he says it.*) INFERENTIAL: DETERMINE CHARACTERS' EMOTIONS

Page 168 Have a volunteer read page 168. Ask students to listen to find out what Murphy is thinking. Ask: **Why do you think Murphy is concerned about Al's campaign?** (Possible response: *He doesn't think Al is taking the election seriously.*) CRITICAL: INTERPRET STORY EVENTS **Why would Lincoln's portrait help Murphy decide to stand up for what was right?** (Possible response: *because Lincoln also stood up for what was right*) CRITICAL: CONNECT IDEAS ACROSS TEXTS

Page 169 Ask students to look at the illustration and predict what will happen. INFERENTIAL: MAKE PREDICTIONS Have them read page 169 to confirm their predictions. Ask: **How does Murphy feel about the school and its students? How do you know?** (Possible response: *He cares about the school and its students. He erases graffiti and picks up trash, and he gives Al ideas for ways to improve things for students.*) METACOGNITIVE: INTERPRET CHARACTERS' MOTIVATIONS

Page 170 Have students read page 170 to find out what happens after lunch. Ask: **What does Murphy notice other students doing?** (*They are staring, giggling, and whispering about him.*) INFERENTIAL: IMPORTANT DETAILS **Why do you think they are doing this?** (Possible response: *Maybe they're making fun of Murphy for being so serious.*) CRITICAL: SPECULATE

Page 171 Have students read page 171 to find out how the story ends. Ask: **What does Al do?** (*He withdraws from the election and tells students to vote for Murphy.*) INFERENTIAL: SUMMARIZE **What do you think Al was doing earlier when he whispered to students about Murphy?** (*He was campaigning for Murphy.*) CRITICAL: DRAW CONCLUSIONS **Who do you think won the election, Casey or Murphy? Why?** (Responses will vary. Accept reasonable responses.) CRITICAL: SPECULATE

SUMMARIZE THE SELECTION Ask students to think about what happened on the first, second, and third days of the school election campaign. Then have them write three sentences to summarize the story.

Page 172

Answers to Think About It Questions

1. Murphy sees that his friend Al is unwilling to work to improve the school. Al's only campaign promise is no homework. SUMMARY
2. He probably feels worried about what they're saying. He must think the other kids are making fun of him. INTERPRETATION
3. Webs and paragraphs should describe Murphy as an honest person who is willing to work hard to help others. WRITE A PARAGRAPH

Page 173 For instruction on the Focus Skill: Predict Outcomes, see page 173 in *Timeless Tales*.

Name ________________________________

REPRODUCIBLE STUDENT ACTIVITY PAGE

Certain Steps

Write one or two sentences in each box below to summarize the selection. Be sure to write the events in correct order.

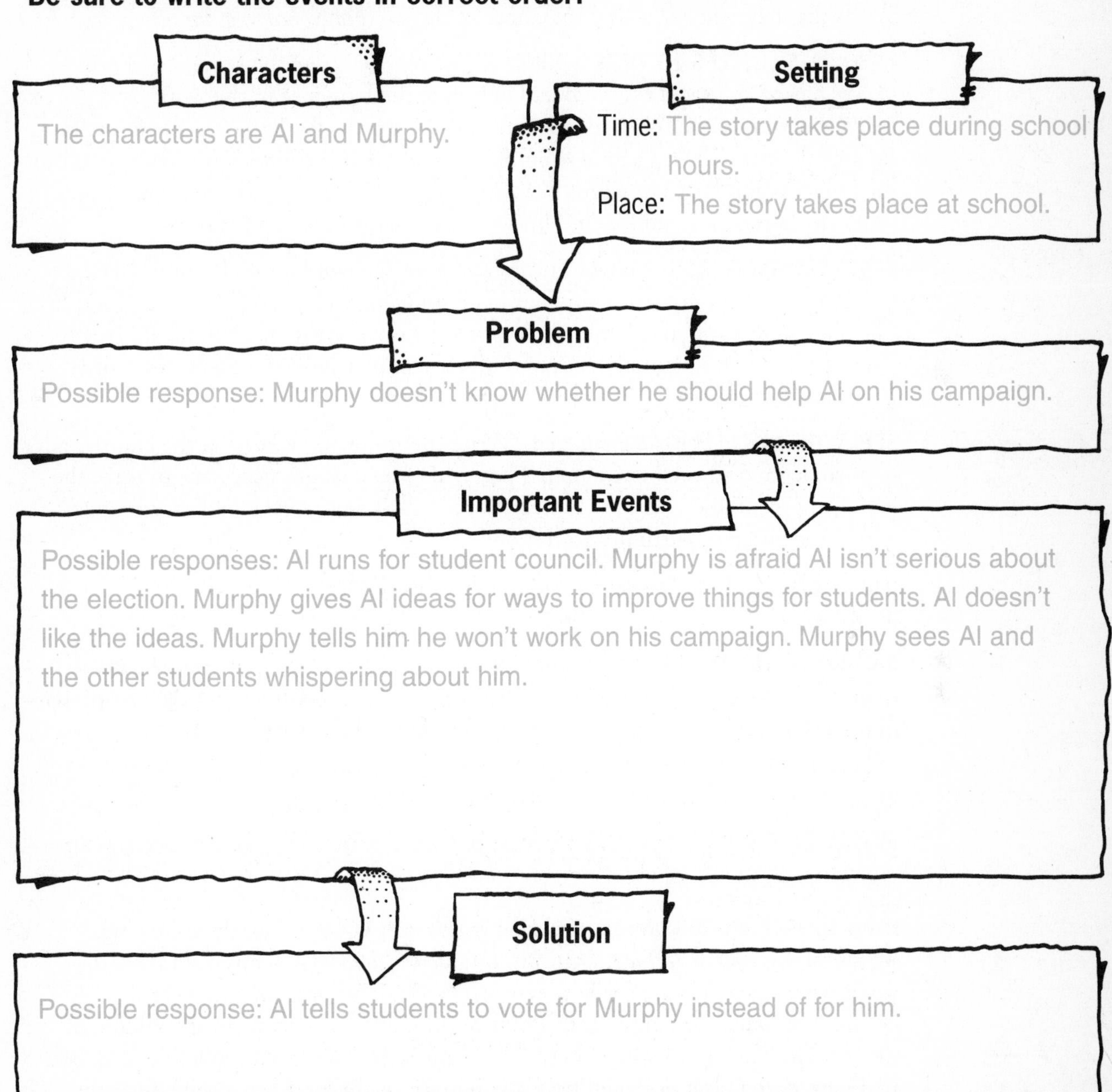

Now write a one-sentence summary of the story.

Possible response: Murphy tells Al he won't help him run for student council, but instead of becoming angry with Murphy, Al tells everyone to vote for him.

Harcourt

Quest for a Healthy World

by Carol Storment **Use with *Timeless Tales*, pages 174–181.**

Preteaching Skills: Short Vowel /e/ea

Teach/Model

IDENTIFY THE SOUND Have students repeat the following sentence aloud three times: *A heavy shower is heading toward the meadow.* Ask students to identify the words that have the /e/ sound they hear in *thread.* (*heavy, heading, meadow*)

ASSOCIATE LETTERS TO THEIR SOUND Write on the board the sentence *A heavy shower is heading toward the meadow.* Underline the letters *ea* in the words *heavy, heading,* and *meadow.* Tell students that in these words, the letters *ea* stand for the /e/ sound, or the short *e* sound. Remind students that the letters *ea* usually stand for the long *e* sound heard in words like *each* and *beach.* Explain, however, that sometimes the letters *ea* stand for the short *e* sound heard in *head* and *meadow.*

WORD BLENDING Model how to blend and read the word *bread.* Point to *b* and say /b/. Point to *r* and say /r/. Slide your hand under *ea* and say /e/. Point to *d* and say /d/. Slide your hand under the whole word as you elongate the sounds /bbrreedd/. Then say the word naturally—*bread.* Follow a similar procedure with the words *spread* and *instead.*

Practice/Apply

APPLY THE SKILL *Vowel Substitution* Write the following words on the board, and have students read each one aloud. Then make the changes necessary to form the words in parentheses. Ask a volunteer to read each new word aloud. Try to give every student an opportunity to respond.

had (head)	sweet (sweat)	broth (breath)
deed (dead)	throat (threat)	father (feather)

DICTATION AND WRITING Have students number a sheet of paper 1–8. Dictate the following words, and have students write them. After students write each word, display the correct spelling so students can proofread their work.

1. healthy*	2. instead	3. ahead*	4. dreaded
5. dead*	6. threat*	7. wealthy	8. spread*

**Word appears in "Quest for a Healthy World."*

Dictate the following sentence for students to write: *I spread a serving of healthful jam on my bread.*

READ LONGER WORDS *Review Breaking Words with VCCV* Write the following words on the board: *deafness, breakfast, threadbare, dreadful.* Remind students that when two consonants appear between two vowels, the word usually is broken into syllables between the consonants. Point out the two consonants in the middle of the word *deafness.* (*f, n*) Then cover the ending *-ness,* and have a volunteer read the first part, *deaf.* Cover *deaf,* and have a volunteer read *ness.* Then draw your hand under the entire word as students read it aloud. Follow a similar procedure with the remaining words.

REPRODUCIBLE STUDENT ACTIVITY PAGE

INDEPENDENT PRACTICE See the reproducible Student Activity on page 129.

Name ____________________

REPRODUCIBLE STUDENT ACTIVITY PAGE

Quest for a Healthy World

Circle and write the word that answers each riddle.

1. I have the same vowel sound as in *tread.*
I am at the top of your body. What am I? head

hair **head** **spread**

2. I have the same vowel sound as in *dead.*
I am a word for rain, snow, or storms. What am I? weather

forecast **sweat** **weather**

3. I have the same vowel sound as in *spread.*
I am the opposite of *sick*. What am I? healthy

healthy **strong** **instead**

4. I have the same vowel sound as in *bread.*
I am something you use with a needle. What am I? thread

thimble **tread** **thread**

5. I have the same vowel sound as in *sweat.*
I am hard to lift. What am I? heavy

heavy **large** **thread**

6. I have the same vowel sound as in *breath.*
I am a part of a bird. What am I? feather

feather **beak** **claw**

7. I have the same vowel sound as in *head.*
I have a lot of money. What am I? wealthy

feather **rich** **wealthy**

8. I have the same vowel sound as in *thread.*
You might dig me out of the ground.

What am I? treasure

treat **treasure** **measure**

9. I have the same vowel sound as in *health.*
I am one of three daily meals. What am I? breakfast

lunch **treads** **breakfast**

10. I have the same vowel sound as in *deaf.*
I am something you might do while jogging. What am I? sweat

sweat **eat** **health**

Harcourt

Introducing Vocabulary

Apply word identification strategies.

LOOK FOR FAMILIAR SPELLING PATTERNS Display the vocabulary words, and ask students to identify the ones they know. Remind students that they can sometimes figure out a new word by looking for familiar spelling patterns. Point out the CVC pattern in both syllables of *hubbub.* Call on volunteers to read the word aloud and to tell how they were able to figure it out. (*A vowel between two consonants usually has the short sound.*) Help students read the remaining vocabulary words aloud, providing clues as necessary: exciting (*dramatic*); teacher (*instructor*); a procedure (*method*); a search (*quest*); hard to carry (*unwieldy*). If students misread a word, encourage them to try again by saying, **Look at the word again. Does it look as though the word you said could be that word?**

VOCABULARY DEFINED

dramatic exciting

hubbub noisy confusion

instructor teacher

method a way of doing something

quest a search for something valuable or important

unwieldy hard to handle or carry

Discuss the meanings of the vocabulary words. Then ask students to make up sentences using at least two of the vocabulary words. (Possible response: *The instructor gave a dramatic speech.*) Continue until all the vocabulary words have been used at least once and every student has had an opportunity to respond.

Check understanding.

Have students write the vocabulary words on a sheet of paper. Ask them to name the word that answers each of the following questions and to circle that word on their papers.

- **Which word means "a search"?** *(quest)*
- **Which word describes the noise that's made by a lot of people talking at the same time?** *(hubbub)*
- **Which word means the opposite of "easy to handle"?** *(unwieldy)*
- **What is another word for *teacher*?** *(instructor)*
- **Which word might describe the effect of a big scientific discovery?** *(dramatic)*
- **Which word means "a way of doing something"?** *(method)*

REPRODUCIBLE STUDENT ACTIVITY PAGE

INDEPENDENT PRACTICE See the reproducible Student Activity on page 131.

NOTE: The following vocabulary words from "Little by Little" are reinforced in "Quest for a Healthy World." If students are unfamiliar with these words, point them out as you encounter them during reading: *polio, immobility, decipher, astonished, dismayed* (p. 177); *despised* (p. 178).

Name ______________________________

Quest for a Healthy World

Read the fact sheet for the true story titled "Quest for a Healthy World."

Important Events in Dr. Salk's Life

Dr Salk went to medical school, where he made a **dramatic** discovery.
His **instructor** said that a vaccine for viruses could not work.
Dr. Salk showed that he could use killed viruses to make a virus vaccine.
He followed this **method** to develop a vaccine for the flu.
Dr. Salk decided that his next **quest** would be to develop a polio vaccine.
He knew that many people had died from polio.
Other polio victims had to use **unwieldy** leg braces and crutches to walk.
Dr. Salk finished the polio vaccine in 1955.
There was a big **hubbub** over the vaccine, but Dr. Salk didn't want to make money on it.

Now answer these questions. Use each word in dark type one time.

1. What did Dr. Salk do while he was at medical school? He made a **dramatic** discovery.
2. Who claimed that vaccines could not be used against viruses? his **instructor** at medical school
3. How did Dr. Salk develop a vaccine for the flu? He followed a **method** that uses killed viruses.
4. What happened after he developed the flu vaccine? He decided that his next **quest** would be to develop a polio vaccine.
5. What were some effects of polio on people? They died or had to use **unwieldy** leg braces and crutches to walk.
6. What happened after Dr. Salk finished the polio vaccine? There was a big **hubbub**, but he didn't want to make money on it.

Harcourt

Directed Reading

Page 174 Ask a volunteer to read the title. Explain that this selection tells the true story of a famous doctor who made many important discoveries. Have students read page 174 to find out something about Jonas Salk's early life. Ask: **What did Jonas Salk first plan to be?** (*a lawyer*) LITERAL: NOTE DETAILS

Page 175 Have students read page 175 to find out what Salk became. (*medical scientist*) INFERENTIAL: IMPORTANT DETAILS Ask: **What did one of Salk's instructors claim?** (*that the method for preventing bacterial illnesses wouldn't work for illnesses caused by viruses*) INFERENTIAL: SUMMARIZE

Page 176 After students read page 176, ask: **Did Salk agree with his instructor? How do you know?** (*No; he tried using a killed-virus vaccine again.*) METACOGNITIVE: DRAW CONCLUSIONS **What did Salk make?** (*a vaccine that stops the flu*) INFERENTIAL: IMPORTANT DETAILS

Page 177 Read page 177 aloud, having students listen to find out what Dr. Salk decided to do next. (*develop a polio vaccine*) INFERENTIAL: IMPORTANT DETAILS Ask: **Was the vaccine successful? How do you know?** (Possible response: *Yes; there was a big hubbub, and Dr. Salk became famous.*) INFERENTIAL: DRAW CONCLUSIONS

Page 178 Have a volunteer read aloud the first sentence. Ask students to read the rest of page 178 to find out why Salk never applied for a patent. (*He believed it was wrong to make money from something that people need.*) INFERENTIAL: MAIN IDEA Ask: **Do you think it is wrong to make money from something that people need? Why or why not?** (Responses will vary.) CRITICAL: MAKE JUDGMENTS

Page 179 Have students read page 179 to learn about the people who were important to Dr. Salk. Ask: **Who did Dr. Salk feel was his best teacher, and why?** (Possible response: *His mother; she taught him that it is important to work hard and to go to school.*) INFERENTIAL: SYNTHESIZE

Page 180 Have students read page 180 to find out how Dr. Salk thinks people should choose a career. (*by figuring out what they can give to life on earth and what they care about, and then working for that dream*) INFERENTIAL: SYNTHESIZE Ask: **What words might you use to describe Dr. Salk?** (Possible responses: *kind, smart, generous, hard-working*) **Why?** (Responses will vary.) INFERENTIAL: DETERMINE CHARACTERS' TRAITS

SUMMARIZE THE SELECTION Ask students to think about Salk's life before, during, and after developing the flu and polio vaccines. Then have students write three sentences to summarize the selection.

Page 181

Answers to Think About It Questions

1. Possible response: Salk developed vaccines for influenza and polio. SUMMARY
2. Possible response: Salk felt it was important to help humanity. He may have felt he could help more people by doing medical research than by treating patients. INTERPRETATION
3. Letters should follow the business-letter format and should express appreciation for Dr. Salk's hard work and accomplishments. WRITE A LETTER

Name ______________________________

Quest for a Healthy World

Write one sentence in each box below to tell about Jonas Salk.

Pages 174–175

Main Idea: Possible response: Jonas Salk became a medical scientist.

Page 176

Main Idea: Possible response: He showed that it was possible to make a vaccine against the flu virus.

Pages 177–178

Main Idea: Possible response: He developed a polio vaccine that made him famous, but he didn't want to make money on it.

Pages 179–180

Main Idea: Possible response: He believed that his mother was his best teacher and that people should help others as well as themselves.

Write a one-sentence summary statement about the selection.

Possible response: Dr. Jonas Salk helped many people by developing flu and polio vaccines.

Harcourt

Pete's Great Invention

by Linda Lott **Use with *Timeless Tales*, pages 182–189.**

Preteaching Skills: Long Vowel /ā/*ea, ei, eigh*

Teach/Model

IDENTIFY THE SOUND Have students repeat the following sentence aloud three times: *Sam took a snapshot of his cat.* Ask students to identify the words with the /a/ sound they hear in *hat.* (*Sam, snapshot, cat*) Then have students repeat the following sentence aloud three times: *My neighbor unveiled a great work of art.* Ask students to name the words with the same /ā/ sound they hear in *vein.* (*neighbor, unveiled, great*)

ASSOCIATE LETTERS TO THEIR SOUND Write on the board the two sentences above. Point out the words with the CVC pattern in the first sentence. (*Sam, snapshot, cat)* Remind students that words with this pattern usually have a short vowel sound. In the second sentence, underline the letters *ea* in *great.* Point out that in the word *great,* the letters *e* and *a* together stand for the long *a* sound. Then underline the *eigh* in *neighbor* and *ei* in *unveiled,* and tell students that the letters *eigh* and *ei* also can stand for the long *a* sound. Explain that the letters *gh* in *eigh* are silent.

WORD BLENDING Model how to blend the sounds and letters to read the word *freight.* Point to *f* and say /f/. Point to *r* and say /r/. Slide your hand under *eigh* and say /ā/. Point to *t* and say /t/. Slide your hand under the whole word as you elongate the sounds: /ffrrāātt/. Then say the word naturally—*freight.* Repeat the procedure with *break* and *veil.*

Practice/Apply

APPLY THE SKILL ***Letter Substitution*** Write the following words on the board, and have students read each aloud. Make the changes necessary to form the words in parentheses. Have a student read each new word aloud.

van (vein) ran (rein) stack (steak)

Have students form a generalization about words with two vowels between two consonants. (*When two vowels come together in a word, they often stand for a long vowel sound.*)

DICTATION AND WRITING Have students number a piece of paper 1–8. Dictate the following words, and have students write them. Have them draw a line through a misspelled word and write the correct spelling beside it. After students write each word, display it so they can proofread their work.

1. steak*	2. breakable	3. veil*	4. reindeer
5. eight*	6. freight*	7. neigh	8. paperweight

**Word appears in "Pete's Great Invention."*

Dictate the following sentence, and have students write it: *I had great chow mein at my neighbor's house.*

READ LONGER WORDS ***Introduce Breaking Words with* eigh** Write *weightless* on the board. Have a volunteer identify the letters that come together to form the long *a* sound. (*eigh*) Tell students that when reading a longer word with the long *a* sound spelled *eigh,* they should always say the two vowels as one sound, /ā/. Draw your hand under the entire word as students read it. Repeat the procedure for the word *sleighing.*

REPRODUCIBLE STUDENT ACTIVITY PAGE

INDEPENDENT PRACTICE See the reproducible Student Activity on page 135.

Name ______________________________

REPRODUCIBLE STUDENT ACTIVITY PAGE

Pete's Great Invention

Read the story. Then read each question. Decide which is the best answer. Mark the letter for that answer.

Diana's neighbor Seth owns eight Great Danes. Great Danes are very large dogs. They can weigh up to 175 pounds! Seth's dogs can lick his face when they stand up on their hind legs.

Seth told Diana that together the dogs weighed more than a thousand pounds. After that Diana started calling the dogs the "heavyweights." Diana likes to tease Seth about his dogs. One day Seth told Diana that he feeds the dogs raw steak. Diana asked if the dogs' food had to be delivered by freight train.

At daybreak Seth takes his eight dogs for a walk. Diana likes to watch them from her window. She thinks the dogs' leashes look like reins. Once she told Seth that he should make fake antlers for his dogs. Then they could be his very own reindeer! "Seth driving a sleigh—how funny!" she said to herself. Seth didn't think it was such a great idea. It did make him laugh, however.

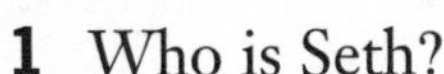

1 Who is Seth?
- **A** Diana's great-grandfather
- **B** a sleigh driver
- **C** a lightweight boxer
- **(D)** Diana's neighbor

2 What does Seth own?
- **F** eighteen Great Lakes
- **(G)** eight Great Danes
- **H** a freight train
- **J** eight reindeer

3 Why does Diana call the dogs the "heavyweights"?
- **A** They weigh eight tons.
- **B** They break sleighs.
- **(C)** Together, they weigh more than a thousand pounds.
- **D** They neigh like horses.

4 What does Seth feed the Great Danes?
- **F** chow mein
- **G** paperweights
- **H** reins
- **(J)** raw steak

5 Diana asked if the dogs' food is delivered by
- **(A)** a freight train.
- **B** a sleigh.
- **C** a neighbor.
- **D** a great supermarket.

6 When do the dogs go for a walk?
- **F** after a great meal
- **G** while unveiling a statue
- **(H)** at daybreak
- **J** every eight days

Harcourt

Introducing Vocabulary

Apply word identification strategies.

LOOK FOR FAMILIAR SPELLING PATTERNS Display the vocabulary words, and ask students to identify the ones they know. Remind students that they can sometimes figure out a new word by looking for familiar spelling patterns. Point out the vowels between consonants in *racket* and *success.* Call on volunteers to read these words aloud and tell how they were able to figure them out. (*A vowel between two or more consonants usually stands for a short vowel sound.*) Help students read the remaining vocabulary words aloud, using clues as necessary: this tells what something looks like (*description*); an inventor makes this (*invention*); what you call something that has never been made before (*original*); what you call something that can't be explained (*mysterious*). If students misread a word, encourage them by saying, for example, **You read ___ and then changed it to ____. Why? How did you know to do that?**

VOCABULARY DEFINED

description a statement that tells what something looks like or how it works

invention a new and useful device

mysterious puzzling

original entirely new

racket a loud, unpleasant noise

success a result that was hoped for

Discuss the meanings of the vocabulary words. Then ask students to invent a story using each of the vocabulary words, having each student add a sentence to build the story. You may want to begin the story with this sentence: *Maria has a new invention.* Continue building the story until all students have had a chance to respond and all the vocabulary words have been used at least once.

Check understanding.

Have students write the vocabulary words on a sheet of paper. Then ask the following questions. Have students name the word that best answers the question and circle that word on their papers.

- **What kind of noise might a train make as it goes by your house?** *(racket)*
- **When you describe what something looks like, what are you giving?** *(description)*
- **Which word is related to the word *mystery*?** *(mysterious)*
- **Which word has the smaller word *invent* inside it?** *(invention)*
- **Which word describes something entirely new that has never been made before?** *(original)*
- **Which word names a kind of victory?** *(success)*

REPRODUCIBLE STUDENT ACTIVITY PAGE

INDEPENDENT PRACTICE See the reproducible Student Activity on page 137.

NOTE: The following vocabulary words from "Dear Mr. Henshaw" are reinforced in "Pete's Great Invention." If students are unfamiliar with these words, point them out as you encounter them during reading: *refinery, muffle* (p. 183); *insulated* (p. 185); *prowls, partition* (p. 186); *submitted* (p. 187).

Name ______________________

REPRODUCIBLE
STUDENT
ACTIVITY PAGE

Pete's Great Invention

These sentences are about "Pete's Great Invention." Write the word from the box that makes sense in each sentence.

success	description	invention	original	mysterious	racket

1. Almost everyone wakes up to the ___racket___ an alarm clock makes.
2. But when Pete is sleeping, a ___mysterious___ thing happens. He can't hear the alarm!
3. Maybe a new ___invention___ could solve Pete's problem.
4. Pete wants to invent something ___original___ and useful.
5. Pete has an idea for an invention that he thinks will be a great ___success___.
6. Pete writes a ___description___ of what he plans to make.

Answer these questions to tell what you think might happen in "Pete's Great Invention."

1. What do you think Pete will want his invention to do?

   Responses will vary.

2. Do you think Pete's invention will be a success? Explain why or why not.

   Responses will vary.

Harcourt

Directed Reading

Page 183 Have students read aloud the title of the story. Ask a volunteer to look at the picture and identify Pete. Then have students read page 183 to find out why Pete's face is so red. (*He feels embarrassed.*) INFERENTIAL: DETERMINE CHARACTERS' EMOTIONS Ask: **Why does Pete feel this way?** (*Mark teased him about being late eight days in a row and everyone laughed.*) INFERENTIAL: CAUSE-EFFECT **Why can't Pete get up in the morning?** (Possible response: *The alarm clock doesn't make enough noise to wake him up.*) INFERENTIAL: DRAW CONCLUSIONS

Page 185 Have volunteers describe what they see in the picture. Ask: **What do you think Pete will invent?** (Possible response: *a really loud alarm clock*) INFERENTIAL: MAKE PREDICTIONS Then have students read page 185 to confirm their predictions. Ask: **What two problems does Pete hope his invention will solve?** (*having to make an invention for the class invention fair and being late to school*) INFERENTIAL: SYNTHESIZE Have students summarize the steps Pete took, in sequence, to build his invention. (*First, he insulated the bedroom wall. Then he threaded a rope through a hook and attached pots and pans to the rope. Then he tied a weight to the other end of the rope and set the weight on top of the alarm clock's switch.*) INFERENTIAL: SUMMARIZE/SEQUENCE **How does the invention work?** (*When Pete tries to turn off the alarm, he'll knock over the weight, and the rope will jangle the pots and pans.*) INFERENTIAL: SUMMARIZE

Page 186 After students read page 186, ask: **What problem does Pete have to solve to make sure his invention works?** (*He has to make sure the cat doesn't set it off.*) INFERENTIAL: IMPORTANT DETAILS **Does his mom stop grumbling about his using her pots and pans? Why?** (*Yes, she probably decides it is more important for Pete to get up on time.*) INFERENTIAL: DRAW CONCLUSIONS

Page 187 Have students read page 187 to find out what happens at the class invention fair. (*Pete's invention is a great success.*) INFERENTIAL: IMPORTANT DETAILS Ask: **Has Pete already used his invention at home? How do you know?** (*Yes, Miss Deighton says that Pete hasn't been late once since he invented it.*) METACOGNITIVE: DRAW CONCLUSIONS **Do you think Pete's invention is a good one? Why or why not?** (Possible responses: *Yes, it was easy to make and solved his problem; no, it uses up a lot of pots and pans and is very loud.*) CRITICAL: MAKE JUDGMENTS

SUMMARIZE THE SELECTION Have students think about what happened at the beginning, middle, and end of "Pete's Great Invention." Then help them summarize the selection in three sentences.

Page 188

Answers to Think About It Questions

1. Pete invents an alarm clock that makes a lot of noise. Miss Deighton knows the invention is a success because Pete has stopped being late for class. SUMMARY
2. Accept reasonable responses. Possible response: No one else would be interested because his alarm clock takes up too much space and makes too much noise. INTERPRETATION
3. Accept reasonable responses. Ads should describe the invention accurately and should make the alarm clock seem attractive and effective. WRITE AN AD

Page 189 For instruction on the Focus Skill: Author's Purpose and Perspective, see page 189 in *Timeless Tales*.

Name ____________________

REPRODUCIBLE STUDENT ACTIVITY PAGE

Pete's Great Invention

Complete the sequence chart about "Pete's Great Invention." Write a sentence in each box. The first one is done for you.

Event 1:

Pete is late to school again because his alarm clock can't wake him up.

Event 2:

Possible response: He decides to invent a super alarm clock.

Event 3:

Possible response: He writes a description and draws a diagram of his invention.

Event 4:

Possible response: He builds the super alarm clock in his bedroom.

Event 5:

Possible response: He shows the alarm clock to his parents.

Event 6:

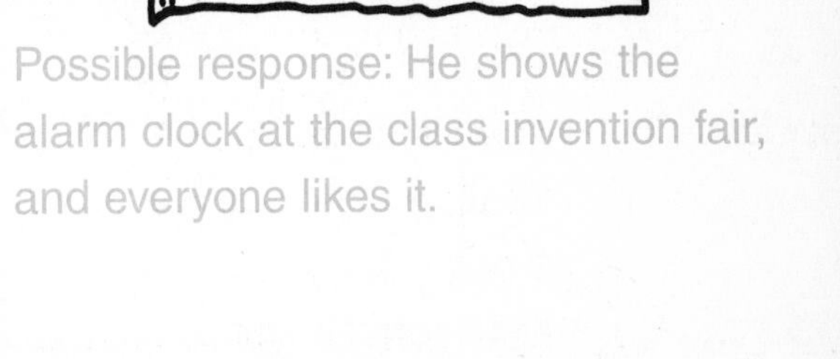

Possible response: He shows the alarm clock at the class invention fair, and everyone likes it.

Write a one-sentence summary statement about the selection.

Possible response: Pete invents a super alarm clock so that he won't be late to school anymore.

Harcourt

The Mystery of the Crimson Cards

by Pam Zollman **Use with *Timeless Tales*, pages 190–197.**

Preteaching Skills: Letter Pattern *ough*

Teach/Model

IDENTIFY THE SOUNDS Have students repeat the following sentence aloud two times: *He bought enough flour to make lots of dough.* Ask students to identify a word that rhymes with *thought*. (*bought*) Have them name a word that rhymes with *stuff*. (*enough*) Ask students which word rhymes with *go*. (*dough*)

ASSOCIATE LETTERS TO SOUNDS Write on the board the sentence *He bought enough flour to make lots of dough.* Underline the letters *ough* in *bought*, *enough*, and *dough*. Explain to students that the letters *ough* can stand for several different sounds: *ough* stands for the /ô/ sound in *bought*, the /uf/ sound in *enough*, and the /ō/ sound in *dough*. Explain to students that the letters *ough* also can stand for the /o͞o/ sound in *through*.

APPLY THE SKILL ***Sorting the Sound*** Write *bought*, *tough*, and *dough* on the board. Have a volunteer read the words aloud and identify the sound that *ough* stands for in each word. Have students sort the following words by writing each in a column under the word that has the same *ough* sound: *cough*, *enough*, *thought*, *though*, *rough*, *although*, and *trough*. Have them line up the letters *ough* in each column.

Practice/Apply

APPLY THE SKILL ***Letter Substitution*** Write each of the following words on the board, and have students read it aloud. Then make the changes necessary to form the words in parentheses. Have a volunteer read each new word aloud. Try to give each student an opportunity to respond.

cuff (cough)	both (bought)	toad (tough)	dug (dough)
enroll (enough)	though (thought)	throat (through)	those (though)

DICTATION AND WRITING Have students number a sheet of paper 1–8. Dictate the following words. Tell students that the vowel sound in each word is spelled *ough*. After students write each word, display it so they can proofread their work.

1. rough	2. tough	3. dough	4. ought*
5. bought*	6. through*	7. bough	8. though*

**Word appears in "The Mystery of the Crimson Cards."*

Dictate the following sentence, and have students write it: *Jon thought his sister played rough.*

READ LONGER WORDS ***Introduce Breaking Words with* ough** Write these words on the board: *doughnut*, *thoughtful*. Explain to students that in a word with the letter pattern *ough*, this combination of letters stays together when the word is broken into syllables. Point to *doughnut*, and ask students which part of the word stands for /dō/ and which part stands for /nut/. Follow a similar procedure with *thoughtful*. Then ask students to read *afterthought* and *sourdough* and explain how they figured them out.

REPRODUCIBLE STUDENT ACTIVITY PAGE

INDEPENDENT PRACTICE See the reproducible Student Activity on page 141.

Name ______________________________

REPRODUCIBLE STUDENT ACTIVITY PAGE

The Mystery of the Crimson Cards

Read the story, and circle all the words with *ough*.

Maya and Alden thought they saw something flash in a tree. "Look, it went through those branches," said Maya. "We ought to find out what it is." They could see the tiny object move through the leaves. Finally, the small blur got close enough to be identified.

Alden was thoroughly delighted. "It's a hummingbird!" he exclaimed. The bird was tiny, but it was as bright as a jewel.

The little bird zipped out of sight behind a branch. The children sought to find it among the leaves. "Tough luck," Maya said. "We lost sight of it."

"It must be rough to be so small in this gigantic world," said Alden. "I hope that little bird has enough to eat. Maybe we can help. We could put up the hummingbird feeder that my mom bought."

Maya and Alden brought the feeder with them on their next trip to the park.

Now write the word with *ough* that best completes each sentence.

1. The hummingbird ___thoroughly___ delighted Alden.
2. Alden's mom had ___bought___ a hummingbird feeder.
3. The friends ___brought___ the feeder with them next time.
4. Maya said they ___ought___ to find out what the flash was.
5. Alden said he hoped the bird had ___enough___ food.
6. Maya thought it was ___tough___ luck when they lost sight of the bird.
7. Alden thought it must be ___rough___ to be so small.
8. The hummingbird flew ___through___ the branches.

Harcourt

Introducing Vocabulary

Apply word identification strategies.

LOOK FOR FAMILIAR SPELLING PATTERNS Display the vocabulary words, and ask students to identify the ones they know. Remind students that they can sometimes figure out new words by looking for familiar spelling patterns. Point out the familiar CVC pattern in the first syllable of *crimson*, *hesitate*, and *timid.* Call on volunteers to read these words aloud and tell how they were able to figure them out. Help students read the remaining vocabulary words aloud, using clues as necessary: a display in an art museum (*exhibition*); means "beautiful decorations or shapes" (*designs*); means "worthwhile" (*worthy*). If students misread a word, encourage them by saying, for example, **You said ___ and then changed it to ___. Why? How did you know to do that?**

VOCABULARY DEFINED

crimson red

designs drawings or decorations

exhibition a public display of objects

hesitate to pause out of uncertainty or fear

timid shy; fearful

worthy deserving

Discuss the meanings of the vocabulary words. Then ask students to create a sentence using two or more vocabulary words. (Possible response: *Timid people sometimes hesitate to speak in public.*) Continue until all the vocabulary words have been used at least once and each student has had a chance to respond.

Check understanding.

Ask students to write the vocabulary words on a sheet of paper. Then ask each of the following questions. Have students name the word that best answers the question and circle it on their papers.

- **Which word describes something that has value?** *(worthy)*
- **What do you do if you pause before entering a room?** *(hesitate)*
- **What might you call decorative tiles on a building?** *(designs)*
- **What is another word for a display of an artist's paintings?** *(exhibition)*
- **Which word might you use to describe the color of a ripe red apple?** *(crimson)*
- **Which word means "shy"?** *(timid)*

REPRODUCIBLE STUDENT ACTIVITY PAGE

INDEPENDENT PRACTICE See the reproducible Student Activity on page 143.

NOTE: The following vocabulary words from "The Hundred Dresses" are reinforced in "The Mystery of the Crimson Cards." If students are unfamiliar with these words, point them out as you encounter them during reading: *incredulously* (p. 190); *stolidly, jaunty* (p. 191); *exquisite, impulsively* (p. 192); *accord* (p. 193).

Name ______________________________

The Mystery of the Crimson Cards

Read each sentence. Write the word from the box that makes sense in the sentence.

designs	timid	exhibition	crimson	worthy	hesitate

Some of the students in class got ___crimson___ cards on their desks. Mrs. Benson got one, too. "What fine ___designs___!" she exclaimed. "Whoever made this card has artistic talent." She thought the cards were ___worthy___ of an art ___exhibition___. Carla and Hector thought that whoever made the cards might be too ___timid___ to speak up. They decided they would try to catch the card person. "Let's not ___hesitate___. I want to find out who the mystery person is," said Carla. Now more students have cards. Each card has something on it that the person getting the card likes.

Answer these questions to tell what you think will happen in the story.

1. Why do you think the person making the cards doesn't want anyone to know who he or she is? Possible response: The person may be too shy to sign the cards or say anything.

2. Do you think the students will find out who is making the cards? Possible response: Yes, they will figure out the clues.

Harcourt

Directed Reading

Page 190 Ask students to look at the illustration on pages 190–191. Then have them read page 190. Ask: **What strange thing is happening in this classroom?** (*Students are getting red homemade cards with personalized designs on them.*) INFERENTIAL: MAIN IDEA **Do you think the students know who the cards are from? Why or why not?** (*no, because the cards aren't signed*) INFERENTIAL: DRAW CONCLUSIONS

Page 191 After students have read page 191, ask them how the students in the class feel about getting the cards. (*They are excited.*) **Does Carla wish she would get a card?** (*yes*) LITERAL: NOTE DETAILS **How do Yen, Jake, and Tim seem to feel about not getting cards on their desks?** (Possible response: *They don't seem to care. Yen just shakes her head, Jake smiles, and Tim keeps on drawing.*) INFERENTIAL: DETERMINE CHARACTERS' EMOTIONS

Page 192 Ask a volunteer to read page 192 aloud as students listen to find out what Carla and Hector plan to do. Ask: **Why do you think Carla and Hector want to catch the card person?** (Possible response: *Maybe they are curious about who has the wonderful talent.*) INFERENTIAL: SPECULATE **At first Hector thinks Mrs. Benson is making the cards. Why does he change his mind?** (*because just then Mrs. Benson gets a card, too*) INFERENTIAL: CAUSE-EFFECT

Page 193 Have students read page 193. Ask: **What events on this page might be clues to the identity of the mystery person?** (Possible responses: *Tim drops his books, Jake falls over them, and Yen bumps into Carla. Maybe one of them is the card person.*) INFERENTIAL: SPECULATE

Pages 194–195 As students read pages 194–195, tell them to look for more clues to the artist's identity. After they read, ask: **What other clues about the artist's identity did you find?** (Possible response: *The mystery person is thoughtful, because he or she has learned something about each person in the class.*) LITERAL: NOTE DETAILS **Why do the students think that the person making the cards won't get one?** (Possible response: *because it would be silly to make a card for yourself*) INFERENTIAL: CAUSE-EFFECT

Page 196 After students have read page 196, ask them to identify the mystery person. (*Yen*) Ask: **Why do you think Yen made the cards?** (Possible responses: *She likes her teacher and classmates; she wanted to do something that would make people happy.*) CRITICAL: INTERPRET CHARACTERS' MOTIVATIONS **Why do you think she didn't sign the cards?** (Possible responses: *She is shy. She likes mysteries.*) INFERENTIAL: DETERMINE CHARACTERS' TRAITS

SUMMARIZE THE SELECTION Discuss the surprises in the story. Then ask students to summarize the story in three sentences.

Page 197

Answers to Think About It Questions

1. Yen makes the cards. She is too timid to start talking with the other students, so she makes cards for them. SUMMARY
2. Possible response: They think the cards are beautiful, and they like the fact that each card shows something about the person it is made for. INTERPRETATION
3. Accept reasonable responses. Cards should describe and have messages related to students' special interests. CREATE A CARD

Name ______________________________

REPRODUCIBLE STUDENT ACTIVITY PAGE

The Mystery of the Crimson Cards

Write one or more sentences in each box below to sum up the story. Be sure to write the events in correct order.

Characters

The characters are Carla, Hector, Yen, Tim, Jake, and Mrs. Benson.

Setting

Time: It is a school day.

Place: The story takes place in a school.

Problem

Possible response: The students wanted to find out who was giving out handmade cards.

Important Events

Possible response: Carla and Hector talk about who the card-giver might be. They think it might be Mrs. Benson, but then she gets a card too. Carla and Hector decide to catch the mystery person.

Solution

Possible response: Yen raises her hand and says that she made the cards.

Now write a one-sentence summary of the story.

Possible response: Everyone tries to guess who is giving out beautiful handmade cards, and finally Yen says that she made them.

Harcourt

One of a Kind

by Ann W. Phillips **Use with *Timeless Tales*, pages 198–205.**

Preteaching Skills: Silent Letters *b, h, t, n*

Teach/Model

IDENTIFY THE SOUND Have students repeat the following sentence aloud three times: *Honestly, those boys often climb that column.* Ask: **What sound does the word *climb* end with?** (/m/) **What sound do you hear in the middle of *often?*** (/f/) **What sound does the word *column* end with?** (/m/) **Does the word *honestly* begin like *honey*, or like *on*?** (*on*)

ASSOCIATE LETTERS TO SOUNDS Write the sentence *Honestly, those boys often climb that column* on the board. Underline the letter *H* in *Honestly*, the *t* in *often*, the *b* in *climb*, and the *n* in *column*. Ask students what sound each of these letters stands for in these words. (*None; they are silent.*) Tell students that in the letter combinations *mn* and *mb*, the *n* and *b* are usually silent. *H* is silent at the beginning of a few words, such as *honest* and *honor*; and *t* is sometimes silent after *s* and *f*, as in *listen* and *often*.

WORD BLENDING Write the words *thumb, honor, soften*, and *solemn* on the board, and model how to blend and read them. Point to *th* in *thumb* and say /th/. Touch *u* and say /u/. Point to *mb* and say /m/, pointing out that *b* is silent. Slide your hand under the whole word as you elongate the sounds: /thuumm/. Then say the word naturally—*thumb*. Repeat the process for the remaining words.

Practice/Apply

APPLY THE SKILL ***Letter Substitution*** Write the following words on the board, and have students read each aloud. Make the changes necessary to form the words in parentheses. Have a volunteer read each new word. Try to give every student an opportunity to respond.

soft (soften) plum (plumber) list (listen) number (numb)

DICTATION AND WRITING Have students number a sheet of paper 1–8. Dictate the words below, and have students write them. After they write each one, display the correct spelling so students can proofread their work.

1. comb*	2. dumb*	3. limb	4. listening*
5. whistle*	6. solemn*	7. condemn	8. honor*

**Word appears in "One of a Kind."*

Dictate the following sentence, and have students write it: *I listened to the lambs.*

READ LONGER WORDS ***Review Breaking Words with VCCV*** Write these words on the board:

glisten often condemn

Remind students that when two or more consonants appear between two vowels, the word usually is broken into syllables between the consonants. Point to the word *glisten*. Cover the word part *ten*, and have a volunteer read *glis*. Then cover *glis*, and ask a volunteer to read *ten*. Point out that in this word, *t* is silent. Draw your hand under the whole word as students read it aloud. Call on volunteers to read the remaining two words, and have them tell how they figured them out.

REPRODUCIBLE STUDENT ACTIVITY PAGE

INDEPENDENT PRACTICE See the reproducible Student Activity on page 147.

Name ________________________________

REPRODUCIBLE STUDENT ACTIVITY PAGE

One of a Kind

Do what the sentences tell you.

1. Marty is sitting on a tree limb. Draw the limb he is sitting on.
2. Noni will climb the tree next. Add a rope to help her climb.
3. Marty is eating a cookie. Draw some crumbs falling from the cookie.
4. A lamb followed Noni and Marty to the tree. Give the lamb a name tag and a name.
5. Noni asks Marty if he reads her column in the class paper. Draw a speech balloon next to Noni, and write in her question.
6. Marty is honest. He says, "No." Draw a speech balloon next to Marty, and write "No" in it.
7. There is a beehive in the tree! Draw bees next to the honeycomb.
8. Noni sees the bees and whistles to Marty. Draw a whistle for her to use.
9. Marty is not listening. Put an X over his ear to show that he does not hear Noni.
10. A bee stings Marty's thumb. Draw the bee.
11. Noni feels bad that Marty got stung. She gives the thumbs-down signal. Draw it.
12. Marty does not cry often, but he starts to cry now. Draw tears on his face.

Now circle the words that have silent *b, t, n,* or *h*.

Harcourt

Introducing Vocabulary

Apply word identification strategies.

LOOK FOR FAMILIAR SPELLING PATTERNS
Display the vocabulary words, and ask students to read them silently and to identify the ones they know. Remind students that they can sometimes figure out a new word by looking for spelling patterns they know. Point out the long vowel pattern in *bait.* Call on a volunteer to read this word aloud and tell how he or she was able to figure it out. (*Two vowels together in a word often stand for a long vowel sound.*) Help students read the remaining vocabulary words aloud, using clues as necessary: what you use when you think hard (*concentration*); not joking (*serious*); tell what something is (*identify*); what homework can be called (*assignment*); looked up at the bright light (*squinted*). When students self-correct, encourage them by saying, for example, **First you read ___, and then you changed it to ___. How did you know which word was right?**

VOCABULARY DEFINED

assignment a task or job that a person is told to do

bait something that lures or entices

concentration focused attention

identify to say or show what something is or who someone is

serious earnest

squinted looked at with eyes squeezed partly closed

Discuss the meanings of the vocabulary words. Then give students a clue for each word. Have them name the word that the clue describes. (Possible clue: *I'm thinking of a word that names a job that someone else gives you to do.*) Continue until all the vocabulary words have been used at least once and each student has had an opportunity to respond.

Check understanding.

Tell students to write the vocabulary words on a sheet of paper. Ask them to name the word that answers each of the following questions and to circle that word on their papers.

- **Which word has to do with a duty or a job?** *(assignment)*
- **What did someone do when he narrowed his eyes?** *(squinted)*
- **What is the condition of thinking hard about something?** *(concentration)*
- **What can you use to catch fish?** *(bait)*
- **What do you do when you name the correct answer?** *(identify)*
- **What is the opposite of funny?** *(serious)*

REPRODUCIBLE STUDENT ACTIVITY PAGE

INDEPENDENT PRACTICE See the reproducible Student Activity on page 149.

NOTE: The following vocabulary words from "Frindle" are reinforced in "One of a Kind." If students are unfamiliar with these words, point them out as you encounter them during reading: *reputation, sidetrack, oath* (p. 199); *aisle* (p. 202); *absorbed* (p. 203); *beaming* (p. 204).

Name ______________________

REPRODUCIBLE STUDENT ACTIVITY PAGE

One of a Kind

Read the ad.

Meet Jenna and Her Friends!

Every Friday afternoon, instead of working on an **assignment,** Jenna's class played the widget game. Jenna, Holly, and Peter were on the same team. Mr. Lee was their teacher. Andy was the head of the other team. To play the widget game, Mr. Lee would choose an object. The teams would have to ask questions to **identify** it. Each time a team won, it earned points toward a pizza party. Jenna knew that the pizza was **bait**. It was good bait. Jenna's team was **serious** about winning. Mr. Lee gave the first clue: "The widget doesn't whistle!" Jenna **squinted** her eyes. She chewed her thumb. She listened silently. She knew her powers of **concentration** must be very sharp to get the answer first. Was it smaller than the room? Yes. Was it bigger than a book? Yes. Did it have hair? No. Was it one of a kind? Yes. The questions went on and on.

Will Jenna's team identify the widget first and win a pizza party? Read the story to find out!

Write a word from the ad to complete each sentence. Choose from the words in dark type.

1. On Friday afternoons, the class did not work on an assignment.
2. Instead, the students played a game. They asked questions to identify an object.
3. Mr. Lee promised the winning team a pizza party as bait.
4. When she was thinking hard, Jenna squinted her eyes.
5. Jenna, Peter, and Holly would need great concentration to win.
6. Jenna and her team members were very serious about winning.

What do you think will happen in "One of a Kind"? Will Jenna's team guess the answer and win the pizza party?

Responses will vary.

Harcourt

Directed Reading

Pages 198–199 Ask a volunteer to read the title of the story. Then help students identify Mr. Lee, Jenna, Jenna's teammates Holly and Peter, and Andy, the head of the opposite team, in the illustration on pages 198–199. Have students read page 198. Ask: **How is the widget game played?** (Possible response: *The teacher thinks of an object, and teams ask questions until someone guesses what it is.*) INFERENTIAL: MAIN IDEA **What is the prize for winning the widget game?** (*a pizza party*) LITERAL: NOTE DETAILS

Page 200 Have a volunteer read page 200 while other students listen to find out what happens when a class member thinks he or she knows the answer. (*To guess the answer, a team member has to blow his or her kazoo. If the guess is wrong, the team is out of the game.*) As the volunteer reads the questions and answers on page 200, have students listen to find out what kinds of questions are asked during the widget game. **At this point in the story, what do you think the object might be?** (Encourage speculation. Answers will vary.) INFERENTIAL: SPECULATE

Page 202 Have students look at the illustration on page 202 and describe what they think is happening. (Possible response: *Jenna looks as if she wants to guess the answer, because she is diving for her kazoo.*) INFERENTIAL: DRAW CONCLUSIONS Have students read page 202 to find out what happens. **Do you predict that Jenna will know the correct answer?** (Responses will vary.) INFERENTIAL: MAKE PREDICTIONS

Page 203 Have students read page 203 to find out whether Jenna makes a guess. **What do you think of Jenna's answer? Could it be correct? Explain your thinking.** (Responses will vary.) CRITICAL: EXPRESS PERSONAL OPINIONS

Page 204 Before students read page 204, have them look at the illustration and make a prediction about whether Jenna's guess is correct. Then have them read to see whether they predicted correctly. **Is the ending of the story believable? Could you have guessed correctly, from the clues given?** (Responses will vary.) CRITICAL: MAKE JUDGMENTS

SUMMARIZE THE SELECTION Ask students to think about what happened during the beginning, middle, and end of the widget game. Then have students write three sentences to summarize the story.

Page 205

Answers to Think About It Questions

1. When Mr. Lee says that the widget is one of a kind, the answer comes to her. She puts together the fact that Mr. Lee is one of a kind with the other facts. SUMMARY
2. Possible response: Before she gives her answer, she worries that she could be wrong. After she gives her answer, she feels proud of herself. INTERPRETATION
3. Accept reasonable responses. Statements should identify classroom objects. Questions should elicit information useful to the game. WRITE SENTENCES

Name ______________________________

One of a Kind

Write sentences in the boxes below to summarize the selection. Be sure to write the events in correct order.

Characters

The characters are Mr. Lee, Jenna, Peter, Holly, Andy, Colin, and other classmates.

Setting

The setting is Mr. Lee's classroom.

Problem

Possible response: Jenna's team must figure out what object Mr. Lee is thinking of in order to win a pizza party.

Important Events

Possible response: Each team asks Mr. Lee questions about the object. He answers "no" to almost every question. Someone asks if the object is one of a kind, and he says it is.

Solution

Possible response: Jenna realizes that the object Mr. Lee is thinking of is himself. She wins the game for her team.

Harcourt

Now write a one-sentence summary of the story.

Possible response: Jenna wins a pizza party for her team by figuring out that the one-of-a-kind object Mr. Lee is thinking of is himself.

A Safe Harbor

by Susan McCloskey **Use with *Timeless Tales*, pages 206–213.**

Preteaching Skills: Prefixes *un-*, *re-*, *dis-*

Teach/Model

IDENTIFY THE MEANING Have students repeat the following sentences aloud two times: *I stared in disbelief at my little brother's untied shoes. I had just retied them for the sixth time!* Ask: **What does *retied* mean?** (*"tied again"*) Ask: **Which word is the opposite of *belief*?** (*disbelief*) **Which word is the opposite of *tied*?** (*untied*)

ASSOCIATE PREFIXES TO MEANINGS Write the sentences from above on the board. Explain to students that a prefix is a word part added to the beginning of a word that changes its meaning. Underline the prefixes in the words in which they appear. Then use the word *retied* to explain how a prefix changes the meaning of a word. Cover up the prefix *re-*, and ask a volunteer to identify the word that remains. (*tied*) Then cover up the word *tied*, and have a volunteer identify the prefix. (*re-*) Explain that this prefix means "again" and that *retied* means "tied again." Repeat the procedure for the remaining prefixes.

Practice/Apply

APPLY THE SKILL ***Prefix Addition*** Write the following words on the board, and have students read each aloud. Make the changes necessary to form the words in parentheses. Have a volunteer read each new word aloud and explain its meaning. Try to give each student an opportunity to respond.

pay (repay)	reliable (unreliable)	placed (displaced)	heated (reheated)
united (reunited)	undid (did)	satisfied (dissatisfied)	rewarded (unrewarded)

DICTATION AND WRITING Have students number a sheet of paper 1–8. Dictate the words below, and have students write them. After students write each word, display the correct spelling so students can proofread their work. Have them draw a line through a misspelled word and write the correct spelling beside it.

1. distaste	2. reheated	3. unmatched	4. unsteady*
5. unsafe*	6. disliked*	7. unhappy*	8. repay*

**Word appears in "A Safe Harbor."*

Dictate the following sentences, and have students write them: *I was displeased with Nan. She would not repay the cash I had loaned her. Nan was unreliable.*

READ LONGER WORDS ***Introduce Breaking Words with Prefixes*** Write this word on the board: *dissatisfied*. Tell students that in a word with a prefix, the letters of the prefix stay together when the word is broken into syllables. Point to *dissatisfied*, and ask students which part of the word stands for /dis/, which part stands for /sat/, which part stands for /əs/, and which part stands for /fīd/. Make sure students understand that the prefix forms the first syllable of the word. Then ask them to read these words and explain how they figured them out: *unrewarded, recaptured, reunited, distasteful, unbelievable, disenchanted.*

REPRODUCIBLE STUDENT ACTIVITY PAGE

INDEPENDENT PRACTICE See the reproducible Student Activity on page 153.

Name ______________________________

A Safe Harbor

Circle and write the word that best completes each sentence.

1. Alvin's mother was ___displeased___ when she saw his room.
   displayed **disproved** **(displeased)**

2. "I've been too busy ___reassembling___ my bicycle to clean my room," Alvin said. **repackaging** **(reassembling)** **reconsidering**

3. "No more work on your bike until you ___reorganize___ your belongings," his mother said. **(reorganize)** **reopen** **replace**

4. "But that's ___unfair___!" Alvin cried. "I need to fix my bike so I can
   unfriendly **unwise** **(unfair)**
   ride with the bike club today!"

5. "Enough," said Alvin's mother. "When I ___reappear___ in one hour, your room had better be clean." **(reappear)** **reconsider** **remake**

6. Alvin sat down on his bed and stared at the mess ___unhappily___.
   unavoidably **(unhappily)** **uncontrollably**

7. "You could start by ___restacking___
   (restacking) **releasing** **redirecting**
   your books on the shelves," said his sister Ella.

8. "Why are you being so helpful?" asked Alvin ___uncertainly___.
   unstoppably **unluckily** **(uncertainly)**

9. "I know how important it is to you to fix your bike so you can ___rejoin___ the bike club," Ella explained.
   (rejoin) **replay** **rejoice**

10. "Boy, do I owe you one!" Alvin exclaimed as they started to ___reorder___ his toys.
    remodel **redesign** **(reorder)**

Harcourt

Introducing Vocabulary

Apply word identification strategies.

LOOK FOR FAMILIAR SPELLING PATTERNS Display the vocabulary words, and call on volunteers to identify the ones they know. Remind students that they can sometimes figure out a new word by looking for familiar spelling patterns. Point out the familiar vowel pattern in the first syllable of *seeping*. Ask students to use what they know about this pattern to read the word aloud. Help students read the other words aloud, using clues as necessary: a safe place for ships (*harbor*); how someone who is tired feels (*weary*); means "standing up" (*upright*); what a captain uses to keep a boat in one place (*anchor*); describes still water (*calm*). As students read each word, encourage them by saying, **That's right. Look at the word again. What made you think that could be the word?**

VOCABULARY DEFINED

anchor a device made of metal attached to a boat by a cable and cast overboard to hold the boat in place

calm still, quiet

harbor a part of a body of water protected from waves and deep enough so that ships can anchor

seeping flowing or passing slowly through small openings

upright in a position in which the main part is perpendicular to the ground

weary tired

Discuss the meanings of the vocabulary words.
Then ask students to make up a story about boats or other watercraft. Have them take turns saying sentences that contain one or more vocabulary words. (Examples: *The captain sailed the boat into the calm harbor. Water is seeping into the leaky canoe.*) Continue until all the vocabulary words have been used at least once and each student has had an opportunity to contribute.

Check understanding.

Have students write the vocabulary words. Read aloud the following clues. Call on students to answer each one, and circle that vocabulary word on their papers.

- **Which word means "tired"?** *(weary)*
- **Which word can describe water that is leaking into a boat?** *(seeping)*
- **Which word begins like *harden* and is a safe place for ships?** *(harbor)*
- **Which word names something that keeps a boat from drifting?** *(anchor)*
- **Which word contains the smaller words *up* and *right*?** *(upright)*
- **Which word has almost the same meaning as *peaceful*?** *(calm)*

Provide vocabulary support.

Students may have trouble with names such as Manolo Sanchez, Palos, Santa Maria, Pinta, and Nina (p. 206). Introduce the words by writing them on the board and pronouncing each. As students come across the words in the selection, offer assistance as needed.

REPRODUCIBLE STUDENT ACTIVITY PAGE

INDEPENDENT PRACTICE See the reproducible Student Activity on page 155.

NOTE: The following vocabulary words from "Across the Wide Dark Sea" are reinforced in "A Safe Harbor." If students are unfamiliar with these words, point them out as you encounter them during reading: *settlement* (p. 206); *vast* (p. 208); *beams*, *lurked* (p. 209); *rigging*, *furled*, *huddled* (p. 210).

Name ____________________

REPRODUCIBLE STUDENT ACTIVITY PAGE

A Safe Harbor

Read the story.

Manolo Sánchez likes to go with his papá to the **harbor** in Palos, Spain. They look at Christopher Columbus's ships. Papá is a cook on one of Columbus's ships. Manolo says, "Let me go, too. I will work hard even when I am **weary**!" Mamá says, "I don't want you to go. How will the ship stay **upright** all the way around the world?" Mamá lets Manolo go with Papá. They wave to Mamá as the ship lifts **anchor** and sets sail. Manolo scrubs the deck on days when the water is **calm**. One day there is a bad storm. Water is **seeping** through the beams! How can Manolo help?

Write a story word to complete each sentence. Choose from the words in dark type.

1. When the water is ____calm____, Manolo can work on the deck.
2. The ship lifts its ____anchor____ before it sets sail.
3. Manolo looks at the ships in the ____harbor____.
4. When water starts ____seeping____ in, the ship can be harmed.
5. Mamá thinks the ship might not stay ____upright____ if it goes around the world.
6. Manolo says he will work hard even if he is ____weary____.

Tell what you think will happen next in "A Safe Harbor".

Possible response: Manolo will find a way to stop the ship from sinking.

____

Harcourt

Directed Reading

Page 206 Read aloud the title of the story, and preview the illustrations with students. Explain that this story is a work of *historical fiction:* it is a made-up story based on an event that really happened. Read aloud page 206 as students follow along. Ask: **Which famous person is mentioned in the story?** (*Christopher Columbus*) INFERENTIAL: IMPORTANT DETAILS

Page 207 Ask students to read page 207 to find out whether Manolo gets to sail with Christopher Columbus. Remind them to pay attention to quotation marks to follow the speakers' exact words. Ask: **Does Manolo get to sail with Columbus? How?** (*Yes. His father is hired as a cook on the ship, and Manolo gets to go along to help.*) LITERAL: MAIN IDEA **Why do you think Mamá doesn't want Manolo to go on the voyage?** (Possible response: *She is worried that the trip won't be safe.*) INFERENTIAL: SUMMARIZE

Page 208 Call on volunteers to read page 208 aloud. Ask students to listen to find out what happens when the ship sets sail. Ask: **What does Manolo do on the ship?** (Possible response: *He helps Papá cook, scrubs the deck, ties and unties ropes, and carries buckets of water.*) INFERENTIAL: SUMMARIZE **Do you think Manolo wants to be treated like a real sailor? Why or why not?** (Possible response: *yes, because he helps the sailors*) INFERENTIAL: DRAW CONCLUSIONS

Page 209 Discuss the illustration with students, and then have them read page 209 to find out what happens during the storm. Ask: **Why is the storm dangerous?** (*It might cause the ship to sink.*) INFERENTIAL: CAUSE-EFFECT **What is the meaning of the phrase "danger from the storm lurked everywhere"?** (Possible response: *The danger is like a scary animal that is waiting to attack.*) INFERENTIAL: UNDERSTAND FIGURATIVE LANGUAGE

Page 210 Ask students to read page 210 to find out who saves the ship. Ask: **Who saves the ship?** (*Manolo*) LITERAL: MAIN IDEA **What does he do that no one else on the ship will do?** (*He is the only person brave enough to climb the rigging and lower the sails.*) INFERENTIAL: MAKE COMPARISONS

Page 211 Read aloud page 211. Remind students to think about how Manolo is feeling. Ask: **How would you feel if Columbus thanked you for saving the ship?** (Possible response: *I would feel proud and would remember the day forever.*) CRITICAL: IDENTIFY WITH CHARACTERS

SUMMARIZE THE SELECTION Ask students to discuss what happens during Manolo's voyage with Columbus and what he learns. Then have them summarize the story in two or three sentences.

Page 212

Answers to Think About It Questions

1. Manolo saves the Santa María and its crew when he climbs the mast and lowers the sails during a storm. SUMMARY
2. Possible response: They don't feel bad because the teasing was just in fun. It had not discouraged Manolo. INTERPRETATION
3. Accept reasonable responses. Diary entries should be written in the first person, from the point of view of Manolo's father. They should describe the storm and Manolo's actions. WRITE A DIARY ENTRY

Page 213 For instruction on the Focus Skill: Summarize/Paraphrase, see page 213 in *Timeless Tales.*

Name ___________________________

REPRODUCIBLE STUDENT ACTIVITY PAGE

A Safe Harbor

Complete the sequence chart about "A Safe Harbor." Write a sentence in each box. The first box has been done for you.

Event 1

Manolo's father is hired as a cook on Christopher Colombus's ship, and Manolo gets to go on the trip and help out.

Event 2

Manolo helps out in many different ways, and he doesn't mind it when the sailors tease him.

Event 3

One day a terrible storm comes up and the ship is in danger of sinking because the sails are not lowered.

Event 4

Manolo is the only crew member brave enough to climb up the rigging and lower the sails, and he saves the ship.

Now use the information from the boxes to write a one-sentence summary of the selection.

Possible response: When Manolo gets to sail on Christopher Columbus's ship, he proves his bravery by saving the ship in a storm.

Harcourt

Who Was Poor Richard?

by Jennifer Lien

Use with *Timeless Tales*, pages 214–221.

Preteaching Skills: Prefixes *im-*, *non-*, *pre-*

Teach/Model

IDENTIFY THE MEANING Have students repeat the following sentence aloud two times: *Nick found it impossible to put down the new nonfiction book about prehistoric animals.* Ask: **What does *impossible* mean?** ("not possible") Ask: **Which word means "not fiction"?** (*nonfiction*) Have a volunteer identify the word that means "before recorded history." (*prehistoric*)

ASSOCIATE PREFIXES TO MEANINGS Write the sentence *Nick found it impossible to put down the new nonfiction book about prehistoric animals* on the board. Explain to students that a prefix is a word part added to the beginning of a word that changes its meaning. Underline the prefixes in the words in which they appear. Then use the word *impossible* to explain how a prefix changes the meaning of a word. Cover up the prefix *im-*, and ask a volunteer to identify the word that remains. (*possible*) Then cover up the word *possible*, and have a volunteer identify the prefix. (*im-*) Explain that this prefix means "the opposite of" or "not" and that *impossible* means "not possible." Repeat the procedure for the remaining prefixes.

Practice/Apply

APPLY THE SKILL ***Prefix Addition*** Write the following words on the board, and have students read each aloud. Make the changes necessary to form the words in parentheses. Have a volunteer read each new word aloud and explain its meaning. Try to give each student an opportunity to respond.

heat (preheat)	stop (nonstop)	perfect (imperfect)	pay (prepay)
fat (nonfat)	patient (impatient)	set (preset)	polite (impolite)

DICTATION AND WRITING Have students number a sheet of paper 1–8. Dictate the words below, and have students write them. After students write each word, display the correct spelling so students can proofread their work. Have them draw a line through a misspelled word and write the correct spelling beside it.

1. nonfat	2. improper	3. impractical*	4. presuppose
5. impossible*	6. nonsense	7. preschool	8. nonexistent*

**Word appears in "Who Was Poor Richard?"*

Dictate the following sentences, and have students write them: *Ashley talked nonstop during the movie previews. Carl told her she was being impolite.*

READ LONGER WORDS ***Review Prefixes*** Write these words on the board: *imbalance*, *nonverbal*. Remind students that in a word with a prefix, the letters of the prefix stay together when the word is broken into syllables. Point to *imbalance*, and ask students which part of the word stands for /im/, which part stands for /bal/, and which part stands for /ən(t)s/. Follow a similar procedure with *nonverbal*, asking students which part of the word stands for /non/, which part stands for /vər/, and which part stands for /bəl/. Then ask them to read these words and explain how they figured them out: *immovable*, *nonexistent*, *prepackage*, *replacement*, *dissatisfied*.

REPRODUCIBLE STUDENT ACTIVITY PAGE

INDEPENDENT PRACTICE See the reproducible Student Activity on page 159.

Name ______________________________

Who Was Poor Richard?

Read the story. Circle each word that has one of these prefixes: *im-*, *non-*, or *pre-*.

"Are you ready to go shopping for our party?" asks Tanya.

"Why are you so impatient to get started?" asks Luis.

"It's impractical to wait until the last minute," Tanya says. "That's why having a prepared list is such a good idea."

"Let's add prepackaged foods to the list," said Luis. "They are easy to preheat. They will be hot when the guests arrive."

"Nonsense!" snaps Tanya. "Home-cooked food is immeasurably better than the store-bought kind."

"Okay, you cook," replies Luis.

"Fine," says Tanya. "Now, should we order preprinted invitations? I think they might be too impersonal."

"It will be impossible to write them all by hand!" cries Luis. "We'd have to work nonstop for hours to make them!"

Circle and write the word that best completes each sentence.

1. Tanya and Luis have a ___prepared___ shopping list.

prepared **previewed** **prepaid**

2. Tanya is ___impatient___ and wants to get going.

impartial **impolite** **impatient**

3. Luis wants to add ___prepackaged___ foods to the list.

predated **preheated** **prepackaged**

4. "___Nonsense___," argues Tanya.

nonstop **nonfiction** **nonsense**

5. "Should we send ___preprinted___ invitations?" asks Tanya.

presupposed **preprinted** **prepackaged**

6. Luis thinks it will be ___impossible___ to write all the invitations all by hand.

immobile **impossible** **immaterial**

Harcourt

Introducing Vocabulary

Apply word identification strategies.

LOOK FOR FAMILIAR SPELLING PATTERNS Display the vocabulary words, and ask students to read them silently. Remind students that they can sometimes figure out a new word by looking for spelling patterns they know. Point out the *are* and *or* patterns in *carelessly* and *inventor.* Call on volunteers to read those words aloud and tell how they were able to figure them out. Help students read the remaining vocabulary words aloud, using clues as necessary: right away (*immediate*); good for laughs (*humorous*); fact-filled book (*almanac*); a very specific study (*specialty*). When students read and then self-correct, encourage them by saying, for example, **At first you read ___, and then you changed it to ___. How did you know which word was right?**

VOCABULARY DEFINED

almanac a book published once a year containing calendars, dates of holidays, weather forecasts, and other information

carelessly done without much thought or attention

humorous funny; full of humor

immediate taking place now or very soon

inventor a person who creates new things or ways of doing things

specialty a unique feature, interest, or field of work

Discuss the meanings of the vocabulary words. Then ask students to order the words so that they could be used to tell a round-robin story. Have students take turns building the story by making up sentences using the vocabulary words. (Possible opening sentence: *I started the morning by opening up my trusty almanac and reading the weather predictions.*) Continue until all the vocabulary words have been used at least once and each student has had an opportunity to contribute.

Check understanding.

Tell students to write the vocabulary words on a sheet of paper. Ask them to name the word that answers each of the following riddles and to circle that word on their papers.

- **I am someone's main interest or skill.** *(specialty)*
- **I describe something that tickles your funny bone.** *(humorous)*
- **I dream up new technologies.** *(inventor)*
- **I am the opposite of *carefully*.** *(carelessly)*
- **I mean "without any delay."** *(immediate)*
- **I am a book that contains facts about weather, stars, and tides.** *(almanac)*

REPRODUCIBLE STUDENT ACTIVITY PAGE

INDEPENDENT PRACTICE See the reproducible Student Activity on page 161.

NOTE: The following vocabulary words from "What's the Big Idea, Ben Franklin?" are reinforced in "Who Was Poor Richard?" If students are unfamiliar with these words, point them out as you encounter them during reading: *contraptions* (p. 215); *edition, suspended* (p. 216); *honors, repeal, treaty* (p. 219).

Name ______________________________

REPRODUCIBLE STUDENT ACTIVITY PAGE

Who Was Poor Richard?

Read the story. Then fill in the web. Use all the words in dark type in your answers.

In the early 1730s, books were rare. Most readers read the Bible, the newspaper, and the **almanac**. Many almanacs were published in those days. Benjamin Franklin's main job at the time was publishing a newspaper. Franklin is best known as an **inventor**, but writing was his **specialty**. He decided to publish an almanac himself. He used the pen name Richard Saunders and called his book *Poor Richard's Almanack. Poor Richard's Almanack* was **humorous.** It became an **immediate** best-seller. In the almanac, Poor Richard told stories, described solar eclipses, and **carelessly** predicted the weather. *Poor Richard's Almanack* was also filled with sayings. Here's one:

Fish and visitors stink in three days.

Who he was and what he was good at

Franklin was a publisher and **inventor**. Franklin's **specialty** was writing.

What he wrote using a pen name

Poor Richard's **Almanack**

Ben Franklin

What people thought of the almanac

Poor Richard's Almanack was an **immediate** best-seller.

What he did in his almanac

wrote **humorous** stories and proverbs, predicted weather **carelessly**

What else do you think Benjamin Franklin did in his life?

Answers will vary. Accept reasonable responses.

Harcourt

Directed Reading

Page 214 Ask a volunteer to read the title of the story. Help students identify the colonial American setting in the illustration on page 214. Ask: **What is the family reading?** (*a newspaper*). Have a volunteer read page 214 while other students listen to find out what American colonists read in the early 1700s. **What is an almanac?** (Possible response: *An almanac is a book containing calendars, lists of holidays, weather forecasts, and other interesting bits of information.*) LITERAL: NOTE DETAILS

Page 215 Ask students to read page 215 to find out more about Benjamin Franklin. Ask: **What is a pen name, and who was Richard Saunders?** (Possible response: *A pen name is a name that an author uses to disguise his or her true identity. Richard Saunders was a name and character made up by Franklin.*) INFERENTIAL: IMPORTANT DETAILS

Page 216 Have students read page 216 to find out what the character Richard Saunders was like. **What was "Poor Richard's" reason for starting an almanac?** (Possible response: *His wife was nagging him to do something useful, and they needed the money.*) LITERAL: NOTE DETAILS

Page 217 Ask volunteers to read the proverbs on page 217. Ask: **What is a proverb?** (Possible response: *a short humorous saying that gives advice*) INFERENTIAL: DRAW CONCLUSIONS

Page 218 Read page 218 aloud. Ask students to listen to find out more about the history of *Poor Richard's Almanack*. Ask: **How do you know that *Poor Richard's Almanack* was popular with colonial Americans?** (Possible response: *The author says on page 216 that the book was an immediate hit. On page 217 the author says that the proverbs brought nods and smiles from readers.*) METACOGNITIVE: SYNTHESIZE

Page 219 Read page 219 aloud to students so they can find out more about Benjamin Franklin's other accomplishments. Ask: **What made Benjamin Franklin an important person during colonial times?** (Possible response: *He was an inventor and a good diplomat. He helped draft the Declaration of Independence.*) INFERENTIAL: SUMMARIZE

Page 220 Have volunteers read the text and proverbs on page 220. Ask: **What proverb listed here do you like best? Why do you think this is good advice for people?** (Answers will vary.) CRITICAL: EXPRESS PERSONAL OPINIONS/MAKE JUDGMENTS

SUMMARIZE THE SELECTION Ask students to think about the events of Franklin's life before, during, and after the years he published *Poor Richard's Almanack*. Then have students write three or four sentences to summarize Franklin's life and contributions.

Page 221

Answers to Think About It Questions

1. Benjamin Franklin used the pen name Richard Saunders to write and publish *Poor Richard's Almanack*, in which he told stories, described eclipses, predicted the weather, and gave advice. SUMMARY
2. Accept reasonable responses. Possible response: He knew that people were more likely to read and remember short, humorous sayings than serious statements or long explanations. INTERPRETATION
3. Accept reasonable responses. Newspaper articles should explain that the last edition is being published and that it contains a special preface. They should discuss the popularity of all the editions of the almanac and should give some basic information about "Richard Saunders." WRITE A STORY

Name ____________________

REPRODUCIBLE STUDENT ACTIVITY PAGE

Who Was Poor Richard?

Write one sentence in each box below to answer the questions.

Page 214

What were almanacs, and why were they popular in colonial America?

Possible response: They were books containing tidbits of information, and they were popular because there wasn't much else to read.

Page 215

How was Benjamin Franklin's almanac different from the rest?

Possible response: It was humorous, it contained proverbs, and he wrote it under a pen name.

Page 219

What is Benjamin Franklin also famous for?

Possible response: He was a writer, inventor, and diplomat, and he helped write the Declaration of Independence.

Write a one-sentence summary of the selection.

Possible response: In addition to playing an important role in the American Revolution, Ben Franklin was also a famous inventor and writer who created *Poor Richard's Almanack.*

Harcourt

Frontier Children

by Kana Riley **Use with *Timeless Tales*, pages 222–229.**

Preteaching Skills: Suffixes *-ly, -ful, -able, -less*

Teach/Model

IDENTIFY THE MEANING Have students repeat the following sentence aloud two times: *After examining the bike thoroughly, Sandy said the problem was fixable.* Ask: **What does *thoroughly* mean?** ("in a way that is thorough") Which word describes something that can be fixed? (*fixable*) Then have students repeat this sentence aloud twice: *I'm hopeful that this visit to the dentist will be as painless as the last one.* Ask: **Which word means "full of hope"?** (*hopeful*) **Which word describes something that is without pain?** (*painless*)

ASSOCIATE SUFFIXES TO MEANINGS Write the sentences from above on the board. Explain to students that a suffix is a word part added to the end of a word that changes its meaning. Cover up the suffix *-ly* in the first sentence, and ask a volunteer to identify the word that remains. (*thorough*) Then cover up *thorough*, and have a volunteer identify the suffix. (*-ly*) Slide your hand under the entire word as students read it aloud. Then explain that the suffix *-ly* means "in a way that is" and that *thoroughly* means "in a way that is thorough." Follow a similar procedure for the suffixes *-able* ("able to be"), *-ful* ("full of" or "with"), and *-less* ("without").

Practice/Apply

APPLY THE SKILL ***Suffix Addition*** Write each of the following words on the board, and have students read it aloud. Then make the changes necessary to form the words in parentheses. Have a volunteer read each new word aloud and explain its meaning. Try to give each student an opportunity to respond.

delight (delightful)	read (readable)	fear (fearless)	safe (safely)
help (helpful)	treat (treatable)	help (helpless)	permanent (permanently)

DICTATION AND WRITING Have students number a sheet of paper 1–8. Dictate the following words, and have students write them. After they write each word, display the correct spelling so students can proofread their work.

1. quickly*	2. trustingly*	3. careful	4. pailful*
5. unbreakable	6. comfortable*	7. useless*	8. endless*

**Word appears in "Frontier Children."*

Dictate the following sentence and have students write it: *The watchful teacher quickly grabbed the breakable vase before the careless student could knock it off the table.*

READ LONGER WORDS ***Review Breaking Words with Suffixes; Introduce Breaking Words with Prefixes*** Write these words on the board: *restful, weightless.* Explain to students that the letters of a suffix stay together when the word is broken into syllables. Point to *restful*, and ask students which part of the word stands for /rest/ and which part stands for /fəl/. Follow a similar procedure with *weightless.* Then remind students that the letters that make up a prefix also stay together when a word is broken into syllables. Write these words on the board: *reclaim, unaware, disadvantage, unexpected.* Have volunteers read the words aloud and explain how they figured out each one.

REPRODUCIBLE STUDENT ACTIVITY PAGE

INDEPENDENT PRACTICE See the reproducible Student Activity on page 165.

Name ______________________________

Frontier Children

Write the word that answers each riddle.

1. You can wash me. What am I? washable

   washable **unwashable** **watchful**

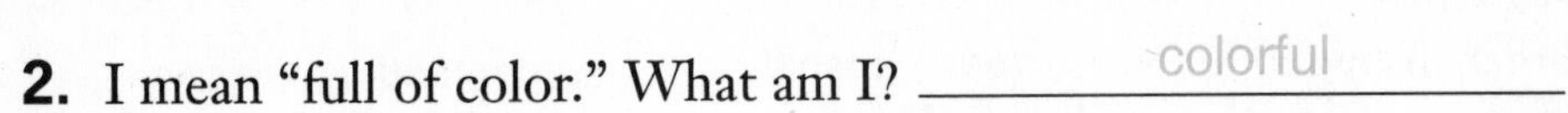

2. I mean "full of color." What am I? colorful

   uncolorful **coloring** **colorful**

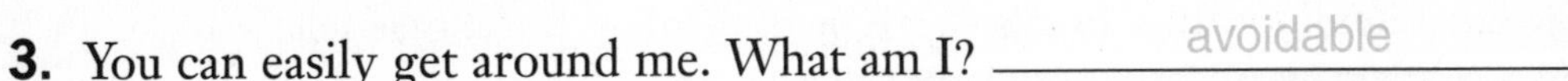

3. You can easily get around me. What am I? avoidable

   avoidance **unavoidable** **avoidable**

4. I mean "in a way that is honest." What am I? honestly

   honesty **honestly** **dishonestly**

5. I mean "without thought." What am I? thoughtless

   thoughtful **thoughtless** **thoughtfully**

6. I mean "very sad." What am I? sorrowful

   unsorrowful **sorrily** **sorrowful**

7. You enjoy having me around. What am I? enjoyable

   enjoyable **joyless** **unenjoyable**

8. I mean "in a sad way." What am I? sadly

   sad **sadly** **saddle**

9. I mean "without end." What am I? endless

   endless **ending** **ended**

10. I am filled with respect if I act this way. What am I? respectful

    disrespectful **returned** **respectful**

Harcourt

Introducing Vocabulary

Apply word identification strategies.

LOOK FOR FAMILIAR SPELLING PATTERNS Display the vocabulary words, and invite students to identify the ones they know. Remind students that they can sometimes figure out a new word by looking for familiar spelling patterns. Point out the familiar CVC*e* pattern in the first syllable of *homesteading*. Also point out the *ea* spelling for the short *e* sound in the second syllable of this word and the *-ing* ending. Ask a volunteer to read the word aloud. Help students read the other words aloud, using clues as necessary: what you call an area's weather throughout a year (*climate*); what you call a group of people who live and work together (*community*); what a person did when he repainted and fixed up an old building (*restored*); the opposite of *populated* (*desolate*); a type of building material (*adobe*). When students self-correct, encourage them by saying, **You read ___ and then changed it to ___. How did you know which word was right?**

VOCABULARY DEFINED

adobe brick made of sun-dried earth and straw; a house made from this material

climate the average weather of a place over a period of years

community people who live in a certain area and share common interests or duties

desolate empty of humans, animals, or trees; deserted

homesteading settling on public lands through a homestead law

restored brought back into its original state

Discuss the meanings of the vocabulary words. Then have students take turns creating sentences that contain one or more of the words. (Example: *The prairie seemed <u>desolate</u> before people started <u>homesteading</u>.*) Continue until all the vocabulary words have been used at least once and each student has had a chance to respond.

Check understanding.

Have students write the vocabulary words on a sheet of paper. Read aloud the following riddles. Call on students to answer each one by using a vocabulary word. Then have them circle that word on their papers.

- **I am made of sun-dried earth and straw, and I can be used to build homes. What am I?** *(adobe)*
- **I begin like *homework*, and I mean "settling on public lands." What am I?** *(homesteading)*
- **I begin like the word *communicate*, and I name people who live in the same area. What am I?** *(community)*
- **I begin like *destination*, and I have almost the same meaning as *deserted*. What am I?** *(desolate)*
- **I name the usual weather in a place. What am I?** *(climate)*
- **I end like *bored*, and I mean "brought back to its original condition." What am I?** *(restored)*

REPRODUCIBLE STUDENT ACTIVITY PAGE

INDEPENDENT PRACTICE See the reproducible Student Activity on page 167.

NOTE: The following vocabulary words from "Black Frontiers" are reinforced in "Frontier Children." If students are unfamiliar with these words, point them out as you encounter them during reading: *designated* (p. 223); *exodus, migrated, burrowing* (p. 224); *installment* (p. 225).

Name ______________________________

REPRODUCIBLE STUDENT ACTIVITY PAGE

Frontier Children

You are about to read a story titled "Frontier Children." Read the story fact sheet.

Who is in the story:
a frontier family: mom, dad, sister, brother
a **community** of frontier farmers

Where the story takes place:
a sod house; a schoolhouse

What happens:
Some frontier farmers lived in homes made of **adobe** bricks. At first, life on the prairie seemed **desolate**. There were few trees and few people. After a while, the prairie felt more like home. The family in this story makes its home in a **restored** sod house. What was life like for a family that lived in a sod house more than one hundred years ago?

The family is **homesteading** on the land. One fall day, the children do chores. It is chilly. In the fall, the **climate** is cool. The girl milks the cow, and the boy feeds the animals.

Now answer these questions. Use each word in dark type one time.

1. To what larger group does the family belong? Possible response: The family is part of a farming **community** on the frontier.

2. What is it like outside in the fall? Possible response: In the fall the **climate** is chilly.

3. What is the family doing on the land? Possible response: The family is **homesteading** on the land.

4. How did the prairie look when the family arrived there? Possible response: The prairie looked **desolate.**

5. What can frontier families use to make their homes? Possible response: They can use **adobe** bricks or sod.

6. What kind of house does the family live in? Possible response: The family lives in a **restored** sod house.

Harcourt

Directed Reading

Page 222 Read aloud the title of the story, and tell students that the story is based on historical events. Read aloud page 222 as students follow along. Ask: **How do the children help out in the mornings?** (*They do chores.*) INFERENTIAL: NOTE IMPORTANT DETAILS **What chores do you think they have to do?** (Possible response: *Maybe they have to make breakfast or take care of animals.*) INFERENTIAL: MAKE PREDICTIONS

Page 223 Ask students to read page 223 silently. Ask: **How are the girl's chores different from the boy's chores?** (*The girl has indoor chores; the boy has outdoor chores.*) INFERENTIAL: MAKE COMPARISONS/CONFIRM PREDICTIONS **How can you tell that the children like going to school?** (Possible response: *They hurry to get their chores done; they will be sad when it is too snowy to go to school.*) METACOGNITIVE: DETERMINE CHARACTERS' EMOTIONS

Pages 224–225 Ask volunteers to read pages 224–225 aloud. Remind students to pay attention to the time-order words. Ask: **Why did the family come to the West?** (*They wanted to find good farming land.*) INFERENTIAL: SUMMARIZE **Did the children like the land at first?** (*No, they thought it was desolate and useless.*) INFERENTIAL: DRAW CONCLUSIONS **Would you like living in this place? Why or why not?** (Possible responses: *Yes, it would be an adventure; no, I would miss my friends.*) CRITICAL: EXPRESS PERSONAL OPINIONS **How can you tell that frontier life is difficult?** (Possible response: *The family has to make a home out of sod, take care of animals, plow the fields, harvest crops, and pay back a loan.*) METACOGNITIVE: DRAW CONCLUSIONS **Why doesn't the family build an adobe house or a log cabin?** (Possible response: *The plains regions doesn't have the resources to build these kinds of houses.*) INFERENTIAL: SUMMARIZE

Page 226 Ask students to read page 226 to learn how the children get ready for school. Ask: **What is special about the food the children eat?** (*The girl picked the berries for the jam they are having for breakfast. The boy gathered the eggs they will have for lunch.*) INFERENTIAL: SUMMARIZE **What do children use instead of mules to get to school today?** (Possible response: *They walk, ride in cars, or ride the bus.*) CRITICAL: CONNECT TO PERSONAL EXPERIENCES **How can you tell that the children like living on the frontier now?** (*They like playing with their friends at school.*) INFERENTIAL: DRAW CONCLUSIONS **Why is it important for frontier families to form a community?** (Possible response: *They can help each other out and feel less lonely.*) CRITICAL: INTERPRET THEME

SUMMARIZE THE SELECTION Ask students to discuss how the children get used to living in a frontier community. Then have them summarize the story in three sentences.

Page 228

Answers to Think About It Questions

1. Their old house was in a town in the East. Their frontier house is made of sod and is on a farm, miles away from the next house. SUMMARY
2. Possible response: They don't mind doing the chores because they can see that they are a real help to the family. INTERPRETATION
3. Accept reasonable responses. Letters should follow the friendly-letter format and should describe the family's new home and way of life from the girl's point of view. WRITE A LETTER

Page 229 For instruction on the Focus Skill: Main Idea and Supporting Details, see page 229 in *Timeless Tales*.

Name ______________________________

Frontier Children

Write one sentence in each box below to show what you learned about frontier life.

Pages 222–223

What is life like for frontier children? Possible response: The children rise early in the morning to do chores.

Pages 224–225

What challenges do newcomers to the frontier face? Possible response: They must adapt to the unfamiliar and desolate landscape, build a home out of sod, and start a farm.

Pages 226–227

What do the frontier children like about their new home? Possible response: They enjoy eating fresh food from the farm and making new friends at school.

Harcourt

Now use the information in the boxes to write a one-sentence summary of the selection.

Possible response: Although it was difficult to adjust to life on the frontier, families who settled there found ways to make it feel like home.

Black Cowboys

by Sydnie Meltzer Kleinhenz

Use with *Timeless Tales*, pages 230–237.

Preteaching Skills: Word Parts/Suffixes /shən/-*tion*, -*sion*; /yən/*ion*

Teach/Model

IDENTIFY THE SOUNDS Have students repeat the following sentence aloud three times: *In your opinion, is the action movie about the space mission worth seeing?* Ask students to identify the words with the /shən/ sound they hear in *caution.* (*mission, action*) Read the sentence again, and ask students to identify the word with the /yən/ sound they hear in *trillion.* (*opinion*)

ASSOCIATE LETTERS TO SOUNDS Write the sentence from above on the board. Point out the *sion* pattern in *mission* and the *tion* pattern in *action.* Tell students that these letter patterns usually stand for the /shən/ sound. Explain that *-tion* and *-sion* are suffixes, and remind students that suffixes change the meanings of words. Also point out that the *ion* pattern in *opinion* stands for the /yən/ sound.

WORD BLENDING Write these words on the board: *devote, devotion; decide, decision.* Read aloud the word *devote.* Then model how to blend and read *devotion.* Point to *de* and say /di/. Point to *vo* and say /vō/. Slide your hand under *tion* and say /shən/. Then model how to blend the syllables together to read the entire word. Follow a similar procedure with the words *decide* and *decision.*

Practice/Apply

APPLY THE SKILL ***Suffix Substitution*** Write the following words on the board, and have students read each aloud. Make the changes necessary to form the words in parentheses. Have a volunteer read each new word.

note (notion) institute (institution) decide (decision) tense (tension)

DICTATION AND WRITING Have students number a sheet of paper 1–4. Write the word *perfection* on the board. Tell students that the first word you will say has the suffix *-tion* as in *perfection.* Dictate the word, and have students write it. After they write each one, display the correct spelling so students can proofread their work. Then write *mission* on the board. Tell students that the next two words you will say have the suffix *-sion* as in *mission.* Dictate words 2–3, and have students proofread as before. Then write *opinion* on the board. Tell students that the last word you will say has the word part *-ion* as in *opinion.* Dictate the last word, and have students proofread as before.

1. completion 2. passion 3. procession* 4. dominion

**Word appears in "Black Cowboys."*

Dictate the following sentence, and have students write it: *An expression of pure elation crossed the champion's face.*

READ LONGER WORDS ***Review Suffixes*** Write these words on the board: *collection, intention.* Remind students that the letters that make up a suffix stay together when the word is broken into syllables. Point to *collection* and ask students which part of the word stands for /kəl/, which part stands for /lek/, and which part stands for /shən/. Repeat this procedure with the word *intention.* (/in/ + /ten/ + /shən/)

REPRODUCIBLE STUDENT ACTIVITY PAGE

INDEPENDENT PRACTICE See the reproducible Student Activity on page 171.

Name ______________________

REPRODUCIBLE STUDENT ACTIVITY PAGE

Black Cowboys

Mark the letter in front of the sentence that best describes the picture.

1 **A** Margaret uses caution when exploring.
B Margaret has a passion for the sea.
C Margaret visited the ranger station.

2 **A** She often takes vacations on her boat.
B She studies bird migration.
C She has a superstition about traveling.

3 **A** She planned an expedition down the coast.
B She wrote letters on her best stationery.
C She ignored the information.

4 **A** She followed the whale's migration.
B She worked for the coastal institution.
C She sailed to a far-off nation.

5 **A** She won the racing championship.
B Her face showed her happy emotions.
C Sometimes her boat is tossed by the waves.

6 **A** On occasion the waves are huge.
B She felt elation when the storm passed.
C She had to ration her supplies.

7 **A** In her opinion, sailing is boring.
B Margaret made it back in good condition.
C Margaret couldn't reach her destination.

Harcourt

Introducing Vocabulary

Apply word identification strategies.

LOOK FOR FAMILIAR SPELLING PATTERNS
Display the vocabulary words, and ask students to read them silently. Remind students that they can sometimes figure out a new word by looking for spelling patterns they know. Point out the consonant and short vowel pattern in *duds* and *mustangs* and the long vowel pattern in *strays.* Call on volunteers to read those words aloud and to tell how they were able to figure them out. (*A vowel between two consonants usually has the short sound; I remember that* ay *usually has the long* a *sound.*) Help students use the sounds that letters stand for to read the remaining vocabulary words aloud, using clues as necessary: strong and thin (*wiry*); grassy plains (*prairie*); enjoyed very good growth and health (*flourished*). When students read a word correctly, encourage them by saying, for example, **That's right. How did you know that was the correct word?**

VOCABULARY DEFINED

duds a slang term for clothing

flourished was a success, prospered

mustangs a small, strong horse of the western plains of North America

prairie an area of wide, flat, or rolling grasslands

strays animals, such as cattle, that have wandered away from their herds or are lost

wiry slender but tough

Discuss the meanings of the vocabulary words. Then ask students to use each word in a sentence having to do with cowboys of the Wild West. (Possible response: *Cowboys rode their horses across the western prairie.*)

Check understanding.

Ask students to write the vocabulary words on a sheet of paper. Ask them to name the word that answers each of the following questions and to circle that word on their papers.

- **Which word names a kind of horse?** *(mustangs)*
- **Which word describes the clothes cowboys wear?** *(duds)*
- **Which word describes a place where cattle might graze?** *(prairie)*
- **What could you call cattle that get separated from the herd?** *(strays)*
- **What did a successful business do?** *(flourished)*
- **Which word describes a person who is slim as well as strong?** *(wiry)*

Provide vocabulary support.

Students may have trouble with names such as Bose Ikard (p. 231), Charles Goodnight (p. 231), Bill Pickett (p. 237), Myrtis Dightman (p. 237), and Charles Sampson (p. 237). Introduce the words by writing them on the board and pronouncing each. As students come across these words in the sentence, offer assistance as needed.

REPRODUCIBLE STUDENT ACTIVITY PAGE

INDEPENDENT PRACTICE See the reproducible Student Activity on page 173.

NOTE: The following vocabulary words from "Cowboys of the Wild West" are reinforced in "Black Cowboys." If students are unfamiliar with these words, point them out as you encounter them during reading: *discharged, wranglers* (p. 231); *stampedes, prospering* (p. 233); *domesticated* (p. 235); *descended* (p. 237).

Name ______________________________

Black Cowboys

These sentences are about "Black Cowboys." In each sentence, write the correct word from the box.

duds	mustangs	prairie	wiry	flourished	strays

1. Renata and Dad were dressed in their Western ___duds___. They were getting set for an eighty-seven-mile trail ride into Houston.

2. Dad told Renata stories about black cowboys who rode the ___prairie___ in the days of the Wild West.

3. Cowboy Bose Ikard helped rancher Charles Goodnight run a cattle business that ___flourished___.

4. Another cowboy, Nat Love, was great at taming wild ___mustangs___.

5. Nat Love took many risks while hunting for ___strays___ on the open range.

6. Bill Pickett was a small, ___wiry___ cowboy. He was well-known for rodeo skills such as wrestling steers.

Answer these questions to tell what else you might read about in "Black Cowboys."

7. What dangers do you think there might have been to cowboys during cattle drives?

____

____

8. Why do you think freed slaves and men who fought in the Civil War might want to go west and become cowboys?

____

____

Harcourt

Directed Reading

Pages 230–231 Ask a volunteer to read the title of the selection. Have students look at the illustration on page 230, and help them identify Renata and Dad. Point out that all the trail riders are African American and that the setting is modern-day Houston. Explain that the riders are taking part in a two-week trail ride to honor and remember the contributions of black cowboys in the 1800s. Have students read page 231 to find out more about Renata and her father. Ask: **Where did Renata and Dad start their ride, and where will they end up?** (*They started in Prairie View, Texas, and are going to the Houston Livestock Show and Rodeo.*) INFERENTIAL: IMPORTANT DETAILS

Page 232 Have students look at the illustration on page 232. Explain that this is a mental image of the story Dad tells. Ask them to predict what is happening in Dad's story. (Possible response: *There was a stampede and a cowboy was trying to calm the cattle.*) INFERENTIAL: MAKE PREDICTIONS

Page 233 Have students read page 233 to find out how the story about Bose Ikard and Charles Goodnight ends. Ask: **What cowboy does Dad tell her about next, and what is that cowboy known for?** (*Nat Love, a cowboy known for taming wild mustangs*) INFERENTIAL: MAIN IDEA

Page 234 Ask students to look at the map and read the captions on page 234. Ask: **What are the names of the two trails traveled by Bose Ikard and Nat Love?** *(Goodnight-Loving Trail, Chisholm Trail)* INFERENTIAL: IMPORTANT DETAILS

Page 235 Have a volunteer read page 235 while students listen to find out what Nat Love did as a cowboy. (Possible response: *He won every event at a rodeo in Deadwood, South Dakota.*) INFERENTIAL: RETELL

Page 237 Have students read page 237 to find out about Bill Pickett and more about Renata and Dad's trail ride. **Who was Bill Pickett?** (Possible response: *He was a rodeo star and the first black cowboy to be inducted into the National Cowboy Hall of Fame.*) INFERENTIAL: SUMMARIZE Then have students look back at the map on page 234. Ask volunteers to retell the stories told by Dad, using information shown on the map. INFERENTIAL: RETELL

SUMMARIZE THE SELECTION Ask students to think about what they learned about Renata and Dad, Bose Ikard, Nat Love, and Bill Pickett. Then have students write four sentences to summarize the information in the selection.

Page 237

Answers to Think About It Questions

1. Working as a cowboy was a good way for a black man to earn money and respect. SUMMARY
2. Possible response: He has learned a lot about black cowboys and he wants to share what he knows with Renata. INTERPRETATION
3. Postcards should be written in the first person, from Renata's point of view. They should describe the fun she had riding with her dad and listening to his stories. WRITE A POSTCARD

Name ______________________________

REPRODUCIBLE STUDENT ACTIVITY PAGE

Black Cowboys

Write one sentence in each box below to show what the narrator tells about African American cowboys in the story.

Pages 231–233

Who was Bose Ikard?

Main Idea: Possible response: He was a former slave and a talented cowboy who worked faithfully for a wealthy cattle rancher for many years.

Pages 233–235

Who was Nat Love?

Main Idea: Possible response: He was a mustang tamer who lived a life of adventure as a cowboy and rodeo wrangler.

Pages 236–237

Who were the black rodeo cowboys?

Main Idea: Possible response: Nat Love, Bill Pickett, Myrtis Dightman, and Charles Sampson were among the best black rodeo cowboys.

Harcourt

Write a one-sentence summary statement about the selection.

Possible response: Black cowboys have been an important part of American history since the end of the Civil War.

The Mystery Guest

by Kaye Gager Use with *Timeless Tales*, pages 238–245.

Preteaching Skills: Review Syllable Patterns

Teach/Model

IDENTIFY THE SYLLABLES Remind students that a syllable is a word part that can be said by itself and that every syllable has one vowel sound. Say the following words aloud, and have students hold up one, two, three, or four fingers to show how many syllables each word has: *carpet, weightlessness, coolly, pointer, graphics, poise, distastefully, replace, powerlessness, schoolhouse, found, bicep, polar, puppet, fine, necktie.*

ASSOCIATE LETTERS TO SOUNDS Write *carpet* on the board. Ask students which part of the word stands for /cär/ and which part stands for /pət/. Remind students that when two consonants come together in the middle of a two-syllable word, the word is usually broken between the two consonants. Also remind them that when *r* follows a vowel, the *ar* stays together when the word is divided. Then write *portray* on the board, and have students divide it into syllables.

Follow a similar process with the words below. Write each word on the board, and guide students in identifying the syllables in it, focusing on the points in parentheses.

- **weightlessly** (The letters *eigh* stay together when dividing into syllables.)
- **coolly** (Divide between the double consonants.)
- **graphics** (The letters *ph* stay together.)
- **replace** (The prefix *re-* forms a syllable. *Re-* means "again.")
- **powerless** (The letters *ow* stay together. The suffix *-less* stays together.)
- **bicep, polar** (The first syllable has a long vowel sound; the word is divided after the vowel.)
- **puppet** (The first syllable has a CVC pattern, which usually stands for a short vowel sound; the word is divided between the double consonants.)
- **necktie** (This word is made up of two smaller words, *neck* and *tie*. These two words form the syllables in *necktie.*)

Practice/Apply

APPLY THE SKILL Write the following words on the board, and have students read each aloud and identify its syllable pattern(s): *hitting, win, place, minor, undertow.*

DICTATION AND WRITING Have students number a sheet of paper 1–8. Dictate the following words, and have students write them. After they write each word, display the correct spelling so students can proofread their work.

1. safe*	2. cellar*	3. humanity*	4. needlework*
5. photograph	6. identity*	7. assuredly*	8. accomplishment*

**Word appears in "The Mystery Guest."*

Dictate the following sentence, and have students write it: *Sally found a hammer, a screwdriver, and several nails in the toolshed.*

READ LONGER WORDS ***Review Syllable Patterns*** Write the following words on the board: *humankind, neighborly, prehistoric, nonflammable, successfully.* Have students read each word aloud. Guide them in explaining the syllable pattern or patterns that enable them to figure out each word.

REPRODUCIBLE STUDENT ACTIVITY PAGE

INDEPENDENT PRACTICE See the reproducible Student Activity on page 177.

Name ______________________________

REPRODUCIBLE STUDENT ACTIVITY PAGE

The Mystery Guest

Read the story. Then write the word from the story that best completes each sentence below it.

April and Danny are taking a photography class. April wants to learn how to take better pictures of wildflowers. Danny wants to learn how to develop his photos himself.

Last weekend April and Danny practiced taking pictures. They took a picnic basket to a meadow near their neighborhood. "I can't wait to start!" said April. "I see several flowers I want to photograph."

"I'm famished," said Danny. "I think I'll eat first and take photos later." He unpacked the picnic basket and began to munch on an apple.

Meanwhile, April walked around the meadow, snapping pictures nonstop. She did her best to remain motionless when she took each one, as her teacher had showed her. By the time Danny joined her, she had already gone through two rolls of film. "You're unbelievable!" Danny laughed when she showed him the rolls.

"Not really," April said. "I'm just determined to improve!"

1. April and Danny are taking a pho|tog|ra|phy class.
2. They practiced taking photos last week|end.
3. They went to a meadow near their neigh|bor|hood.
4. When they got there, A|pril started shooting pictures.
5. Danny was fam|ished, so he chose to eat first.
6. The first thing he ate was an ap|ple.
7. Meanwhile, April took pictures non|stop.
8. Danny thought she was un|be|liev|able for working so hard.

Now draw a line between the syllables of each word you wrote.

Harcourt

Introducing Vocabulary

VOCABULARY DEFINED
accomplishment something that has been completed with much effort
assuredly without a doubt
celebrity a famous person
emphatic spoken with or marked by strong feeling
identity the condition of being a specific person
indebted owing thanks to another

Apply word identification strategies.

LOOK FOR FAMILIAR SPELLING PATTERNS Display the vocabulary words, and call on volunteers to identify the ones they know. Point out the long vowel pattern in the first syllable of *identity* and the short vowel pattern in the second syllable. Ask a volunteer to use what he or she knows about these patterns to read the word aloud. Help students read the other words aloud, using clues as necessary: what you might call a famous person (*celebrity*); means "marked by strong feelings" (*emphatic*); what you are if you owe someone thanks (*indebted*); an achievement you are proud of (*accomplishment*). When students self-correct, encourage them by saying, **You read ___ and then changed it to ___. How did you know which word was right?**

Discuss the meanings of the vocabulary words. Then have students take turns making up riddles for each vocabulary word. Examples: *I begin like* celebration *and I name a famous person. Which word am I?* (*celebrity*) *I describe words that are spoken with strong feeling. Which word am I?* (*emphatic*) Continue until all the vocabulary words have been used at least once and each student has had a chance to contribute.

Check understanding.

Have students write the vocabulary words on a sheet of paper. Read aloud the following incomplete sentences. Call on students to complete each one by using a vocabulary word. Then have them circle that word on their papers.

- **I saw a famous** *celebrity* **at the movie's opening night.**
- **His greatest** *accomplishment* **was climbing the mountain.**
- **"This is the shortest way to the park," Sam said** *assuredly*.
- **Randy was** *indebted* **to the firefighter who saved his cat.**
- **A costume hid Manuela's true** *identity*.
- **Rosa was** *emphatic* **when she said, "I don't like asparagus!"**

Provide vocabulary support.

Students may have trouble with names such as Lucretia Mott (p. 238) and Harriet Tubman (p. 238). Introduce the words by writing them on the board and pronouncing each. As students come across these words in the selection, offer assistance as needed.

REPRODUCIBLE STUDENT ACTIVITY PAGE

INDEPENDENT PRACTICE See the reproducible Student Activity on page 179.

NOTE: The following vocabulary words from "Name This American" are reinforced in "The Mystery Guest." If students are unfamiliar with these words, point them out as you encounter them during reading: *suffrage, guarantee, interpreter* (p. 240); *misleading* (p. 242); *stumps* (p. 243); *distinguished, anthem* (p. 244).

Name ______________________

The Mystery Guest

Read each sentence. Write the word from the box that makes sense in the sentence.

indebted	emphatic	assuredly	accomplishment	identity	celebrity

JAMES MOTT: Lucretia, we must be very careful. The accomplishment of this new plan has to happen without any mistakes.

LUCRETIA MOTT: Do you think we are at risk?

JAMES: Our lives will assuredly be at risk if we fail.

BETH: Are we having a guest? What is happening?

LUCRETIA: We are having a guest, but her identity must be kept secret.

BETH: Will I meet the guest?

LUCRETIA: No, you will be asleep.

JAMES: Lucretia, I must be emphatic. Do not tell Beth any more!

BETH: Who is she? Is she a celebrity?

LUCRETIA: You know her name, but I can't tell you who she is.

BETH: Why are we putting food in napkins?

LUCRETIA: I can't tell you, but I am indebted to you for your help.

Answer these questions to tell what you think will happen in the story.

1. What do you think will happen after Lucretia and Beth bring the food outside?
Maybe they will meet the mystery guest.

2. Who do you think the mystery guest is? Maybe it is someone who is running away from danger.

Harcourt

Directed Reading

Pages 238–239 Read aloud the title of the story. Discuss the conventions of a play. Have students read page 238 silently. Ask: **Who are the characters?** (*Lucretia Mott, James Mott, Beth, Harriet Tubman, three or four escaped slaves*) LITERAL: NOTE DETAILS **If necessary, tell students that Harriet Tubman was a real person who risked her life to help enslaved people escape to freedom. Where and when does the play take place?** (*at the Motts' home in Pennsylvania, in 1850*) LITERAL: NOTE DETAILS

Page 240 Read page 239 aloud as students follow along. Then have volunteers reread the characters' dialogue aloud. Ask: **What does Beth want to know?** (*She wants to know whether something is wrong and if they're having a guest.*) LITERAL: SUMMARIZE **Why do you think Lucretia keeps the guest's identity a secret?** (Possible response: *Perhaps it is dangerous for a young girl to know who the guest is.*) CRITICAL: SPECULATE

Page 241 Follow the same procedure for page 241 as for page 240. Ask: **How does James feel about Beth becoming involved in the plans?** (*He is upset.*) INFERENTIAL: DETERMINE CHARACTERS' EMOTIONS **Why do you think he is going to the cellar?** (Possible response: *Perhaps that is where the guest is going to stay.*) INFERENTIAL: MAKE PREDICTIONS

Page 242 Call on new volunteers to read aloud page 241. Remind students to follow the stage directions, too. Ask: **Why do you think Lucretia is making food bundles?** (Possible response: *Perhaps the guest is hungry and needs to eat in secret.*) CRITICAL: SPECULATE

Page 243 Ask students to read page 242 Ask: **What do Lucretia and Beth do with the food bundles?** (*They take them outside and set them by the woodshed.*) LITERAL: NOTE DETAILS **Why do you think they go outside without a light?** (Possible response: *Maybe they don't want to be seen.*) CRITICAL: SPECULATE **What happens after James comes out of the cellar?** (*Lucretia, James, and Beth go inside the house.*) INFERENTIAL: SEQUENCE

Page 244 Read aloud page 244. Ask: **Who is the distinguished guest?** (*Harriet Tubman*) INFERENTIAL: NOTE IMPORTANT DETAILS **What do you think is the message of this play?** (Possible response: *It is important to take risks to help people in need.*) CRITICAL: INTERPRET AUTHOR'S VIEWPOINT

SUMMARIZE THE SELECTION Ask students to discuss how Lucretia and James get ready for the mystery guest and how Beth helps. Then have them summarize the play in two or three sentences.

Page 245

Answers to Think About It Questions

1. The mystery guest is Harriet Tubman. She and the escaped slaves with her have to remain in hiding, so they are going to stay in the cellar. SUMMARY
2. Possible response: She slips out because she wants to see who the mystery guest is. When Beth sees Harriet Tubman, she is probably excited. INTERPRETATION
3. Accept reasonable responses. Compositions should be written in play format. They should present a discussion of the previous night's events and perhaps plans for activities to come. WRITE A SCENE

Name ______________________

REPRODUCIBLE STUDENT ACTIVITY PAGE

The Mystery Guest

Complete the sequence chart about "The Mystery Guest." Write a sentence in each box. The first one is done for you.

Event 1 (page 240):

Lucretia and James Mott are risking their lives to help a guest, but they won't tell their niece Beth who the guest is.

Event 2 (page 241):

Possible response: Lucretia tells Beth when the guest is coming, but James urges Lucretia not to say any more in order to protect Beth.

Event 3 (page 242):

Possible response: Beth is very curious to know more. She helps her aunt prepare food for the guest even though Lucretia won't tell her more.

Event 4 (page 244):

Possible response: Beth is sent to bed, but later she sneaks outside and sees her aunt and uncle greet Harriet Tubman and three escaped slaves.

Now use the information from the boxes to write a one-sentence summary of the play.

Possible response: Aunt Lucretia and Uncle James won't tell Beth who their mystery guest will be, but Beth sneaks outside and learns that her aunt and uncle have risked their lives to help Harriet Tubman.

Harcourt

Index of Phonics/ Decoding Elements